The Lords of Yester
Charles Nettlefold

Pewsey Press

2nd edition

First published 2014 by
Pewsey Press
Avebrick House, Pewsey, Wiltshire SN9 5NT

Text copyright © Charles Nettlefold 2013

Charles Nettlefold asserts the moral right to be identified as the author of this work.

Copy Editor Tara O'Sullivan
Designer Claire Rogers
Cover design Nicky Collings

A CIP catalogue record for this book is available from the British Library

ISBN 978-0-9929242-0-1

DTP by Duncan Petersen Publishing Ltd
Printed by Imprint Digital, Devon

The Fell Types are digitally reproduced by Igino Marini. www.iginomarini.com

Giff and Marjorie Tweeddale on their wedding day, March 1945.

To my grandmother, Marjorie

Contents

INTRODUCTION

In November 1905, William George Arthur Montagu Hay, the Earl of Gifford, was pulled in an open landau up the drive of Yester House by his estate workers on the occasion of his 21st birthday. He was joined by his father, the 10th Marquis of Tweeddale, the descendant of those who had lived at Yester since the 13th century. Yester stands ten miles from Haddington in East Lothian in Scotland and Tweeddale's estate there comprised 40,000 acres of farmland and moorland. The Marquis sat in the House of Lords as Baron Tweeddale and Queen Victoria had appointed him a Knight of the Thistle and Brigadier-General of the Royal Company of Archers. He was a classic representative of the comfortable Edwardian gentleman, possessed of a grand title and extensive lands whose country seat was considered one of the most beautiful in Scotland. The ceremony celebrating his eldest son's birthday represented the natural, inevitable and secure succession to a line descended from the Norman families of Giffard and de la Haya, who had come over to England with William the Conqueror and who had been joined together in marriage in 1373. His ancestors had served their adopted country for over 800 years with some playing important, and often leading, roles in many of the great events that shaped the history of both Scotland and England. Three were Lord Chancellors of England, and one of Scotland; two had been directly involved in the deaths of English kings; and from one branch had descended the Earls of Erroll, hereditary High Constables of Scotland.

Yet within ten years Tweeddale and one of his three sons would be dead and William, who was always known as Giff, was to be the last Marquis of Tweeddale to live at Yester. In 1970 his second wife, my grandmother Marjorie, would drive down the same drive alone, leaving Yester to its new owner, breaking the hereditary line first granted by King Malcolm of Scotland 800 years before.

Yester House stands a mile from the small village of Gifford where an avenue of 300-year-old lime trees leads to an iron gateway flanked by stone pavilions. An arch spans the twin columns of the gateway and, at its apex, sits a Marquis's coronet. Beyond stretches the long straight drive, flanked on the left by a steep bank filled with great stands of beech, ash, chestnut, larch and fir, some of them planted by the 1st Marquis at the end of the 17th century. On the right the ground is flat and grassed until it reaches a ribbon of trees which follow the bank of the burn called Gifford Water, which runs shallow and fast towards the village. The bank beyond rises steeply and again is full of ancient trees, some of which are Scotland's oldest and tallest.

When Giff's landau reached the end of the long straight stretch of road it followed the drive round to the right and was pulled over the 18th century bridge spanning the burn fifty feet below.

From there Yester House can be seen a quarter of a mile to the left, standing on a small rise beyond the banks where the burn cuts and curves through undulating parkland. Yester is a beautiful Palladian-style house built during the first half of the 18th century and has been described as 'one of the most perfect Scottish houses'. It gives a sense of great serenity as it stands amidst lovely sylvan parkland. Built of soft pink sandstone ashlar cut from quarries on the estate, its walls, when lit by the setting sun, glow like the embers of a fire. The view of Yester seen from the bridge is of the north front and it is not one of classical perfection as one of the two flanking pavilions was demolished in the 19th century.

To the south, the wide lawn slopes gently upwards towards parkland, uninterrupted by trees or flowerbeds. To the west, the drive ends in a gravel circle around mown grass where stands a stone *porte-cochère* with glassed roof and walls. This is now the main entrance to the house, where beautiful flowers such as datura, lilies, jasmine and geraniums fill the air with their sweet scent. Behind the remaining pavilion on the east side, in a thick cluster of old oaks and chestnuts, stands the chapel of St Cuthbert's, where Giff was buried in 1967.

In 1735 the Irish poet, Samuel Boyse, wrote a long poem about Yester which captures the magic it holds to this day:

> ...Safe in the bosom of a sylvan scene
> Amidst projecting shades of varied green
> Like some fair matron-form in cypress veil'd
> In Solitude sweet Yester lies conceal'd.
> Plain but majestic with proportion'd height
> Equal it rises to the ravish'd sight...
> And from the whole arrangement well-combin'd
> Calls out, a master beauty of the kind
> A modest grandeur dignifies the whole
> Thy palace, Tweeddale, represents thy Soul...

A mile from Yester, deep in thick woodland, stands Yester Castle, built by Sir Hugh Giffard in the 13th century and immortalised by Sir Walter Scott in his poem *Marmion* six centuries later. Little of the castle now stands, but the walls that remain tell of its original strength and size. What the casual visitor does not see, however, is more wonderful: deep beneath the grassed-over remains of the motte lies the famous Goblin Hall, which was rumoured to have been built in one night with the help of spirits.

I knew Yester because my father's divorced mother Marjorie married Giff in 1945. I was christened in St. Cuthbert's in 1951 and I spent most of my summer and Christmas holidays at Yester. It was a house full of history which, as I grew up, was impossible to ignore as wherever I walked the eyes of past Tweeddales and other nobles gazed down from portraits or blindly from busts, whilst ancient swords and spears, breast plates, helmets, pistols and muskets from long past battles hung thickly on its walls.

Thomas Hannan wrote in 1928: 'It is seldom that one may see a more beautiful or more elegant interior than that of Yester House.' There are 85 rooms but the main block is dominated by three great rooms. On the ground floor, the dining room fills the centre of the north front, with three large windows looking on to the steep bank where ancient beeches and larches climb to the sky. On the walls hung portraits of Giff's mother and father, the picture of Lord Charles Hay taunting the French at the Battle of Fontenoy and the portrait of the 7th Marquis, who died in captivity in France with his wife, leaving eleven orphaned children aged under fifteen.

On the south side of the house the double drawing room looks out over the broad sweep of the lawn. Mirrors at each end of the rooms reflected the multiple images of the beautiful chandeliers endlessly and portraits of Charles I and Charles II hung beside those of elegant ladies painted by Lely and Ramsay. A great staircase leads to the first floor which is dominated by the Saloon; designed by Robert and William Adam it is the most magnificent room in the house and, some say, in Scotland.

At the bottom of the staircase hung the portrait of John Hay, the 1st Marquis, sitting with his wife and surrounded by their 10 children, two of whom are shown as angels. His life was the most extraordinary of all of his line. He was an ardent Presbyterian who fought against King Charles in the Civil War and stood as a Member of Parliament under Cromwell. His father had been made bankrupt by debts incurred by his nephew, the Earl of Dunfermline, and he struggled all through his life to pay these back. He was jailed by Charles II but later became the king's key minister in Scotland under the Earl of Lauderdale. He was appointed Lord Chancellor of Scotland by King William, but he signed the authorisation for the Scottish Company whose collapse precipitated Scotland into Union with England. He married into the richest family in Scotland, but was plagued with financial worries all his life. It was he who commissioned the design for Yester and it was he who planted the park, some of whose trees stand to this day.

This book seeks to tell the history of the two families of Giffard and Hay. It focuses on individuals as much as it can, but they are often lost amidst the forces that swept through England and Scotland during almost a thousand tumultuous years. Without trying to describe those forces, it is impossible to understand how those individuals survived and produced the families who achieved such stature and longevity at Yester. Given the frequent ferocity of those forces, it is remarkable that so few family members died other than in their beds. This may be because they shared a consistent vein of loyalty to monarch and country and a sense of honour that kept their reputations high when those of so many of their contemporaries were wracked by greed and treachery.

Chapter 1 – The origins of the Hays and the Giffards

The first account of how the Hays rose to prominence 80 years before the Conqueror's invasion occurs in the *Legend of Luncarty*, written by Hector Boece in his *Scotorium Historia* of 1525, which tells of King Harald of Denmark's invasion of Scotland in 980. Boece's account has been much challenged, but there seems no doubt that a battle did take place at Luncarty in the 10th century and there are enough matters of interest within the Legend to merit its telling here. Harald, called Bluetooth because of his dark complexion, was the descendant of famous Viking kings. He was an aggressive ruler who had converted Denmark to Christianity and he had made several previous attacks on Scotland and England. On this occasion, his army landed in the east of Scotland and took Montrose, massacring its inhabitants and demolishing its castle. The Danes then moved down through Angus, killing and burning as they went.

King Kenneth II of Scotland confronted the invaders at Luncarty, a small village outside Perth. Scotland had suffered greatly from the continued attacks of the Vikings in the 10th century and Kenneth told his men that the fate of Scotland depended on them and promised money to any soldier who brought him a Danish head. The Scots fought fiercely but concentrated more on securing their reward than on defeating the enemy who broke through the Scottish line, routing both wings and isolating the main body led by Kenneth. Those Scots who fled ran down a narrow ravine near where a local farmer, Thomas Hay, was ploughing with his two sons. Hay and his sons quickly stopped the rout with their yokes and led the Scots back against the Danes who soon lost heart and were defeated with great losses.

Kenneth rewarded the Hays and asked them to lead the victory march through Perth, which they did with their bloodied yokes upon their shoulders. Hay was knighted and Kenneth promised him and his sons as much of the land of Gowry as a falcon could cover in one flight. The hawk flew a circuit of seven miles long and four broad around the village of Erroll and this the king gave to the Hays.

Alexander Nisbet, writing in 1722, describes the Legend, saying: 'Hay and his sons being nobilitate, the King gave him ... *Argent three escutcheons Gule* [three red shields on a white background] to intimate that the father and the two sons had been luckily the three shields of Scotland…the circumstances of which story is not only perpetuate by the three escutcheons but by the exterior ornaments ... of the family of Erroll; having for crest on a wreath a falcon proper; for supporters two men in country habit, holding the oxen yokes of a plough over their shoulders, and for motto *serva jugum*' ('keep the yoke').

Sir Iain Moncreiffe of that Ilk, late father of the present Earl of Erroll, dismissed this story. He considered that the first ancestor of the Hays in Scotland was William de Haya, who went there in the 12th century having come originally from France and whose 'arms ... have always been the same as those borne by the ancient Norman family of La Haye ... whose fiefs bordered that of Soules near St Lo.'

In the *arrondissement* of Coutances, on the Cotentin Peninsula of Cherbourg, stand the ruins of the castle of the barons of La

Haye-du-Puits. This dated from 911 when Rollo, the Viking leader who had besieged Paris, pledged allegiance to King Charles of France and converted to Christianity. He was made ruler of Normandy where he was joined by many families from the Nordic and Fleming regions. One of the most prominent of these was Thurstan le Goz (995–1061), Baron of La Haye-du-Puits and Viscount d'Avranches, whose ancestors had been Kings of Kvenland. He was Chamberlain to Richard, 2nd Duke of Normandy (978-1026), the great-grandson of Rollo. Thurstan married one of Richard's sisters, Judith de Montanolier, and their second son was Halduc (Richard) de la Haye (1013-1079) who married Emma, the daughter of Richard of Normandy and they had two sons, Eudo and Ranulf. When Halduc died he was buried at Lessay Abbey, a beautiful Romanesque building in the Cotentin Peninsula, which he had founded in 1056. Eudo (1035–1098) inherited as Baron de la Haye and was appointed Steward to William the Conqueror.

The historian, Beryl Platts, holds a different view of the origin of the de Hayas and distinguishes between the Normans, who served under William at Hastings, and the Flemings, who fought alongside them under the leadership of their liege lord, Eustace II, Count of Boulogne. Platts writes that a number of families called de la Haie lived near La Haye-du-Puits but the origin of William de Haya was rather La Haie near Loos in west Flanders. Its lord 'served the castellans of Lille...the de Insulas ...and his device, *ticturally sable* and *argent*, was shield upon shield, exactly like Scottish Hay except that, as was the early fashion, a singleton was used instead of three'.

Platts writes that members of de Insula's family fought at Hastings and that two of their grandsons, Reynold and Hugo de Lille, married daughters of Count Arnold of Guines, who were descended from Charlemagne. 'They had for arms *azure, an escutcheon argent*-that device echoed by the lord of La Haie, who must have been a kinsman. Is it possible that William de Haya was a second son of the marriage between Reynold and Matilda [of Wavrin], inheriting his mother's *maritagium* of La Haie and her arms, as was the custom, but having to change the tinctures to argent and gules, because he was not Wavrin's direct heir?' If Platts is right then the de la Hayas were originally Flemish and kept their loyalty to those of similar background who tended to live in the east of England after the Conquest and who became close to King David I of Scotland when he married one of their number, Maud, in 1113.

∼

The Giffards came from Normandy where lived Osbern de Bolebec (954-1035) Count of Longueville-de-Giffart and 1st Lord Bolebec. Longueville-de-Giffart is a farming village that stands on the banks of the river Scie in the Haut-Normande region and Bolebec is a small milling and mining town in the same region, close to Le Havre. Osbern married Aveline de Crepon, who was the granddaughter of King Harald Bluetooth and the sister of Gonnor, wife of Richard, 1st Duke of Normandy. Aveline's sister Beatrice married Ranulph de Warenne, and their great-granddaughter, Ada de Warenne (1120-1178), was to transform the destinies of both the de la Haya and Giffard families. Osbern and Aveline had three sons, Walter, Hugh and Richard.

Walter Giffard (1027-1085) is described by the historian Planche as 'the progenitor of a race from which the noblest of families in England may be proud to trace their descent'. Walter fought for William, Duke of Normandy, the future Conqueror, at the battle of Val-es-Dunes in 1047 and at the battle of Mortemer in 1054, where he helped defeat the French King Henry I. He was made Earl of Longueville by William and later fought in Spain against the Moors from where he brought William a war-horse given by the King of Spain, which William rode at the Battle of Hastings.

William learned that Harold had been crowned king of England in January 1066 and he called his barons together, including Walter Giffard and Eudo de la Haye, and told them of his plan to invade England; Walter supported him with thirty ships and one hundred men. On the eve of the battle, Ralph de Conches, William's Standard Bearer, asked to be released because of age and Walter was offered the post, but he refused it since, as he told the Duke, he wanted both hands free to fight.

Eudo de la Haye was probably the 'Sire de la Haye' mentioned by the 12th century Norman poet Wace, who at Hastings 'charged on, and neither spared nor pitied any; striking none whom he did not kill, and inflicting wounds such as none could cure'. Sir Francis Palgrave wrote of him: 'From La Haye-du-Puits came the great Eudo who acquired, whether by force or favour, the largest proportions of robbery, called conquest, in the counties of Sussex, Essex, and Suffolk.' Eudo was indeed richly rewarded by William but he gave much of his fortune to religious foundations. William de Jumiéges cites him 'among the most magnificent of the Norman nobles, who signalised themselves by their zeal in building churches.'

৵

The *Carmen de Hastingae Proelio*, written by Bishop Guy of Amiens shortly after the battle, tells of how William saw that Harold had been separated from his men during the battle:

> [he] called Eustace de Boulogne to him... Hugh, the noble heir of Ponthieu, escorted these two... fourth was Giffard, known by his father's surname; these four bore arms for the destruction of the king... the first, cleaving

his breast through the shield with his point, drenched the earth with a gushing torrent of blood; the second smote off his head below the protection of the helmet and the third pierced the inwards of his belly with his lance; the fourth hewed off his thigh and bore away the severed limb; the ground held the body thus destroyed. The king's two brothers were found lying beside him. He himself, all dignity lost, was recognised not by his face, but by certain indications.

William of Malmesbury wrote that 'Harold fell from having his brain pierced with an arrow... he yielded to death. One of the soldiers with a sword gashed his thigh as he lay prostrate for which shameful and cowardly act he was branded with ignominy by William, and expelled from the army.' However,if one of Walter's sons was responsible, then he was soon forgiven, for the Giffards were richly rewarded for their contribution to William's victory.

Little is known of Walter's brother Hugh, Seigneur de Beuffe, but his son Osbern also fought at Hastings and was granted substantial estates in Wiltshire and Gloucestershire, including the 2,000 acres estate of Brimpsfield, whose lordship he was given and where he built a castle. He died in 1096 and his descendants constituted the main Giffard family line in England.

Walter Giffard was created Earl of Buckingham by William who granted him 107 manors totalling 36,000 acres in six counties, the largest being Crendon in Buckinghamshire, where he built a castle. He married Ermengarde Flaitel and had two sons, Walter and William, and a daughter, Rohaise. He died in 1085 and his son Walter succeeded as 2nd Earl of Buckingham. He was one of the Commissioners who drew up the Domesday survey, and he was appointed William's chief minister as Justiciar of England. His brother William entered the church and held the offices of Dean of Rouen and Prior of Reading Abbey.

Walter's daughter Rohaise was one of the few ladies listed in the Domesday Book. She married Richard Fitz Gilbert de Clare, the son of Gilbert, Count of Brionne and the grandson of Richard I of Normandy. He fought at Hastings and was rewarded by William with 176 lordships and large grants of land in England, including the right to build the castles of Clare and Tonbridge. He served as joint Chief Justiciar and was one of the nobles responsible for defeating the revolt of the earls in 1075. However he was not a supporter of King William II (1056-1100) and rose against him in 1087. He died in 1091 and was buried in St Neot's Priory in Huntingdonshire, which he and Rohaise had founded. They had seven children, from whom descended the earldoms of Pembroke, Gloucester and Hertford and one of whom, Adele, married Walter Tirel.

William II was hunting in August 1100 in the New Forest with a group that included his younger brother Henry, Rohaise's sons, Gilbert and Roger FitzRichard de Clare, and her son-in-law, Tirel, who fired the arrow that killed William during the hunt. It is a matter of great debate if this was accidental, but the circumstances of the death and its immediate aftermath point to a conspiracy in which the de Clares, Tirel and William Giffard were deeply involved. King William's body was left where it fell, and only later taken to Winchester Cathedral on the cart of a local charcoal-burner. Henry had ridden immediately to Winchester, where he appointed William Giffard as Bishop. Although Giffard had been appointed Lord Chancellor of England in 1093 by William II he secured Winchester's substantial treasury for Henry, who was crowned king shortly after. Giffard resigned his position as Chancellor in 1101 and remained Bishop until 1107.

The Giffards and the de Clares were now amongst the greatest landowners in England. Rohaise's son Gilbert inherited as Earl of Clare and his son was made Earl of Pembroke. The influence the Giffards and the de Clares held at court at that time is strikingly shown in the *Liber Eliensis*, which was written at Ely Abbey between 1109 and 1189 and which tells:

How King Henry I, urged on by jealous men, expelled Richard de Clare from his abbacy, and how Richard went to Rome.

His deposition was brought about by the mere malice of those wicked men whose hatred had been kindled by the splendour of his mind and his family; his reputation had grown in many directions, he excelled in power, the number of his kinsmen and the amplitude of his wealth compelled a forced reverence from all; those who could not love him feared him.

Indeed, when he attended the King's court he was feared most of all after the King, surrounded as he was on all sides by a crowd of his kinsmen.

All England came to know the kindred of the Ricardi [the de Clares] and the Giffards who have the reputation of their courage and the size of their families. Whenever there was an assembly of nobles their pomp and magnificence, together with their terrifying numbers, had to be endured and in their presence it was not safe for any of the magnates to oppose them. By their hands men were killed in the court of the king and the royal majesty was shaken by frequent panic.

Walter, 2nd Earl of Buckingham, supported Robert, Duke of Normandy, in his unsuccessful attack on his brother King Henry in 1101, so he had to leave for France, where he died in 1102. He was buried at the Cluniac Priory of Sainte-Foi in Longueville which he had founded in 1093 and on his tomb was written: 'Walter, descended from the noble Giffards... he has the tomb that he deserved when living... He showed himself to be a man of great deeds and a friend to his country. A leader powerful in courage and distinguished for his piety.' He had married Agnes de Ribement and they had one child, Walter, who inherited as 3rd Earl of Buckingham.

CHAPTER 2 – ENTERING SCOTLAND

King Henry I consolidated his position by defeating his brother Robert in France in 1106, assuming his title of Duke of Normandy. In 1100 he had married Matilda, the daughter of King Malcolm III of Scotland. She was also the great-grand-daughter of Edmund Ironside, who had briefly been king of England in 1016, thus the marriage joined the Scottish monarchy with the Norman and Saxon line of English kings. However, when Malcolm died in 1093 his brother Donald seized the Scottish throne and exiled Matilda's brothers to England. One brother, David, married Maud, the Flemish widow of Simon de Senlis, Earl of Northumberland and Huntingdon, whose titles David assumed. She was the daughter of the Conqueror's Flemish niece, Judith, who had become the most powerful woman in the kingdom. Many Anglo-Flemish lords joined David's court and the relationship between the Flemings and the Scots grew when their liege lord, the Count of Boulogne, married one of David's sisters.

David was Malcolm's eighth son and he had no realistic expectation of becoming king but Henry encouraged him to return to Scotland to take the throne after the death of his brother King Alexander in 1124. He was supported by a number of mostly Flemish barons and these helped him win the throne which he held until his death in 1153, but they became a powerful body who tried to control the Scottish monarchs for 400 years. Two of the most powerful were Robert Brus, to whom David gave 200,000 acres in Annandale and from whom descended the great king, Robert the Bruce; and Walter Fitzalan, who David made High Steward of Scotland with responsibility for managing the royal finances and from whom descended the Stuart monarchy.

King Henry made the Earl of Buckingham Marshal of England and he led the king's army at the Battle of Brenneville in 1119 where he defeated Henry's brother Robert. Henry died in 1135 and appointed as his successor his daughter, the Empress Matilda, who had married Geoffrey, Count of Anjou. However, her succession was contested by Stephen du Blois, who was also a grandson of the Conqueror and who had married Matilda, the daughter of the Count of Boulogne and of Mary, King David's sister. Stephen was crowned king in December 1135 and the resulting civil war lasted from 1135 to 1151.

The Empress was supported by the Anglo-Normans, mostly from the west of England, and their leader was her illegitimate brother, Richard of Gloucester. Stephen was supported by the Anglo-Flemings who had their estates mainly in the east of the country. King David was torn between the two parties as he had pledged his allegiance to the Empress but he had married into the Flemish dynasty on whom he relied for his military support. When Stephen was crowned in 1135, David ignored the advice of his Anglo-Fleming barons and declared war on him. The conduct of the Scottish army as it moved into England in 1137 was brutal. A contemporary chronicler, Richard of Hexham, tells of:

> an execrable army, more atrocious than the pagans, neither fearing God nor regarding man, spread desolation over the whole province and slaughtered everywhere people of either sex, of every age and rank, destroying, pillaging and burning towns, churches and houses. Then

they carried off, like so much booty, the noble matrons and chaste virgins, together with other women. These naked, fettered, herded together; by whips and thongs they drove before them, goading them with their spears and other weapons. For the sick on their couches, women pregnant and in childbed, infants in the womb, innocents at the breast, or on the mother's knee, with the mothers themselves, decrepit old men and worn-out old women, and persons debilitated from whatever cause, wherever they met with them, they put to the edge of the sword, and transfixed with their spears; and by how much more horrible a death they could dispatch them, so much the more did they rejoice.

The Scots took Northumberland and were confronted by the English in Yorkshire. The Flemish barons feared the impending battle and Platts writes of the impassioned speech that Robert Brus made to David:

I am here, O king, your faithful liege to offer you coun-sel…It is unwise, O king, at the start of such great matters as this, not to look forward to their likely outcome… Against whom are you taking up arms today?…assuredly against the English and the Normans. O king, will you not also come upon those who…have always offered you wise counsel and prompt help? From whom, my lord, you have been given such loyal support in Scotland that you have been freed from anxiety about the English, been given help in keeping away the Normans, and even been preserved from troublesome Scots.

David ignored his pleas and Brus's worst fears were realised as the Battle of the Standard resulted in the complete defeat of the

Scottish army. A treaty was signed which confirmed Prince Henry, David's son, as Earl of Northumberland and Earl of Huntingdon, but he had to perform homage for his English lands, and David had to promise to remain loyal to Stephen at all times. In order to cement the relationship, Stephen gave Ada de Warenne in marriage to Prince Henry; Ada was the daughter of William de Warenne, 2nd Earl of Surrey, and was distantly related to the Giffards through her great-grandmother Beatrice, whose sister Aveline had married Osbern de Bolebec.

The civil war continued in England and the fighting was extremely fierce, especially in the southern counties. Families were often split in their loyalty or were uncertain about who to support and many left England or sent their sons away for safety. It is well known that William and Hugh Giffard and William de Haya were the founders of their respective lines in Scotland and hence the ancestors of the Lords of Yester but what is not yet certain are the origins of these three young men. In the section below I attempt to establish such origins and thus, for the sake of greater certainty, go further into the genealogy than the average reader might feel warranted but I hope the journey can be justified.

Walter Giffard, Earl of Buckingham, supported Stephen but left for France to secure his estates there. He only returned after peace was declared and founded the Augustinian Abbey of Notley in Long Crendon in 1162, where he was buried in 1164. His only child William predeceased him and so his title and estates were granted to his great nephew Richard de Clare, Earl of Pembroke. Elias Giffard, 2nd - Lord of Brimpsfield, was thus the head of the Giffards who remained in England and was called one of the Empress's 'leading Partisans'.

However, the family may have been split in their loyalties and his brother Gilbert may have supported Stephen and, because of this, may have sent his two sons, Hugh and William, both born between 1125 and 1129, to Prince Henry's and Ada's court in Lincolnshire in the 1140s for their safety. The Giffards would have been known to Ada because Rohaise Giffard's son, Robert FitzRichard, had married King David's stepdaughter and Rohaise's brother, William Bishop of Winchester, had been a religious adviser to King David.

A descendant of Eudo de la Haye, William de Haya, was also at Ada's court. Eudo had married Muriel de Conteville, the sister of the Count of Mortaigne, one of the most powerful of the Anglo-Flemings. Eudo died in 1098, leaving a daughter, also Muriel. Eudo's brother Ranulf was Steward to Mortaigne and he married Olivia, daughter of William d'Albini, Cup Bearer to the Conqueror. Ranulf was killed on the First Crusade in 1099 leaving one son, Robert (1075–1154), who inherited as Baron de la Haye from his uncle Eudo and whose daughter, Muriel, he married and they had four sons, Richard, Ralph, William and Hugh.

Richard (1116–1169) was appointed Constable of Lincoln by Henry II and he was the founder of Barlings Abbey in Lincolnshire and Cammeringham Priory in Norfolk. He married a Norman heiress, Matilda de Vernon, who brought to him the title of Constable of Normandy. They had no son so their eldest daughter, Gillette, passed the Barony of La Haye-du-Puits and the office of Constable to Richard de Hommet on their marriage. His brother Ralph fought in France for Stephen but in 1141 Matilda's husband Geoffrey D'Anjou besieged it and Ralph was forced to give himself up with 'a saddle on his back'. His subsequent history is unknown. His brother William de Haya (1120-1172) was probably named after his grandfather, William d'Albini, and it is he who was serving at Ada's court.

Anthony Wagner, *Richmond Herald*, supports this theory. Writing in 1955 he points out that there were numerous Hays in Normandy, and in the department of La Manche there was a village called La Haye Hue, from where he suggests William came. As evidence he points to the seal of David de Haya of Erroll, who died in 1201, showing *Argent three escutcheons Gules* (three red shields on a white background). He says the 14th century French Roll of Arms assigns the same arms to Jean de la Haye Hue and shows how this device was carried by other de la Hayes into the 15th century. He traces the line of these back to Hugh de la Haye who he says, in my view mistakenly, was William's uncle, instead of, as I believe, his brother. William's wider family were strong supporters of Stephen: his uncle Robert FitzRichard was Stephen's Steward and his cousin, William d'Albini, had been made Earl of Lincoln by Stephen.

Ada took for their safety a number of young Anglo-Flemings and Normans to her husband's court at Haddington in Scotland in about 1150. These included William de Haya, Hugh Giffard and his brother William, who had gained the position of *clericus* in Ada's court. Charles-Edwards supports this, writing: 'The Scots Giffards carried *gules, three bars ermine* and probably arrived in Scotland between 1150 and 1160,' and he points out that this device was similar to that of the Brimpsfield Giffards.

Ada transformed the lives of those she brought to Scotland as she helped them reach important positions. William de la Haya married Juliana de Soulis, niece of Randolph, Lord of Liddesdale, who was King David's Cup Bearer, the first Anglo-Fleming to hold that office. He was likely to have known William's family as his estates had bordered those of the de la Hayes at La Haye-du-Puits. He built Liddel Castle at the junction of the Liddel and Esk rivers, which became one of the most fought-over border areas for the next 350 years. Hugh Giffard settled in East Lothian and married the daughter of Herbert, Chamberlain to King David, who was responsible for overseeing the king's finances; and his brother, William Giffard, continued to serve Ada as *clericus*.

Stephen agreed to accept Matilda's son Henry as his heir

and he became King of England when Stephen died in 1154. He was the first of the Plantagenet kings and he married Eleanor of Aquitaine but spent most of his reign trying to control his family and his Angevin Empire, which covered most of Western Europe.

King David's son Henry predeceased him in 1152, aged only 38, leaving seven children, two of whom were to become kings: Malcolm IV (1129-1165) in 1153 and William the Lion (1143-1214). David himself died in 1153 and de Soulis continued as Cup Bearer to both King Malcolm and William, but he was killed by the English in 1171. His nephew by marriage, William de Haya, inherited his position as Cup Bearer to King William but he died only a year later, and his son, also William, assumed his office, aged 41. His was not a major position but it and other such offices of court gave their holders influence beyond the duties implied by their titles, as they became close confidants and advisors to the monarch. The royal court was highly mobile and its officials accompanied the monarch wherever he went, including into battle.

Hugh Giffard was also becoming more powerful at court and he was knighted. Between 1155 and 1190 he witnessed many Acts and Charters for Kings Malcolm and William, and for Ada de Warrene. A charter signed by Malcolm IV, Ada and Herbert granted Hugh the lands of 'Jhestrith [Yester] by its right marches and that part of Lafditune which Edolf, the son of Ginel held, and the land of the moor of Hadingtun by the marches... and a full toft of Linliqu and Berewaldeston which Herbert the Chamberlain gave to him with his daughter... to be held as freely, and quietly, fully and honourably.' King William confirmed this grant of Yester in 1166 and the wording of the conditions was subtly changed to 'to be held as freely, and quietly, fully and honourably as any other knight holds' and Hugh had to commit a knight's service and pay the king £1,000 a year; he also received lands in West Lothian and in Lincolnshire. The lands of Yester, Linlithgow and Lethington were all close to Haddington where Ada continued to live after Prince Henry's death and which had been created a royal borough. Hugh chose to live at Lethington, which stands just outside the boundaries of Haddington and is now known as Lennoxlove and is the seat of the Dukes of Hamilton.

Eleanor of Aquitaine and three of her sons rebelled against King Henry in 1173 and he left England to fight them in France. William the Lion saw this as his opportunity to regain Northumberland and Sir Hugh Giffard and William de Haya joined his army which marched into England. King William tried to take Newcastle but found it too strongly defended, so he split his forces into three groups to take the castles of Alnwick, Prudhoe and Warkworth simultaneously, believing that the English army at Newcastle was too far away to threaten him. However, a party of 400 English knights set out from Newcastle and reached Alnwick shortly after dawn. There they found William protected by only a small bodyguard and he was captured. The English also captured Scotland's five strongest castles, Roxburgh, Berwick, Jedburgh, Edinburgh and Stirling and King William was taken to Henry in Normandy. There he swore an oath of allegiance to Henry and agreed to the continued garrisoning of the captured Scottish castles by English soldiers at Scottish expense. He also had to surrender Scottish land holdings in England and, to secure his release, he had to provide hostages to Henry to guarantee the terms of the treaty. These included his brother David, Sir Hugh Giffard, William de Haya and eighteen other Scottish earls and barons. The condition for their release was that each had to provide a legitimate son as a hostage who was to be held until all terms of the treaty had been met.

As a result Sir Hugh had to forfeit his Lincolnshire estates but King William compensated him by granting him the lands of Fintry, north of Glasgow. On his release, he returned to live at Lethington, which remained a Giffard property until it was sold to the Maitland family in 1345. Sir Hugh had his own Sheriff during this period called Alexander de Saint Martin, who was another of the Anglo-Flemings brought to Scotland by Ada. The Sheriffs dealt with the administration, finance and military affairs of local government and held courts to which all tenants-in-chief could be summoned. Saint Martin owned land at Duncanlaw, which adjoined Giffard's lands at Yester and 150 years later their respective descendants, Sir John Giffard and Euphemia Morham, would marry.

Sir Hugh died in 1195 and was succeeded by his son William who was also knighted and given lands by King William in 1196. These stretched from the Firth of Forth to Aberdeen and included Kincardine, Pollgawie, Forres, and Kintore; that most of these were on the east coast shows how important the role of the knights were in countering Viking invasions. Sir William was sent to London in 1200 as an envoy of the king to arrange a meeting with King John of England, where he was accompanied by the Abbot of Arbroath and William Comyn, Earl of Buchan and Justiciar of Scotia, the most senior royal officer in the Kingdom. The Comyns were one of the dominant Anglo-Norman families in Scotland.

Sir William's Brimpsfield English relations did not have a good relationship with King John as Elias, 4th Lord Brimpsfield, and his brother Osbert fought against him in the First Barons' War in 1216. Their animosity may have been caused by King John having an illegitimate child, Osbert, by Mathilda Giffard, the daughter of Elias's uncle, Richard, who had been Justiciar to Henry II. Elias and Osbert were taken prisoner and John seized Brimpsfield Castle. He sequestered their estates and Elias and Osbert were both excommunicated. However John's death in 1216 changed their fortunes and they swore allegiance to the new King Henry III and had their estates returned.

When William de Haya was released from captivity in 1174, he married Eva de Pitmilly, the Celtic heiress of lands in Fife. King

Henry II confirmed his ownership of this estate 'with all the privileges competent to a barony' and he was also given the lands of Lochloy by King William. De Haya and Eva had six sons, all of whom went on the Third Crusade in 1189 led by Richard I and King William, where all but two were killed. The survivors were the eldest, David (1162–1241), from whom descended the Earls of Erroll, and Robert (1165–1240), from whom descended the Marquises of Tweeddale. Each adopted his own heraldic device: David's was *Argent three escutcheons Gules* (three red shields on a white background) and Robert's was *Azure three inescutcheons Argent* (three white shields on a blue background).

David married Ethna, the daughter of the 3rd Earl of Strathearn, and was appointed Sheriff of Forfar from 1211 to1214. Little is known of Robert but his son, John (1200-1262), married Margaret, daughter of Robert de Lyne, who brought to her husband the estate of Locherworth in Midlothian. John was knighted and his descendants lived in Locherworth Castle until they moved to Neidpath Castle in 1335.

King William's son inherited in 1214 as King Alexander II but he was effectively the vassal of the king of England. However, the peace with England enabled him to focus on securing his kingdom both from the Vikings and from the rebellious magnates in the Highlands. This he did with the help of the barons whose relative strength is shown by the fact that, of the 120 castles built in Scotland in this period, only 30 were regal; all the others were built by the barons.

Sir William Giffard died in 1215, leaving two sons, Sir John and William. Little is known of either of them except that in 1225 William was given 'Nether Yestred by Thomas de Yestred'. Sir John died in 1225 and his son Hugh, who inherited aged only five, became the most famous of the Giffard Lords of Yester. He has been described as a wizard, a necromancer and a magician, and legends tell of his ability to exercise magic powers, including raising a ghostly army through his pact with the Devil.

Hugh was knighted and he built Yester Castle ten miles from Lethington. It was completed by 1267 and was one of the earliest castles built by an Anglo-Norman baron. King Alexander III stayed there in May 1278, from where he wrote a letter to King Edward I of England. The castle stands on a natural defensive position on a curved, steep-sided peninsula between two burns, one called the Hopes Water to the east and the other called Newland to the west. A ditch 50 feet across and 20 feet deep was cut from one burn to the other creating a three-sided moat. The upper part of the castle, which was rebuilt and extended in the 14th century, now lies in ruins, but its extent can be seen from the height and width of the parts of the walls still standing. It contained a tall tower, beneath which lies the famous Goblin Hall, which is entered through a small door hidden in the castle's mound. A long arched tunnel containing a flight of 24 steps descends to the Hall which is 37 feet long, 13 feet wide, and rises 19 feet to a beautiful Gothic-arched vaulted roof. It is a wonderful room, unique in Scotland and astonishingly well preserved. It originally held two floors, each with its own arched entrance at the south end, and the top floor contained a fireplace at the north end. From the Hall another stairway of 36 steps descends to the Hopes Water.

Sir Hugh and the castle were immortalised by Sir Walter Scott in his poem *Marmion*. In Canto III he describes Sir Hugh being summoned by King Alexander to join in the battle against Haco of Norway who invaded Scotland in 1263.

> A clerk could tell what years have flown
> Since Alexander filled our throne,
> Third monarch of that warlike name,
> And eke the time when here he came
> To seek Sir Hugo, then our lord;
> A braver never drew a sword;

A wiser never, at the hour
Of midnight, spoke the word of power:
The same, whom ancient records call
The founder of the Goblin Hall.
I would, Sir Knight, your longer stay
Gave you that cavern to survey.
Of lofty roof, and ample size,
Beneath the castle deep it lies:
To hew the living rock profound,
The floor to pave, the arch to round,
There never toiled a mortal arm
It all was wrought by word and charm;
And I have heard my grandsire say,
That the wild clamour and affray
Of those dread artisans of hell,
Who laboured under Hugo's spell,
Sounded as loud as ocean's war
Among the caverns of Dunbar.

The king Lord Gifford's castle sought,
Deep labouring with uncertain thought:
Even then he mustered all his host,
To meet upon the western coast:
For Norse and Danish galleys plied
Their oars within the firth of Clyde.
There floated Haco's banner trim,
Above Norwayan warriors grim,
Savage of heart, and large of limb;
Threatening both continent and isle,
Bute, Arran, Cunninghame, and Kyle.
Lord Gifford, deep beneath the ground,
Heard Alexander's bugle sound,
And tarried not his garb to change,

But, in his wizard habit strange,
Came forth – a quaint and fearful sight:
His mantle lined with fox-skins white;
His high and wrinkled forehead bore
A pointed cap, such as of yore
Clerks say that Pharaoh's Magi wore:
His shoes were marked with cross and spell,
Upon his breast a pentacle;
His zone, of virgin parchment thin,
Or, as some tell, of dead man's skin,
Bore many a planetary sign,
Combust, and retrograde, and trine;
And in his hand he held prepared
A naked sword without a guard.

Sir Hugh is supposed to have picked a wild pear off a tree on the way to St Cuthbert's church and given it to his daughter Marion as a dowry on her marriage to Sir David Broun of Colstoun. He told her that as long as the pear was undamaged the owners of Colstoun would flourish. In 1966 Marion's descendant, Lady Broun-Lindsay, showed me the pear which was shrivelled yet well preserved, but it bore the teeth marks where Sir George Colstoun's wife had bitten it in 1692, triggering the curse. Sir George was a gambler and he soon suffered large losses and had to be bought out by his brother, Robert. Later, in 1703, when Robert was driving with his family, he tried to ford the swollen Colstoun Water but their carriage overturned and Robert and his two sons were drowned. From that time there were no direct male heir until Lady Edith's husband, Sir Colin, was born in 1926. A family tradition of the Hays holds that Sir Hugo also laid a curse that any of his descendants who dug at Yester Castle for treasure would die and George, Earl of Gifford was fatally injured when excavating the ruins to open the stairway to the

34

Goblin Hall in 1862.

Sir Hugh played an increasingly important role in Scottish government. During the minority of the young King Alexander III and his wife Margaret, daughter of King Henry III of England, a Council of Regents had proposed to manage the government and act as guardians for the young couple. The first Council was lead by members of the Comyn family and included Gamelin, Bishop of St. Andrews. King Henry favoured an alternative group which included Robert Brus, Lord of Annandale (the grandfather of the future King Robert the Bruce); the earls of Carrick, Fife, Strathern, and Dunbar; the bishops of Dunkeld and Aberdeen; Gilbert de Haya of Erroll (despite his being married to William Comyn's daughter, Idonea); and Sir Hugh. Henry called this group his 'beloved friends' and gave them his protection and support. In 1255 they were appointed Regents for seven years by Alexander and Sir Hugh was issued letters of protection by Henry; we can assume the same protection was granted to all the other Regents.

The following year, Gamelin went to Rome to meet Pope Alexander IV and asked him to excommunicate the new Regents, which the pope did in 1257. William Comyn immediately seized the young king and forced him to depose the Regents. To avoid civil war, a compromise Regency was formed in 1258 controlled by Comyn, but it excluded Sir Hugh and ten of his former colleagues. He turned instead to improving his estate and, in 1265, his neighbour Adam de Morham gave him and 'his heirs at Nether Yester for the formation of his park all the side of my wood which is beside the Castle of Yester with the land and all contained therein... as the formation of the said park is designed by the said Sir Hugh... namely from the ford of the burn called Yester... as it descends towards Duncanlaw.' Sir Hugh died in 1280 and left three children: Sir John, Margaret, who married Adam de Seton, who was a Master Clerk for Alexander III, and Marion Broun.

The Viking threat was finally resolved when Alexander defeated King Haakon of Norway at the battle of the Largs in 1263, after which Haakon died. By the Treaty of Perth in 1266 his heir, King Magnus, ceded all his lands in Scotland to Alexander, save for Orkney and Shetland. Alexander's two sons both died young and their only daughter, Margaret, married Magnus's son Eric. Alexander's queen died in 1274 and her daughter followed her in 1283, giving birth to her only child, who was also named Margaret and who became known as the Maid of Norway. The Maid's father Eric then married Isabella, sister of Robert the Bruce. This complicated series of marriages, births and deaths had dramatic consequences for Scotland.

Alexander III did not mourn the death of his queen for long. *The Lanercost Chronicle* tells how 'he used never to forbear on account of season nor storm, nor for perils of flood or rocky cliffs, but would visit none too creditably nuns or matrons, virgins or widows as the fancy seized him, sometimes in disguise.' The Scottish Parliament recognised the Maid of Norway as his heir in 1284. Alexander then fell in love with Yolande de Dreux, a 22-year-old lady of the French Capetian dynasty, and married her in October 1285. In March 1286 he was at Edinburgh Castle for a meeting with his advisors, but did not want to stay the night as he wanted to see Yolande, who had just become pregnant and whose birthday was the next day. He was advised by his nobles not to make the journey across the Firth of Forth to Fife because the weather was so bad but he ignored them and rode into the night. He became separated from his men and was found dead on the southern shore the following morning. Yolande suffered a miscarriage and the Maid of Norway became Queen of Scotland at the age of three. Alexander's death and the subsequent period of instability in Scotland were lamented in an early Scots poem recorded by Andrew of Wyntoun in his *Orygynale Cronykil of Scotland:*

Quhen Alysandyr oure kyng was dede,
That Scotland led in luve and le,
Away wassons of ale and brede,
Of wyne and wax of gamyn and glee.
Oure gold was changed into lede,
Cryst, born into vyrgynyte,
Succoure Scotland and remede,
That stat is in perplexyed.

Sir Hugh Giffard's fame in Scotland was surpassed only by those of his relations living in England. It is worth a detour to examine these as they demonstrate both the heights that the Giffards reached in England but, more tellingly, the fate of those who would not accept the rule of their monarch. In all the annals of the direct lines of the Giffards and Hays of Yester only one senior member fought against his monarch and he was John Giffard, 2nd Lord Giffard.

His father, Sir John Giffard, was the son of Elias, 4th Lord of Brimpsfield and he was born in 1232 at Brimpsfield Castle. Between 1257 and 1299 he was in continuous military service and was described as being both valiant and prudent. He joined Simon de Montfort in his revolt against King Henry III in the second Barons' War and he led the forces that took Gloucester in 1264, where Henry's son, Prince Edward, negotiated a truce. However Edward reneged and Sir John retaliated by capturing Warwick Castle. In 1265 he and de Montfort quarrelled and Sir John joined Edward's forces and led the attack on de Montfort at Monmouth Castle. At the subsequent battle of Evesham, de Montfort was killed and King Henry pardoned Sir John for all his offences and made him 1st Lord Giffard. He was later ordered to capture Llywelyn, the last Prince of an independent Wales, and in 1282 he sent Llywelyn's head to the king. He died in 1299, leaving four daughters and one son.

It was this son, John 2nd Lord Giffard, who was to be the last of the Brimpsfield Giffards. He was born in 1287 and in 1323 he married Aveline, granddaughter of Sir Hugh Despense, Justiciar of England. He had been taken prisoner at Bannockburn in 1314 but was soon released and made keeper of the estate of the Earl of Gloucester, who had been killed in the battle. Giffard then joined the Earl of Lancaster who led the western barons in revolt against King Edward II in 1321. Edward ordered Giffard's Brimpsfield Castle to be demolished and he attacked the king's retinue in revenge. Lancaster's forces were defeated in 1322 and Lancaster was immediately executed. Giffard was captured and taken to Gloucester where he was condemned and hanged on gallows outside the city walls. He was then decapitated and his body quartered. His remains lie in Boyton church in Wiltshire and he was survived by his four half-sisters. Edward III gave the Giffard estates to Sir John Maltravers, one of the men who had killed Edward II.

Another line of the Giffards in England achieved much greater prominence but also produced no male heirs. Sir Hugh Giffard, Lord of Boyton, the third son of Elias 2nd Lord of Brimpsfield was born in 1185 and lived in Boyton Castle. Sir Hugh was appointed Constable of the Tower of London in 1236 and three years later he was made guardian to Prince Edward while his father Henry III was fighting in France. Sir Hugh married Sybil de Corneilles and she took over the responsibility of looking after the royal children when Sir Hugh died in 1248. They had two sons, Walter and Godfrey and a daughter, Agatha, who became the Prioress of Elstow Abbey and Abbess of Shaftesbury Abbey.

Walter was born in 1225 and studied at both Cambridge and Oxford Universities. He took holy orders and became Archdeacon of Wells and a papal chaplain. He was elected Bishop of Bath and Wells in 1264 and, as the Archbishop of Canterbury, Boniface of Savoy, was in France, Walter travelled to Paris to be consecrated at Notre-Dame. The service was performed by the Bishop of Hereford, with Walter having first sworn that he would support King Henry, who was facing de Montfort's rebellion. The barons were angered that Walter had gone abroad against their wishes and, when he made his pledge, they ravaged his estates. After the Battle of Evesham, Henry made Walter Lord Chancellor and in 1266 he was appointed Archbishop of York. He resigned as Lord Chancellor and Henry appointed Walter's younger brother Godfrey in his place and Prince Edward appointed Walter as one of the tutors to his sons. When Henry died in 1272, Walter was appointed First Lord of the Council and, with Sir Roger Mortimer, was appointed to govern England until Edward returned from France. Walter died at York in 1279 and he was buried in York Minster.

His brother Godfrey had been born in 1235. He was Lord Chancellor from 1266 to 1268, when he was appointed Bishop of Worcester, a position he held for 33 years. He was one of the four men chosen by King Edward to negotiate the marriage of his son to the Maid of Norway. Godfrey died in 1302 and was buried in Worcester Cathedral. Neither Walter nor Godfrey had children and thus the death of John 2nd Lord Giffard ended the main Giffard line in England. Only three decades later the same fate overtook the Giffard line in Scotland.

Chapter 3 – Robert the Bruce

Sir William de Haya of Locherworth and Nicolas de Haya of Erroll sat in the Parliament at Brigham in July 1290. Sir William was one of the two representatives of the county of Edinburgh and he had succeeded his father Sir John in 1262 aged 32. Parliament ratified the Treaty of Salisbury which proposed that the Maid of Norway should marry Prince Edward of England; but the Maid died in October and fourteen individuals then claimed the Scottish throne. These included John Balliol, Nicholas de Soulis and Robert Bruce 5th Earl of Annandale, who nominated Sir William to represent his claim.

Edward set up the Assembly of Norham, a Court of 104 nobles, 24 chosen by him, and 40 each by Annandale and Balliol, to judge between the claimants in the formal contest for the crown in November 1292. The Assembly included the 1st Lord Giffard of Brimpsfield, Sir John Giffard of Yester, Sir William de Haya, Nicolas de Haya of Erroll and his son Gilbert de Haya, all of whom, save Lord Giffard, supported Annandale, but the Court chose Balliol. Edward accepted this but quickly sought to undermine Balliol's position by treating Scotland as a feudal vassal state, demanding that Balliol pay homage to him and join the war against France. Balliol was unable to stand up against him and a Council of Twelve was appointed to act as his advisers. One of these was John Comyn, Earl of Buchan and Constable of Scotland, the cousin of John Comyn, Lord of Badenoch and the father-in-law of Gilbert de Haya. The Council made a treaty with France in 1295 and Edward immediately invaded Scotland, taking Berwick in March 1296, slaughtering thousands of its inhabitants and imprisoning the garrison commander, Sir William Douglas. Balliol renounced his homage and refused to meet Edward, who retorted, 'O foolish knave! What folly he commits. If he will not come to us we will go to him.'

The Comyns responded by attacking Carlisle, which was defended for Edward by Annandale's son, Robert Bruce, Earl of Carrick. The attack failed and the Comyns joined the main Scottish army at Haddington. Edward ordered John de Warenne, 6th Earl of Surrey and John Balliol's father-in-law, to attack the Earl of March's castle at Dunbar, a few miles from Haddington. March supported the English but his wife, Marjory Comyn, Buchan's sister, had refused to surrender the castle. Balliol, who was at Haddington, sent part of his army to support the garrison but did not march with them. At the battle of Dunbar in April the Scots were easily defeated and many of their nobles were captured and imprisoned, including Sir John Giffard, Sir William de Haya and his cousin Gilbert de Haya. Sir William's lands were forfeited and he was imprisoned at Berkhampsted Castle, the Earl of Cornwall's castle in Hertfordshire. None of the captives were released until they had agreed to sign the Ragman Rolls pledging loyalty to Edward; there were 11 Hays who signed these. Sir William was released and his lands at Locherworth were restored in 1297, on the condition that he accompanied Edward and his army to Flanders and that the Earl of Atholl stood surety for him.

The spirit of the Scots was broken by their defeats at Berwick and Dunbar. Roxburgh and Stirling castles were surrendered without a fight and Edinburgh Castle resisted for only a week.

Balliol fled north, confessed to rebellion, prayed for forgiveness and abdicated and Edward returned to England, taking with him the Stone of Scone. The treaty with the French was abrogated and Balliol and his son Edward were sent to France, where Balliol died in 1314. Edward appointed a group of English nobles to run Scotland under the Earl of Surrey, who was made Governor, and Hugh Cressingham, who became Treasurer.

It was the Scottish people themselves who resolved to take revenge on the English as their nobles had failed them and many were still in prison. A new champion was needed and William Wallace emerged as that leader. He had strong support from Andrew Moray, Badenoch's nephew, who had escaped from the Tower in 1297, and they retook northern Scotland from Edward in the name of King John Balliol. Sir William Douglas, who had been freed from imprisonment at Berwick, was summoned to London to join Edward on an expedition against the French, but he joined Wallace instead, as did James the Steward. The rebels seized the English treasury at Scone and this helped them raise the army that defeated Surrey and Cressingham at Stirling Bridge in September 1297. Cressingham was killed and it is said that Wallace flayed his skin and wrapped it round the handle of his sword.

After the battle, Moray and Wallace assumed the titles of Guardians of Scotland but Moray died soon after from his wounds. Edward ordered Robert Bruce, Earl of Carrick, still governor of Carlisle, to march against Wallace but Bruce, who was only 22, refused and joined the rebels, saying: 'I must join my own people and the nation in which I was born.' However he, and a number of other barons who had supported the rebels, reached agreement with Edward soon after and in 1298 Wallace was defeated at Falkirk, where it was considered that the Comyns, who commanded the Scottish cavalry, had failed to give Wallace full support. The English then invaded Scotland and Wallace resigned as Guardian in favour of Bruce and Badenoch. Badenoch was the principal supporter of Balliol, thus the Guardians were not natural allies, and they soon fell out.

Sir William de Soulis, 7th Lord Liddesdale, the son of Margaret Comyn, Buchan's daughter, was appointed sole Guardian in 1301 and he tried to bring back Balliol as king. Wallace was betrayed to the English by a Scottish knight in 1305 and he was tried for treason in Westminster Hall. Found guilty, he was stripped naked and dragged through the city by a horse to Smithfield where he was hanged, drawn, castrated and had his bowels burnt in front of him. He was then quartered and beheaded, and his head put on a spike on London Bridge.

These events had effects that significantly increased the wealth and power of the Giffards. Sir John Giffard's son, also John, married Euphemia Morham, who was the granddaughter of the Adam de Morham who had given the Giffards his lands near Yester in 1265. Euphemia was a very wealthy heiress as she was the sole surviving child of Sir Thomas Morham. The story of the Morhams shows how Scottish families were torn between loyalty to the Scottish or to the English kings over this period.

Sir Thomas Morham, Baron of Dunipace, was a Scottish patriot who was betrayed to the English in 1297 and sent to the Tower of London. His eldest son, Thomas II, served in the English army from 1296 until he was killed in 1317. His second son, Herbert, took after his father and fought for Balliol at Dunbar in 1296, where he was one of the many Scottish nobles captured. He was imprisoned in Nottingham, released in 1297, agreed to serve the English and, like his brother, was knighted after Falkirk. The circumstance of these two brothers serving the English and their father's betrayal in 1297 may not be coincidental.

When he was serving in Edinburgh castle in 1298, Herbert kidnapped the young widow Johanna de Clare, Countess of Fife, as she rode from Edinburgh to Stirling on her way to England. He said he wanted to marry her; he seized all her jewels, robes and horses and took her to his brother's house. Unfortunately for him, she had been riding under the full protection of King Edward because her husband, Duncan MacDuff, Earl of Fife, who had been appointed one of the six Regents of Scotland in 1286, had been murdered in 1288 by Sir Walter Percy. Her father, Gilbert de Clare, Earl of Gloucester, was a favourite of Edward, who had appointed him joint Guardian of England and had married him to his daughter, Joan of Acre. Edward was therefore furious at Johanna's abduction and ordered Herbert to stand trial but he fled from Edinburgh, abandoned Johanna and kept her valuables. He joined Robert Bruce, helped him capture Stirling Castle in 1299 and commanded the Scottish army with Sir Simon Fraser in a failed attempt to recapture Bothwell Castle. He was captured in 1303, imprisoned with his father and in 1306 he was beheaded. Herbert's father died in 1314 and Euphemia inherited all the Morham estates, much of which lay close to Yester.

The de Hayas also benefited from the misfortune of the Frasers during these troubled times. Sir William died in 1308 and his son, Sir Gilbert, inherited aged 43. In 1312 he married Margaret Fraser, daughter of Sir Simon Fraser, from whom, as part of his marriage settlement, he gained considerable lands in the county of Peebles, including Neidpath and Oliver Castles. Sir Gilbert quartered the Fraser arms with his own in recognition of the importance of this. He had signed the Ragman Rolls in 1296 and had been rewarded by Edward by being made Forrester of Awne in Argyll and Boyne in East Lothian. He was also given a large estate in Banff in Aberdeenshire.

Fraser had served under Edward I during the seige of Caerlaverock Castle in 1300 but there he stole Edward's horses and armour and became one of his greatest adversaries. He and Badenoch lead the army that defeated the English at Roslin in 1303, supported by Gilbert de Haya of Erroll. In retaliation, Edward burnt Fraser's castle at Neidpath and ravaged Gilbert's lands and sent a team of English knights to capture the rebels. Fraser escaped but he was later captured near Stirling in 1306 and taken to the Tower where, on the same day that Herbert Morham was executed, Fraser was castrated, hung, drawn and quartered and had his head placed on a spike next to Wallace's.

When it became clear that Balliol would not leave France to recover his crown, Bruce became the favoured choice to succeed as king. It is said that Badenoch had agreed to support Bruce in his claim to the throne in exchange for land but in 1306 Bruce met him at the Church of Greyfriars in Dumfries, accused him of treachery and killed him. Bruce was swiftly crowned as King Robert at Scone by Isabella MacDuff, Buchan's wife and the daughter of the Earl of Fife, who held the traditional right of crowning the kings of Scotland. Edward sent an army against him led by Aymer de Valence and, at the battle of Methven, Robert's army was routed. He escaped and was taken north by a group of friends, including Gilbert de Haya of Erroll. The English captured Yester Castle and it was garrisoned by Adam de Welle, Constable of Rockingham Castle.

A neighbour of Sir John Giffard was James Douglas the Good, who had been the signatory of a number of charters granting land to Giffard. He was the eldest son of Sir William Douglas, Wallace's supporter, who had died in the Tower of London. His lands had not been restord by Edward so in 1306 James offered his services to Robert and became his greatest general, being both a ruthless soldier and a brilliant guerrilla tactician. This was evident in his treatment of the English garrison holding his own Douglas Castle which he attacked as they attended the local church on Palm Sunday 1307. He executed all the prisoners, threw their bodies on empty wine casks, set them alight and poisoned the wells with their dead horses.

This showed how vulnerable were the garrisons of the castles held by the English. They typically were comprised of no more than 150 men and depended entirely on receiving supplies from the local area. They were usually far from any supporting forces and communications were poor. They were, however, the only way the English could maintain consistent control of the key border areas of Scotland, so when they fell the only way of regaining control was by large and costly invasions.

In 1307 Edward captured Robert's wife, daughter and sisters, and the Countess of Buchan, who was kept in a cage at Berwick Castle for over three years. This was Edward's last act against Robert, for he died in July and his son succeeded him as Edward II. Robert took advantage of this to regain his authority in Scotland and he destroyed Buchan's army at the battle of Inverurie in 1308 and then pursued Comyn supporters throughout Scotland; Buchan fled to England and by December he was dead.

Robert was now undisputed ruler of Scotland and in 1309 he held his first Parliament at St Andrews. He was lord of the royal states but the magnates held much more land than he did as king. There were 13 earldoms: Fife, Mar, Angus, Buchan, Strathearn, Atholl, Ross, Sutherland, Caithness, Menteith, Lennox, Carrick and March; and there were also three great lordships: his own of Annandale, the MacRuari's Garmoran and Balliol's Galloway. Royal justice was dispensed by the three Justiciars of Scotia, Lothian and Galloway and 28 sheriffs served under them. One tenth of the population were in some kind of clerical order, of which the most powerful were the Cistercians, with abbeys at Melrose, Arbroath, Paisley, Kelso and Holyrood. The Church was led by the two premier bishops of Glasgow and St. Andrews who, with all the other bishops, reported directly to the pope. The Church was, however, controlled by the king as he made all the clerical appointments. The knights were his key military personnel and they swore fealty and gave service to him in exchange for favours and protection.

Gilbert de Haya of Erroll was knighted, made High Constable of Scotland and given the lands of Slains in Buchan and its castle, which had previously been owned by his wife's brother, the Earl of Buchan. Over the next five years, Sir James Douglas and his principal lieutenant, Thomas Randolph, took all the main English-held castles: Linlithgow in 1310, Perth in 1312 and Stirling and Edinburgh in 1314. In 1311 they recaptured Yester Castle and killed de Welles, but Sir John Giffard decided to level the castle to prevent its reoccupation by the English.

Sir Thomas de Haya of Locherworth had succeeded his father Sir Gilbert in 1310 aged 25. He had been knighted by Edward in 1307 but he had joined Robert in 1308 and had his lands forfeited. These were assessed by a court in Edinburgh in 1311 as being worth £15,000[1] in times of peace and half that in time of war and they were given to Sir Robert Hasting, an English knight. In compensation, Thomas was given by Robert lands previously held by the Comyns in Perth. He married Lora, the daughter of Sir William de Cunningesburg, whose dowry included the estate of Tullibody near Stirling.

Edward invaded Scotland again in 1314, supported by a number of Robert's Scottish enemies, including Sir John Comyn of Badenoch, who wanted to avenge his father's murder. The armies met at Bannockburn near Stirling where the Scottish army of 8,000 included Sir Thomas de Haya, Gilbert the Constable and Sir John Giffard. Thomas Randolph, now Earl of Moray, commanded the vanguard, while Robert commanded the rearguard. Robert's brother, Edward, led the third division and the fourth was under the command of the newly knighted Sir James Douglas. The English army was routed and only two Scottish knights were killed. King Edward fled to Dunbar, whence he took a boat to England.

Robert had married Elizabeth de Burg, daughter of the Earl of Ulster in 1302 and he began to pursue his vision of a pan-Gaelic

[1] All monetary rates in this book are given in 2012 equivalent prices calculated by www.measuringworth.com.

Greater Scotia where his lineage would rule over both Ireland and Scotland. His brother Edward invaded Ireland in 1315 and the Irish crowned him as king but he failed to win over the non-Ulster chiefs and he was killed at the battle of Faughart in 1318.

The Declaration of Abroath in 1320, sent to the Pope, declared the independence of Scotland from English rule and the right of King Robert to rule. It declared they would always have a king 'because so long as a hundred of us remain alive we will never be the subject of the English'. It was signed by 38 lords, including the Earl of Moray and Gilbert the Constable.

Sir John Giffard II had inherited from his father in 1315 aged 25 and he restored the family's fortunes and rebuilt Yester Castle. His marriage to Euphemia Morham brought him closer to two of East Lothian's most powerful families, the Earls of Dunbar and the Randolphs, Earls of Moray. Patrick Dunbar, the 9th Earl of Dunbar, married Euphemia's stepsister, Agnes, and witnessed the marriage of Sir John and Euphemia. Euphemia's mother, Isabella, had married, secondly, Thomas Randolph, 1st Earl of Moray, by whom she had two sons and two daughters. Her youngest daughter, also Isabella, married John Dunbar, the nephew of the 9th Earl of Dunbar and they had two sons, one who inherited as 10th Earl of Dunbar and the other who was made 4th Earl of Moray. The Giffards benefitted from these close relationships with such powerful magnates and, as Dunbar was Warden of the East March, Sir John is likely to have treated Dunbar as his liege lord, being obliged to serve in arms under him. In 1322 King Robert granted Sir John and Euphemia her hereditary lands of Morham, Ducanlaw and Dunipace in a charter witnessed by Sir James Douglas, Sir Robert de Keith, Walter the Stewart of Scotland and other prominent Scots.

Sir John raised charters to two of the great Scottish border Abbeys. In the charter to Dryburgh Abbey, he pledged a yearly amount of silver from his village of Bothans that stood near Yester.

In the charter to Melrose Abbey, he states that for 'the weal of his soul and that of my wife Euphemia,' he confirms the original gift of his grandfather Sir Hugh Giffard 'to the House of Melrose, forever one toft and one croft in my town of Yester, and two ox-gangs (120 acres) of land in the tenement of the said town... they can keep six oxen and four cows with their calves of two years, sixty sheep and two horses during the whole year... they can grind freely at my mill... and they shall be first... whenever they come... paying nothing to anyone at anytime because of their prayers.' In a charter of 1327 he settled a long-lasting dispute with the Nuns of Haddington over access to the Nunnery by guaranteeing that he and his heirs would protect and give the nuns free access to the roads and paths leading to the Nunnery lands.

Euphemia may also have got close to her powerful neighbours, but in a different way. Her son Hugh was born in 1321, but Andrew MacEwen believes that she had another son, only not by Sir John. He writes: 'There is reason to believe that he [Hugh Giffard] was the uterine brother of Sir Archibald the Grim 3rd Earl of Douglas, both being sons of Euphemia,' and therefore fathered by their neighbour Sir James Douglas the Good. MacEwan continues: 'Euphemia probably died in 1330, leaving her son [Archibald] to be raised by his paternal uncle, Sir Archibald Douglas the Regent and his wife Beatrice Lindsay.' Sir John died in 1329 aged only 39 and the next year his son Hugh, aged nine, was married to Elizabeth Mure of Rowallan, aged eleven. The marriage was never consummated and Elizabeth later became the mistress and then the wife of the future King Robert II. Hugh was to be the last male Giffard of Yester.

Edward III abandoned any hope of retaking Berwick after he was almost killed by Sir James Douglas in 1327 at the battle of Stanhope Park in Durham. Under the Treaty of Northampton in 1328, he recognised Scotland as an independent kingdom and Robert as its king, but only a year later Robert died and Sir James

Douglas was killed in battle with the Moors in Granada on his way to place Robert's heart in the Church of the Holy Sepulchre in Jerusalem. David, Robert's surviving son, was only six when he became King David II and the magnates of Scotland took advantage of this to pursue their own ambitions. It soon became clear that the Douglases were by far the strongest of them all.

Chapter 4 – The Douglases

For any noble in Scotland, power and wealth came from two principal sources: warfare and land, and the gaining of land was both a result of and a precondition for success in warfare. For most of the 14th century, the war with England was principally fought in the Lowlands and Borders. At the beginning of the century, Edward II divided the English Borders into three Marches and Scotland followed in 1356 when the 1st Earl of Douglas was appointed Lord Warden General of all the Marches. Under him each March was given to one, and sometimes two, nobles to control as Warden, acting as the primary bulwark against the English. These nobles had to raise, maintain and pay for the soldiers serving under them, thus the support of the minor nobles and lairds in each region was crucial as they provided additional military service and men. In exchange, the Wardens gave their supporters grants of land, money and protection against anyone who tried to seize their lands.

The successes of Wallace and Sir James Douglas had shown that guerrilla tactics worked best against the English, but the Scots did not always pursue this form of warfare. From time to time they entered into major battles with the English and these generally resulted in disaster. In addition, the succession of kings who succeeded King Robert over the next two centuries did so as minors and their right to rule was as often challenged by their own magnates as they were by the English. During the 14th century the monarchy remained weak relative to the magnates and each monarch tried to play off one set of magnates against another. The positions of the magnates were well established as many held hereditary offices, known as regalities, such as Sheriffdoms, of which there were 28 throughout the kingdom. Their courts were more important than that of the king as they had the power to deal with all crimes except treason; and the fines resulting went to them as lord of the regality. The income and men-at-arms of the magnates were also increased by the feudal dues from their vassals and tenants.

In comparison, the position of the monarchy was not strong as it held few lands and taxation was seldom levied on a national level. This weakness forced the monarch to play off the rivalries of the great magnates and use the resulting alliances to strengthen his position. Parliament also reflected the ownership of land so, again, the monarch was in a weaker position than the magnates, the bishops and the abbots. However, the monarchy survived because it was a symbol of both permanence and continuity and the presence of a monarch served to prevent the absolute dominance of any one noble faction. The monarchy also represented the system of law and land tenure and it could gain support by creating new earldoms, as with those titles came lands and regalities. However from 1329 to 1603 the monarch was strong for only one third of those years, and between 1406 and 1603 six monarchs out of the seven who succeeded to the throne did so as minors.

Loyalties within Scotland changed frequently as each magnate and king sought to establish his authority through alliances formed to counter the power of the Douglases. The areas below the Forth and the Clyde were the focus of conflict between the Douglases and the monarchy but there was never any certainty as to the dominance of either side as the Douglases were themselves riven by internal conflict. We will focus principally on events in East Lothian and the border counties as the history of the de Hayas and the Giffards in this period can only be understood by the history of the various personalities who pursued their ambitions over these lands. Few Giffards or de Hayas achieved prominence at this time, but their choice of which magnate to support was absolutely crucial to their family's fortunes. That they prospered and emerged stronger from these turbulent times was a tribute to their sagacity, loyalty and courage. Of particular importance were relationships cemented by marriage, and it is significant that a member of both the de Haya and Giffard families married a daughter of a major Douglas noble early in the reign of King David II.

Euphemia Giffard's stepfather, the 1st Earl of Moray, was appointed Guardian to the young King David. The Treaty of Northampton of 1328 had brought to an end over thirty years of war between England and Scotland, but it also left a large group of nobles who had lost lands and influence because of their support of Balliol and the Comyns, who were known as the Disinherited. In the winter of 1331, Henry Beaumont, Earl of Buchan, who had fought against Bruce at Bannockburn and who had inherited John Comyn's title, encouraged Balliol's son, Edward, to leave France. He and Buchan gathered the Disinherited in an armada of 88 ships which sailed to Scotland in July 1332 after Moray's sudden death. They landed in Fife and were confronted near Perth by two Scottish armies. The Earl of Mar, the new Guardian, had taken up position to the north with a strong force on the heights of the Erroll-owned Dupplin Moor, and from the south an army commanded by Euphemia's stepbrother, the 9th Earl of Dunbar, was fast approaching.

Buchan launched a surprise night attack on Mar's army and destroyed it. Over 10,000 may have been killed including Mar; Robert Bruce's illegitimate son, Robert Lord of Liddesdale; the young Earl of Moray; Alexander Fraser, the High Chamberlain; Sir Robert Keith, the king's Marischal; and Sir Nicholas, eldest son of the Constable, Sir Gilbert. No Giffard or de Haya of Locherworth was killed as Hugh Giffard was only twelve and Sir Thomas de Haya was too old to fight. His 22-year-old son, William, had probably been with the Earl of Dunbar's army.

Sir Archibald Douglas, the half-brother of Sir James the Good, became Guardian jointly with Dunbar and they made a truce with Balliol, agreeing that Parliament should decide who the true king should be. This it did, and Balliol was crowned king at Scone. He returned the Disinherited their lands but he recognised who had really put him on the throne and acknowledged that Scotland had always been a fief of England. He promised Edward borderlands, including Berwick, and pledged to serve him for the rest of his life. However he never felt comfortable in his position and he soon left Perth for Galloway, his one area of support. There he was ambushed by Sir Archibald and the new Earl of Moray. Most of his men were killed but he escaped and fled to Carlisle. He appealed to Edward for assistance and promised to cede to him all of the counties of southeast Scotland. Edward sent an army to him with which he besieged Berwick in March 1333, where Edward joined him in May. Sir Alexander Seton defended Berwick bravely and was granted a short truce, but only on the condition that he surrender if not relieved. As a guarantee of good faith, Seton was required to hand over a number of hostages, which included his son, Thomas. A small English army crossed into Dumfries and at the Battle of Dornock defeated a Scottish army led by William Douglas, Knight of Liddesdale, who was captured.

Sir Archibald Douglas responded by crossing the border and destroying Tweedmouth in Northumberland, so Edward ordered the hostages to be hanged, with the first being young Thomas Seton. Sir Archibald then marched north towards Berwick and fought Edward at the Battle of Halidon Hill in July. The Scots were again slaughtered and among those killed were Sir Archibald; his nephew William, Lord of Douglas; the earls of Ross, Lennox, Sutherland and Atholl; and Alexander de Brus, King Robert's illegitimate nephew. Once again William de Haya of Locherworth survived, but all three of his Fraser uncles were killed. The following day Berwick surrendered and Robert Stewart, who had married King Robert's daughter, acted as Regent until King David reached his majority in 1341.

The Constable, Sir Gilbert, died in 1333 and he was succeeded by his young grandson David. Sir Thomas de Haya died two years later leaving two sons, William and John de Haya of Tullibody. John inherited as forester of Awne and he received permission from the king to cultivate the land around the River Spey and his own son, also John, married the King David's niece. Sir William de Haya was 25 when he inherited and he married Agnes Douglas, the daughter of William Douglas, the Knight of Liddesdale. Sir William inherited further Fraser lands in Peebleshire and he decided to use Neidpath Castle as his chief residence and moved his family from Locherworth.

Neidpath stands on the bank of the River Tweed a mile from Peebles. Sir William built the present tall L-plan tower house with roofed battlements on the ruins of the earlier castle destroyed by Edward I. Neidpath was built for war: the walls are almost ten feet thick and there are few windows, all protected by thick iron bars. The main block has five storeys comprising a cellar, a loft, a great hall with a pointed vault and a musicians' gallery, the lord's chambers and a room for other family members. The wing has six storeys including a pit prison, a guardroom, a kitchen and three private rooms above. The keystone bears the Hay crest of a goat's head on a five-pointed coronet, and the archway is decorated with both the goat's head emblem and the strawberries of the Frasers.

King David was sent to France in 1334 under the protection of King Philip and Edward III returned south, having placed his own men in the six key Sheriffdoms in Southern Scotland, those of Lothian, Berwick, Roxburgh, Selkirk, Peebles and Dumfries, protected by the occupied castles of Edinburgh, Dunbar, Berwick, Roxburgh, Jedburgh, Selkirk and Hawick. Some pockets of resistance remained in the south, principally amongst the Lothian lords lead by the Earl of March. Edward had seized most of the Douglas lands apart from those held by two members of the clan: Sir William de Haya's half-brother, Archibald the Grim, and his father-in-law the Knight of Liddesdale. Archibald had succeeded his uncle as the senior member of the clan and he held Douglas lands in trust for Sir James's nephew, William, Lord Douglas, who was in France. Liddesdale joined Sir Alexander Ramsay, Warden of the Middle March, in leading the resistance against the English occupiers and, in the autumn of 1335, they defeated Balliol and Atholl at the Battle of Culblean, which effectively ended Balliol's reign. Edward turned his focus to France, as in 1337 he had claimed the French throne and he took his army to Flanders, beginning the Hundred Years' War. Liddesdale took advantage of this and he captured John Stirling, the English Constable of Edinburgh Castle and Edward's commander over southern Scotland. He also took Hermitage Castle, the key fortress of the Western and Middle Marches which had been a royal castle under King Robert I. It had been forfeited by Sir William's kinsman, Sir William de Soulis, in 1320 because he had tried to betray Robert to the English. He was betrayed by his mistress and was executed by being boiled in molten lead.

Hermitage gave Liddesdale control over much of southern Scotland and he now wanted to gain the support of the king to give him the legitimacy that he lacked. He visited David in France in 1339 and returned with a party of French knights and crossbowmen and the promise of royal favour in return for preparing Scotland for the king's return. Sir Hugh Giffard was also in France, having been sent there to avoid the conflict with England. Whilst returning to Scotland in 1337, aged seventeen, he was captured by the English Admiral, John de Ros, but was soon released.

Liddesdale recaptured Edinburgh Castle in 1341 and the English defenders were slaughtered. Edward released King David later that year and he returned to an impoverished country in need of peace and good government. However he supported his ally King Philip of France during the early years of the Hundred Years' War and led a raid into England shortly after his return, forcing Edward to lead an army north to reinforce the border. David made Liddesdale Earl of Atholl, but only for a few months, later making him resign it to Robert Stewart, after which he took on the title of Lord of Liddesdale. He and Ramsay fell out as Liddesdale was angry that Ramsay had captured Roxburgh Castle when he, Liddesdale, was its titular Constable. He was further angered when the king deprived him in 1342 of his offices of Constable of Roxburgh and Sheriff of Teviotdale and gave them to Ramsay, who he then seized and held in the dungeons of Hermitage Castle, where he starved him to death.

Sir Hugh Giffard married Joanna Douglas in 1345, after the formal annulment of his early marriage to Elizabeth Mure. Joanna was the daughter of Sir James Douglas of Lothian and the sister of the Knight of Liddesdale. Sir Hugh thus became related by marriage to Sir William de Haya, who had married Joanna's niece, Agnes. In the same year Sir Hugh sold Lethington to Sir Robert Maitland, the grandson of William Maitland of Thirlestane, but Sir Robert was killed the following year at the Battle of Neville Cross.

In 1346 the English were threatening to defeat the French, who were desperate for the Scots to create a diversion by attacking England. So King David invaded with 20,000 men including Sir David the Constable and Sir William de Haya. It is very likely that Sir Hugh Giffard served as well. The army plundered parts of Cumberland and Northumberland before entering Durham.

At the Battle of Neville Cross, the Scots were divided into three divisions under the commands of the king, the Earl of Dunbar and Liddesdale and they were once again routed. Sir William de Haya and Liddesdale were captured and Moray was killed, thus ending the line of Sir Thomas Randolph, whose other son had been killed at Halidon Hill. Niall Bruce, an illegitimate son of King Robert, was killed, as were the Earl of Strathearn; Sir Robert Keith, Marischal; Lord Charteris, the Chancellor; and Lord Peebles, the Chamberlain. The Constable was also killed, aged only 28, being the third male member of his family to have died since 1332.

King David was wounded and was held in the Tower for eleven years. In his absence, Scotland was ruled by his nephew, Robert Stewart, who had fled the battle at a very early stage. Stewart had married Sir Hugh Giffard's child bride Elizabeth Mure in 1349. They had twelve children, one of whom married Sir Thomas Hay, the new Constable. However Elizabeth died in 1355, before Robert became king, and the dispute over the competing legitimacy of her children and those of Stewart's second wife, Euphemia Ross, was ultimately to bring down the Black Douglases. Euphemia was the daughter of Hugh de Ross, who in 1327 had given Sir Thomas de Haya land in Angus in exchange 'for paying to us and our heirs a pair of gilded spurs yearly at Pentecost'.

Following the battle of Neville Cross, Balliol returned to Scotland but found no support. Liddesdale also returned after pledging allegiance to Edward. His godson, William Douglas, the heir of Sir Archibald, left France and drove the English from his lands in Lothian and Galloway. Douglas came across Liddesdale hunting on lands in Galloway which Douglas claimed were his by right of inheritance and which he considered Liddesdale had stolen from him. They fought and Liddesdale was killed. King David then granted Douglas all the lands that had been owned by Liddesdale, his uncle Sir James and his father, Archibald. He was thus in complete control of the Douglas clan and was the dominant lord in the Marches and between 1350 and 1380 many members of many Lothian families served him as officers and councillors and provided him with armed followers.

Sir William de Haya was released in 1354 and he appointed a commissioner to negotiate the release of the king. His son Thomas was given as hostage, but in 1355 the truce with England expired and the negotiations to release the king broke down. Douglas defeated an English army at Nesbitt Moor near Duns, took many English nobles prisoner and massacred the soldiers captured. He then attacked Berwick and killed many of its inhabitants. In revenge, Edward laid waste to the Lothians in an event known as the Burnt Candlemass. Edinburgh was attacked and Haddington ravaged, its Abbey and churches burnt and many people killed. This devastation was to be the last major attack on Scotland by the English for 30 years as Scotland ceased to be a threat and this allowed the English to focus on the war in France. Because of this period of peace, the Lowland Scots could earn little from military pay and booty and they had to look elsewhere to make money, which included fighting wars for the French.

Douglas took a large force of Scottish troops to France in 1356, including Archibald the Grim and Sir William de Haya and his three sons. Douglas led this army in support of the French against the Black Prince at Poitiers, where he was knighted by the French king, John II. However, the French were heavily defeated, John captured and the Scots were routed. Douglas escaped but his cousin Archibald was captured. Two of Sir William de Haya's sons, Malitius and James, were killed and only Thomas survived. The following year, aged 25, he succeeded his father, who died at the age of 48. However Thomas was again held hostage for the king, this time by the Sheriff of Northampton, and was only released in 1369.

Douglas returned to Scotland and sat in the Parliament that met at Berwick in 1357 and finalised the release of David through the

Treaty of Berwick for a ransom of £36 million. Douglas was created Earl of Douglas in 1358 and was given the Sheriffdoms of Selkirk and Roxburgh. Scotland was now in a sorry state, ravaged both by war and the Black Death and heavy taxation was needed to pay the king's ransom. The first instalment was paid punctually, the second was late and after that there was no more money. In order to placate Edward, David went to London in 1363 and told the king that, should he die childless, the Scottish crown would pass to him and, in return, David asked that the ransom be cancelled.

Sir Hugh Giffard continued to live at Yester Castle and, in a charter of 1350, he refers to the 'village of Giffardgatis'. This was a village that now stands within the boundary of Haddington and, as this was ten miles from Yester Castle, it shows the extent of the Giffard estate in East Lothian at this time. His father Sir John had referred in a charter of 1327 to 'my town of Yester' and, as Sir John mentions his mill in the same charter, it is likely that this 'town of Yester' was also known as Bothans, as Bothans is mentioned in a charter of 1374 as having both a mill and a hangman. Bothans was thus the village that stood near to the chapel now known as St. Cuthbert's and this was the village that was cleared to make way for the building of Yester House in 1582.

Sir Hugh and Joanna had four daughters: Joanna, Margaret, Euphemia and Alicia. They became the co-heiresses of the Yester estates in their minorities when their father, the last male Giffard of Yester, died in 1365 aged only 43. His widow Joanna married Sir Nigel Cunningham in 1366 and the dynamism with which Sir Nigel added to his estates over the next twenty years was remarkable and ultimately was of tremendous benefit to the Hay family.

In 1368 George, 10th Earl of Dunbar, granted Sir Nigel, 'for his homage and service', the lands of Belton, near Dunbar, and Kilpalet, near Garvald, in the foothills of the Lammermuirs. One year later he received from Sir Gilbert MacLaghlan the lands of Castlehill in Dumfries. In 1373 Sir Gilbert gave him more lands in Dumfries but on condition he rendered 'all services to the King and Justiciar or Sheriff of Dumfries,' and he also had to pay £25,000 in silver to Sir Gilbert. In 1376 he was granted land by Patrick Polwarth, an ancestor of the Earls of Home, and in 1380 his son, Archibald, was granted by Sir Gilbert the Barony of Snaid on the west coast of Scotland near Glasgow. Sir Nigel referred to himself as Lord of Yester in a charter of 1374 and the year before he died in 1387 he was created Lord of Belton.

Thomas de Haya was released as hostage in 1369 by King Edward and he left England for Rome, where he stayed till 1373 when he returned to Scotland, aged 41. He there married Joanna, the eldest of the four Giffard heiresses, thus uniting the two families who had lived and fought beside each other through the three tumultuous centuries since joining Duke William's invasion, and from their union descended the Hays of Yester.

∂

King David was eager to counter the power of the Earl of Douglas and he cultivated Archibald the Grim, who had also been released by the English. Archibald gave the king his support both because it was in the tradition of his father, Sir James, but also because he wanted to regain the lands of Liddesdale he believed rightly belonged to him. He had recently married Joanna Murray, whose father, the Earl of Strathearn, had been killed at Neville's Cross. Her inheritance was considerable and stretched from Roxburghshire to Aberdeen, thus Archibald became a man of considerable wealth. David appointed him Keeper of Edinburgh Castle and Sheriff of Lothian. David also cultivated the Lothian lords as he knew that the Eastern March was where Earl Douglas's support was weakest.

These moves unnerved Douglas and he made an alliance with Robert Stewart, who succeeded to the throne in 1371 when

David died unmarried aged 47. Robert was 55 and not in good health and Douglas used this period of peace and royal weakness to increase his influence in the Middle and Eastern Marches. His sister Eleanor, widowed at Halidon Hill, helped him in this by marrying three Lothian lords in succession, the last of whom was Patrick Hepburn, the ancestor of the Earls of Bothwell. Douglas died in 1384, having been the most powerful man in Scotland for 34 years. He left two sons, his heir James as 2nd Earl and an illegitimate son, George Douglas, by his mistress, Margaret Stewart, Countess of Angus. Both sons had been born at Douglas's massive fortress, Tantallon Castle, which he had built near Dunbar in East Lothian. From these two boys developed respectively the competing lines of the Black and the Red Douglases.

King Richard invaded Scotland in 1385 because Robert had invited French troops to Scotland. They came in a fleet of 180 ships led by Admiral Jean de Vienne, who also brought with him 40,000 francs which he distributed among the Scottish nobles, with Sir Thomas de Haya receiving 400 francs. Richard forced the French to withdraw and burned Melrose, Edinburgh, Perth and Dundee. A Council removed Robert's authority to govern and his two sons were given responsibility for governing Scotland: the elder Earl of Carrick for the south and the Earl of Fife for the north. Fife was later appointed Lieutenant General of the Kingdom, but his power never matched his title. The young James, 2nd Earl of Douglas, was killed in 1388 at the battle of Otterburn fighting against the Percys and Archibald the Grim inherited as 3rd Earl and became the dominant magnate in the kingdom. George Douglas, the 2nd Earl's illegitimate brother, married Carrick's daughter Mary and assumed his mother's title as Earl of Angus and he became the effective liege lord to the Lothian nobles. Between 1350 and 1450 Douglases were Wardens of each of the three Marches and the increasing influence and rivalry between the Black and Red lines dominated Scottish politics for the next 60 years, proving critical to the future of the monarchy and to the Scottish nobles whose fortunes rose or fell with those of the magnates to whom they gave their support.

Sir Thomas de Haya was a canny political animal. He recognised Archibald's dominance, and he may have been aware of his wife's distant relationship to him, but he was also sensitive to Angus's position as the most powerful of the Lothian lords. Archibald initially secured Sir Thomas's allegiance when he appointed him Sheriff of Peebles, a post the family held till 1686, but Sir Thomas died soon afterwards in 1392, aged 57. His son William inherited aged 38, and he followed the example of the Constable and changed his family name to Hay. His three Giffard aunts had all married and each retained their quarter share of the Yester estate. Euphemia married Macdowall of Mackerston; Alicia married Thomas Boyd, Lord Kilmarnock; and Margaret married, first, Maxwell of Fife and, secondly, Sir William Cunningham, the brother of her mother's husband, Sir Nigel.

William Hay cultivated his relationship with Angus, who asked him to attend a meeting at Bothwell Castle with Archibald to try to defuse the feud between Angus and Archibald's kinsman, James Douglas of Dalkeith, over ownership of the lands of Liddesdale. Hay helped broker an agreement whereby Angus's men would end their attacks in exchange for Angus receiving some of the Liddesdale lands.

Robert II died in 1390 and his son Carrick succeeded as Robert III. He was an invalid so his brother Fife continued as Lieutenant General until February 1393 when Robert took control of his kingdom with the support of his fifteen-year-old son David, Duke of Rothesay. Rothesay was appointed Lieutenant General in his own right in 1399 but he was supervised by a Council dominated by Fife, who had been made Duke of Albany. Archibald's influence continued to increase and in 1390 he had arranged the marriage of his heir, also Archibald, to King Robert's daughter Princess

Margaret. In 1399 he arranged the marriage of his own daughter Marjorie to Rothesay, who was however already contracted to marry Elizabeth Dunbar, daughter of George, 10th Earl of Dunbar, who had paid a large sum to secure this. This reflected the reality of power as the historic strength of the Dunbars had been weakening ever since the destruction of their castle in 1338. The peaceful conditions in Scotland had reduced their earnings from military activities and they could not compete with the strength of the Douglases. This had been made brutally clear when Archibald built his great fortress of Tantallon close to Dunbar Castle.

In his anger, Dunbar went to England and pledged his allegiance to Henry IV, who made him Lord of Somerton and paid him an annuity of £60,000; he then joined Henry 'Hotspur' Percy, the son of the Earl of Northumberland, in his invasion of East Lothian in 1401. Robert Maitland of Lethington was the keeper of Dunbar's Castle but he gave it up to the new Earl of Douglas who had succeeded his father Archibald in 1400. Douglas defeated the invaders but later that summer Henry IV invaded Scotland and William Hay helped Douglas defend Edinburgh Castle against him. Henry retreated and he was the last English monarch to invade Scotland in person. Hay was knighted and Rothesay appointed Douglas Keeper of Edinburgh Castle.

Rothesay was arrested by his uncle Albany and Douglas in January 1402 and was held at Albany's Falkland Palace, where he died in March aged 24 amid rumours that he had been starved to death. Albany and Douglas were summoned to appear before Parliament but they were acquitted and Parliament declared that Rothesay had 'departed this life through Divine Providence, and not otherwise'. King Robert retired in despair to the Isle of Bute and Albany resumed his position as Lieutenant General.

Dunbar raided Scotland again in June and defeated a small Scottish force at Nesbit Moor. Douglas led a revenge attack on England supported by the Earl of Moray, Sir William Hay and

Albany's son, Murdoch, and they besieged Newcastle. The earls of Dunbar and Northumberland, and his son, Hotspur, attacked the Scots at Homildon Hill and routed them. Douglas, Angus, Moray, Hay and Murdoch were all captured and King Henry refused to allow any of the hostages to be ransomed. Both Moray and Angus died of the plague in captivity but Hay was able to escape.

Hotspur then supported Owain Glendower in his rebellion against King Henry and he was joined by Douglas and other Scottish hostages when he fought Henry at Shrewsbury in 1403, but again the Scots were on the losing side. Hotspur was killed and Douglas was again captured. Sir William Hay acted as hostage for Douglas in 1409 in a clear sign where his fealty lay, but he must have been released by 1410 as he acted as a commissioner in arranging a treaty with the English, which was signed in 1411. Not until 1413 were most of the other hostages liberated and only then upon payment of a large ransom to the new King Henry V. Murdoch was, however, only released in 1416, when he was exchanged for the Earl of Northumberland, leaving Gilbert Hay, son of the the 8th Constable, serving as hostage for him.

Two of the Lothian lords, the Earl of Orkney and Sir David Fleming, took advantage of Douglas's imprisonment to secure Robert III's remaining son, the twelve-year-old Prince James. They decided to send him to France and in February 1409 they took him through the hostile Douglas territories of East Lothian to take a boat from Dunbar. There they were attacked by James Douglas of Balvenie, the Earl of Douglas's brother, and Fleming was killed. Orkney took the prince to the Bass Rock, a fortress on a great mass of rock standing a mile off the coast from Dunbar. They stayed there for over a month before a ship from Danzig picked them up but the ship was captured by pirates who sold James to the English and he was held captive for eighteen years. The news of his son's capture broke the already despondent king and he died soon after.

Albany now controlled Scotland and refused to pay the ransom for the young King James I. He and Douglas agreed to share control of the kingdom with Albany focussing on the north and Douglas on the south, holding all three Marches and becoming Sheriff of Lothian. Their alliance was further strengthened when Albany's second son, the Earl of Buchan, married Douglas's daughter. Dunbar made his peace with both men and regained his title and castle, but not his estates.

Sir William Hay married and moved his family from Neidpath to Yester Castle and the family became known formally as the Hays of Yester. In East Lothian Douglas gained the support of Borthwick, Hume, Seton, Orkney and Hay who became one his closest advisers, with Douglas referring to him as 'his very dear squire.' Douglas confirmed him as Sheriff of Peebles in 1407 and in 1414 gave him lands in Liddesdale, where later he had to order his men to 'impose distress' on the people of Galloway for refusing to pay Hay the rent due to him.

The marriages of the Hay family at this time show not only the importance of old dynastic relationships but also how the realities of power drove new alliances. Sir William's wife Alicia was the daughter of Sir Thomas Hay, the 7th Constable and his wife Elizabeth, the daughter of King Robert II. William and Alicia had four sons: William, who died young but had been betrothed to Mary, sister of William, 2nd Earl of Angus; Thomas, who inherited but died unmarried; and David, who married Mary Douglas. The youngest son, Edmund of Talla, lived at Oliver Castle and inherited the estate of Linplum, close to Yester. Edmund married his cousin, Annabelle, the sister of Robert 1st Lord Boyd, and from their grandson Sir William descended many cadet branches including the Hays of Linplum, Rannes, Eddleston and Ranfield. One of Edmund's descendants was one of the murderers of Lord Darnley, for which he was hung, drawn and quartered in 1568, being the only descendant of the Hays of Yester to suffer execution.

Sir William's four daughters all married: Margaret to her brother-in-law William, 2nd Earl of Angus; Jean to Sir Alexander Home, whose son was the 1st Lord Home; Alicia to Gilbert Hay of Erroll, and their son became the 1st Earl of Erroll; and Elizabeth to her second cousin Duncan Macdowall, thereby regaining the quarter of the Yester estate he had inherited. The double marriage of David to Mary Douglas and Margaret to Mary's brother, Angus, proved crucial to the fortunes of the family. Sir William continued his father's policy of supporting both lines of the Douglases but his greater connection to Angus and the Red line proved astute as the Black line soon collapsed due to murder and revolt.

Sir William died in 1421, aged 67, just after he had converted the Church of St Cuthbert's into a collegiate establishment for a provost, six prebendaries, and two singing boys, which lasted until the Reformation. His wife Alicia lived till 1450 and endowed St Cuthbert's with the lands of Bales near Haddington. Their son Thomas, who had originally been intended for the Church, inherited aged 24.

Following the death of Albany in 1420, the Scots finally paid the ransom for King James. However he was still not released and Murdoch, who had succeeded his father as 2nd Duke of Albany, took over as Regent. The Earl of Douglas had kept in regular contact with James and they agreed that, in return for James's endorsement of Douglas's position, the earl would pledge James his loyalty. James at last returned to Scotland in 1424 and William, the 8th Constable, and his son Gilbert acted as hostage for him, as did Thomas Hay, with their annual income being valued at £28,000 and £21,000 respectively. King James rewarded the Constable and Thomas with knighthoods. Sir Thomas's brother-in-law Angus was one of the Scottish nobles who had met the king on his return at Durham in 1424 and he too was knighted at James's coronation at Scone in June.

It was not altogether a popular re-entry, as James had fought in

Henry V's army against Scottish forces in France and his large ransom necessitated increased taxes to cover the payments. Later that year, King Charles VII of France asked Douglas for help in his fight against the English. The peace with England had deprived the magnates of their major source of wealth, so they needed to supplement this by military action overseas. Douglas sailed to France with an army of 6,500 men where he was made Duke of Touraine, becoming the first foreigner to be granted ducal status in France. However his ill fortune in battle continued and he was defeated and killed at Verneuil in August 1424, as was his second son, James. Hay's brother-in-law Sir Alexander Home and most of the Scottish forces were also killed.

Important Douglas allies had died in France and some of their heirs now gave their support to rival magnates. This helped improve King James's position and he took advantage of the new Earl Douglas's weakness by asking him to begin a campaign against Albany and his family, who were arrested in 1425. The jury for their trial included Douglas, Angus and a large number of other Douglas nobles. Albany, his two sons and the Earl of Lennox, his father-in-law, were convicted of treason and executed and the widowed Duchess of Albany was held prisoner at Tantallon for eight years. The king seized Murdoch's earldoms of Fife, Menteith and Lennox and the lapsed earldoms of Strathearn and Mar, thereby greatly strengthening the royal estates and beginning the process of increasing the power of the monarchy relative to that of the magnates. James also reduced the threat of Highland insurgency by summoning a number of Highland chiefs to Inverness Castle in 1428 where he executed three of them and imprisoned the others. He was to prove a very different king to his predecessors.

Sir Thomas had again been held a hostage in York in 1426 and he was then sent to the Tower from where he was released in 1429. He died unmarried in 1434 aged only 36 and he was succeeded by his brother David, aged 34, who was to live to 80. Sir David focused on reorganising his inheritance and left his heirs the strong base from which their descendants gained great benefit. He first sold his family's house at Locherworth to Sir William Borthwick, who knocked it down and built a large castle on its foundations. Borthwick was a vassal of the Black Douglases and Sir David became increasingly open in his support of the Red Douglases.

King James made James Douglas the Gross Earl of Avondale in 1437. He was Archibald the Grim's second son, the uncle of the 5th Earl Douglas and he was the murderer of Sir David Fleming in 1409. The king wanted to gain his support so as to increase the pressure on the new Earl Douglas. James also gathered support from the Lothian lords, making the Earl of March Warden of the East March and the Earl of Angus Warden of the Middle March, leaving Douglas only the West March. The Earl of Dunbar had not been given back his lands, however, and he once again turned to the English for help to restore them. Angus took Dunbar Castle in 1435 and was rewarded by the king with lands and fortresses previously held by the Black Douglases, including Hermitage Castle.

King James became, however, increasingly unpopular and he was killed in February 1437. Angus was given responsibility for the capture of his murderers who were led by Sir Robert Graham and the Earl of Atholl, both descendants of Robert II through his second wife Euphemia Ross. The Earl of Douglas was also connected to this line through his marriage to Margaret, the murdered king's sister. Hence the conspiracy was more complicated than one based purely on the ambitions of magnates; it was a direct challenge to the accepted line of royal descent and the murderers were harshly treated. Atholl was executed over three days. On the first, he was dropped by a crane to dislocate his limbs and then was crowned by a red hot ring of metal; on the second, he was dragged around Edinburgh on a hurdle and, on the third, he was disembowelled while still alive, his entrails were burned before his eyes, his heart was then ripped out and his corpse was beheaded and quartered. His grandson was also executed, as were Sir Robert Graham and his son. Thus was the line of the male descendants of Euphemia Ross extinguished, and any credible claim to the throne by the Black Douglases was ended by these executions. Angus was unable to savour his triumph as he died in October, aged only 39 and he was succeeded by his son James as 3rd Earl.

King James II was only six when his father was murdered. The association of Douglas with the conspiritors did not weaken his position and he acted as Regent from 1437 to 1439, supported by his uncle Avondale. After his death in 1439, power was shared between Avondale, Sir William Crichton who was the Lord Chancellor and Governor of Edinburgh Castle, and Sir Alexander Livingston, who was Warden of Stirling Castle. Crichton had been given immediate responsibility for the young king, who lived with him in Edinburgh Castle. These three invited Douglas's two sons, the seventeen-year-old William, 6th Earl, and his fourteen-year-old brother David to Edinburgh Castle in 1440 where they were entertained for two weeks, after which their great-uncle, Avondale, left the castle. Sir Walter Scott tells of what then happened: 'At an entertainment which was served up to the earl and his brother, the head of a black bull was placed on the table. The Douglases knew this to be the sign of death. They were seized by armed men, underwent a mock trial, in which all the insolences of their ancestors were charged against them, and were condemned to immediate execution. The young king wept and implored Livingston and Crichton to show mercy, but in vain. The brothers were led out into the courtyard of the castle and beheaded.'

Avondale thus became the 7th Earl of Douglas, inheriting most of the Douglas estates. But he did not live long to enjoy it for he died in 1443 and was succeeded by his son William as 8th Earl of Douglas, who joined with Livingston to drive Crichton from power. The new Earl of Douglas was made Lieutenant General in 1448 and he consolidated his position as head of the Black Douglases by marrying Margaret, the sister of the two murdered Douglas boys. His own sister, Beatrice, married William Hay, the 10th Constable. The 3rd Earl of Angus died childless in 1446 and his brother George succeeded as 4th Earl, and he was to become known as the Great Earl of Angus.

The rise of the Livingstons demonstrates how the lesser nobility had benefited from the policy of James I to raise them to positions of authority so as to counter the traditional power of the magnates. By 1449 the positions of Judiciar, Comptroller, Master of the Mint, Chamberlain and the Captains of the castles of Edinburgh, Stirling, Dumbarton, Doune and Methven were all held by Livingstons. However, their fall was equally as swift and showed the weaknesses of those lairds who had political power but no great wealth of lands or men to support them. When James II reached adulthood in 1449 he had all the Livingstons arrested and Alexander and his brother Robert were both executed. James, however, continued his father's policy of favouring the lairds by creating a number of them Lords of Parliament. He retained the earldoms of Buchan, Carrick, March, Fife, Lennox, Mar and Strathearn to reward future supporters and he raised some existing nobles to earldoms. These included the Constable Sir William Hay, who became 1st Earl of Erroll, and Argyll, Marischal and Rothes, and he made new creations of the earldoms of Atholl and Caithness. One of the Earl of Douglas's brothers was made Earl of Moray and another Earl of Ormond. James Douglas, 4th Lord of Dalkeith, was made Earl of Morton. His mother was Elizabeth Giffard, the daughter of James Giffard, the nephew of Sir Hugh, the last male Giffard of Yester. Morton was also descended from the Knight of Liddesdale and he married Joan Stewart, the king's daughter, who was both deaf and unable to speak.

Angus joined the earls of Douglas and Ormond on a raid into England in 1448 where they ravaged the countryside as far as

Alnwick. This action would be the last time that the two Douglas branches fought side by side. The Black Douglases were in open conflict with the king by 1450 and they forced him to return them lands which he had previously seized. However the king was determined to gain control of his kingdom and in 1452 he murdered the Earl of Douglas at Stirling Castle, having given him assurances of safe conduct. Thereafter the fall of the Black Douglases was very swift: Douglas's four brothers, James, the 9th Earl, the Earls of Moray and Ormond, and the Lord of Balvenie, rose in rebellion in 1455. It would have been expected that Angus would have joined them, but he joined the king and was given command of the army. The Earl of Douglas went to England to get support from Henry VI, and Angus, with Sir David Hay alongside him, fought the remaining Douglas brothers at the battle of Arkinholm. Moray was killed, Ormond captured and executed and only Balvenie escaped to England to join his brother. The Douglases were attainted and their estates declared forfeit. The 9th Earl continued to make trouble from England until his capture at the battle of Lochmaben Fair in 1484, whereafter he was forced to spend the rest of his days at Lindores Abbey. His estates were divided up between the king's supporters, with Angus taking the lion's share and the power of the Black Douglases was ended forever.

Sir David Hay had sat in the Grand Council of Stirling in 1440, which had ordered the Sheriffs to control the disorders in Scotland. He himself was not innocent of such matters since he and his nephew, Sir William Hay of Talla, were ordered in 1450 to stop harassing John Lindsay of the Byres about the lands and tower of Morham, and in a second judgement Lindsay was declared the rightful owner. A year later Sir David exchanged his Barony of Teyling in Forfarshire for the quarter share of the Yester estate held by Sir Robert Boyd and thus reunited three-quarters of Sir Hugh Giffard's original estate. Sir David then sold his lands at Locherworth to the Chancellor, Lord Crichton, for £40,000 and, seemingly in return, Crichton ordered that the Morham lands be restored to Sir William Hay. Sir David also increased the land he managed by renting Athmure and other lands in Erroll from the Earl of Erroll for £4,000 a year, and he bought land near Yester for the same amount from Sir David Ramsay.

Sir David sat in the Parliament of 1455, where the Act of Revocation was passed authorising the king to own properties throughout his realm, specifically designating as royal the castles of Ettrick, Galloway, Edinburgh, Stirling, Inverness, Urquhart and Dumbarton and confirming as royal titles the earldoms of Fife and Strathearn, and the lordship of Brechin. All crown lands were declared henceforward inalienable, except through Acts of Parliament, and all grants of heritable office made since the death of James I were revoked, except those that James II himself had made. Hereditary Wardenships of the Marches were forbidden, no new regalities were to be created except with the consent of Parliament and all existing regalities were merged into the Sheriffdoms. This Act was crucial to curbing the power of the magnates, which proved crucial as for half the years of the 15th and 16th centuries the crown was held by a minor or an absentee monarch. In addition, the new earldoms created were personal rather than territorial, so they did not increase the wealth and power of the recipients and build up potential problems for the future.

James II was an early supporter of the use of artillery, which he used to besiege Roxburgh Castle in 1460, one of the last Scottish castles still held by the English but he was killed by a cannon exploding beside him. Angus was also wounded but he was able to assume command and take the castle and was later appointed Lieutenant of the Realm by the Queen-Regent, Mary of Guelders. She also made him Warden of the East and Middle Marches, and he officiated at the crowning of the nine-year-old King James III.

The War of the Roses in England caused Henry VI to flee to Scotland in 1461 and he made a pact with Angus to support his fight against Edward of York but Angus died in March 1463 and was succeeded by his son Archibald as 5th Earl, and the Scots made peace with Edward. Sir Robert Boyd, now Lord Kilmarnock, his brother Alexander and a group of other nobles seized the young King James in 1466 and held him at Edinburgh Castle. Kilmarnock was made sole Governor of the Realm and Great Chamberlain for life. His son, Thomas, married the king's sister, Mary, and was made Earl of Arran. Kilmarnock went overseas in 1468 to arrange the marriage between James and Margaret, daughter of the King of Norway and his enemies took advantage of his absence to move against his family and Alexander Boyd was beheaded. Kilmarnock remained overseas and his family's estates were forfeited. Adam Hepburn, Earl of Bothwell, was granted Kilmarnock's estates near Yester, including his quarter share of St. Cuthbert's.

King James took control of his realm and married Margaret in 1469. He was highly intelligent and cultured and he preferred the company of people of lower birth rather than the nobles, who he disliked and mistrusted. James was also eager to have good relations with England and this made him unpopular with a number of the magnates. In 1479 he imprisoned both of his brothers; one, the Earl of Mar, died in captivity and the other, the Duke of Albany, escaped to England and became a supporter of Edward IV.

Sir David Hay died in 1478 aged 80 and his son John inherited aged 54. Sir John married Mary, the daughter of Sir John Lindsay of Byres, by whom he had one son, Thomas. She died in 1468 and he then married Elizabeth Cuningham, only child of Sir George Cunningham of Belton, who was the great-grandson of the Sir Nigel Cunningham, who had married Joanna Giffard in 1366. This family connection resulted in his receiving a great deal of land, much of it being Sir Nigel's original estate, thus bringing those lands back into the Hay family. Their marriage had to receive papal dispensation owing to the mistaken view that there was a fourth degree of consanguinity. They had two sons, John Hay of Snaid and George Hay of Menzion, and two daughters, Margaret, who married the 4th Lord Borthwick, and Isabel, who married Robert Lauder.

Sir John Hay became extremely wealthy due to bequests of lands from existing and new members of his family. Sir William of Talla gave him the tower and land at Morham, his lands at Duncanlaw and his lands at Wester Happrew in Peebles in 1469. One year later, Lord Fleming resolved a long-standing dispute over the Barony of Biggar by resigning the Barony of Oliver Castle and lands in Peebles to Sir John in exchange for all Hay's lands in Biggar and in 1472 Sir George Cunningam gave Sir John, now designated 'of Oliver Castle', the barony of Snaid. These gifts to Hay and his father's acquisitions resulted in his owning an estate worth £10,000 per annum. This was increased in 1478 when Cunningham granted Sir John the barony of Belton and the sheriffdom of Nithsdale on the condition that, if these were not passed on to his son, John of Snaid, then Hay would have to pay £100,000 equally to Cunningham and the king. In 1501 Sir John inherited Cunningham's remaining lands in Dumfries, Fife and Peebleshire.

Sir John's cousin, Angus, was appointed Warden of the East March in 1481 but he later joined a group of nobles who disliked the king's favourite Robert Cochrane. Angus ordered that Cochrane and others of the king's favourites be hanged, thus earning the soubriquet 'Bell the Cat'. He remained loyal to the king, however, and in 1483 he led the army that defeated an invading force from England led by the king's brother, Albany, and James, 9th Earl of Douglas, removing for ever the threat of the Black Douglases. Sir John was created a Lord of Parliament by James in 1488, taking the title of Lord Hay of Yester. The document creating Yester's title described him as sasine of Locherworth, Yester, Duncanlaw, Morham and Ugstoun, all of which were in East Lothian; and of Bankes in Edinburgh; Oliver and Neidpath Castles in Peebles; and of Thankerton, Netherton, and the mills of Strathavin and Glengavill, all in Lanarkshire. Hay's Coat of Arms incorporated those of his ancestors: Quarterly 1st and 4th *Gules three bars ermine* (Giffard of Yester) 2nd and 3rd *Sable three cinquefoils Argent* (Fraser) *an inescutcheon Azure three inescutcheons Argent* (Hay).

Hay's father-in-law, Sir John Lindsay, Robert Crichton and William Ruthven had been enobled with him as all had supported the king's decision to pass over his fifteen-year-old eldest son and name his second son as his heir, creating him Duke of Ross. It is notable that Angus was the leader of those nobles who opposed James in this, and this represents the first time that a Hay had not supported his traditional Douglas liege lord. It is a probable reflection of the fact that Yester was now rich and powerful in his own right and felt that he should now give his support to his monarch directly. Other nobles had opposed James because the king had seized revenues due to them. A major victim of this was Lord Home, whose daughter had married Yester's heir, Thomas. His family traditionally received the revenues from the Abbey of Coldingham in Berwickshire and James demanded that half of these should go to his Chapel Royal.

Parliament ruled in 1488 that these measures could not be opposed and Home, Argyll and the Hepburns joined Angus and took James's eldest son, Prince James, into their care, declaring that the king should be deposed. King James fought the rebels at the Battle of Sauchieburn, where he was supported by the northern nobles Huntly, Marischal, Erroll and Atholl, and by Yester and his recently created fellow peers. Yester's brother-in-law, Sir David Lindsay, presented the king with a 'great grey horse' but it was this horse that threw him during the battle. James was later killed by an unknown priest as he hid in a woodcutter's cottage.

This was the last time that a king of an independent Scotland fought his own subjects in the field. However, the immediate aftermath of Sauchieburn suggested that the traditional control of a young monarch by the magnates would continue. Home became Great Chamberlain, Warden of the East March and Keeper of the castles of Newark and Stirling. Patrick Hepburn became Master of the Household, Constable of Edinburgh Castle and Warden of the West and Middle Marches, and was made Earl of Bothwell. He later swapped his title of Lord Bothwell, but not the earldom, with Angus for the estate of Liddesdale and Hermitage Castle. Another Hepburn became Keeper of the Privy Seal and a third Clerk of the Rolls. Angus became one of the guardians of the young King James IV and made a treaty with Henry VII in 1491, by which he undertook to govern his relations with James according to instructions from England.

Yester decided to substantially rebuild Yester Castle and he demolished the old tower and built a new one, which may have been flanked by two smaller towers. The main tower had a barrel-vaulted first floor and there were probably three floors above. Around these was built a massive wall, six feet thick and up to thirty feet high. He may have done this because he felt vulnerable, as those magnates he had opposed were now in complete control of Scotland.

James IV was sixteen when he succeeded and, by the time he reached his majority in 1493, he was determined not to rely on any magnate but instead to pursue his own policies. He was, like his father, highly intelligent and cultured and was hailed as a Renaissance king. He later employed as the tutor for his son Erasmus who said of the king: 'He had a wonderful intellectual power and astonishing knowledge of everything, unconquerable magnanimity and the most abundant generosity.' In 1496, James showed his independence from Angus's pro-English policy by supporting Perkin Warbeck as pretender to the English throne. However, his support did not translate into any meaningful action and War-beck soon left for England, where he was captured and hanged.

Henry VII, however, wanted to secure relations with Scotland for both strategic and religious reasons and he offered James his daughter Margaret in marriage. James was, however, enjoying himself with many mistresses and felt he was not ready to marry. His favourite lover was Margaret Drummond, with whom he had an affair for six years, but she died in 1501 aged only 26. Her two sisters died with her, supposedly of food poisoning, and they lie together in Dunblane Abbey where the inscription on their grave suggests that Margaret had secretly married James. James now accepted Henry's offer and he married Margaret Tudor in 1503, signing a Treaty of Perpetual Peace with England. The result of the marriage was the Union of the Crowns of England and Scotland exactly 100 years later.

CHAPTER 5 – THE COVENANT

The hold that the Douglases had over Scotland was never replicated by any other clan. The noble families who had influence in the 16th century were of much greater diversity and included the Hamiltons as Earls of Arran; the Highland lords, the Earls of Huntly (Gordon) and Argyll (Campbell); the Western March chiefs, Maxwells and Johnstones; the Middle March families of Ker, Scott and Hepburn (Bothwell); and the Homes in the East March. In the Lowlands the dominant lords were the Kennedys, Earls of Cassillis and the Erskines, Earls of Mar. The Red Douglases retained influence holding the earldoms of Angus and Morton, both of whose holders were related to Lord Yester.

Yester died in 1508 aged 82. His first son Thomas had married Elizabeth, the daughter of Alexander, the 2nd Lord Home, when she was a child. However he later disappeared and was presumed dead, so in 1490 Elizabeth married James Hamilton, who was later made Earl of Arran. He later divorced Elizabeth because he said that Thomas reappeared in 1506 and hence their marriage was illegal. Arran remarried and had a son whose legitimacy was later challenged by the Earl of Lennox in 1526.

Thomas's half-brother, Sir John Hay of Snaid, inherited as 2nd Lord Yester in 1508 aged 38. He married Elizabeth Crichton, daughter of the 1st Lord Crichton and his sisters all married

Lothian nobles: Isabel to Sir Walter Ker, Warden of the Middle March; Margaret to the 4th Lord Borthwick; and Isabella to Robert Lauder of the Bass. In 1512 Yester swapped his estate of Morham for the quarter part of the Yester estate owned by Adam, 2nd Earl of Bothwell. Thus he finally rejoined the estate broken up when Sir Hugh Giffard died in 1365. However he was fated not to have any time to enjoy his new position as in 1513 he marched with James IV to attack England. James's relationship with Henry had been deteriorating and it broke down irrevocably after Henry joined Spain, the pope and the Holy Roman Empire in their League against France. France appealed to James for support after Henry sent an army of 35,000 to Calais and James crossed the border in August with an army of 30,000 supported by significant artillery. He probably only wanted to divert Henry from his war with France, but his strategy was very unpopular in Scotland and he was told by many nobles, including Angus, that he should not fight.

Yester marched with several nobles related to him: his son-in-law Borthwick; his cousin Angus and his two sons, George and William Douglas; Sir William Hay of Talla; the 4th Earl of Erroll and his brother, Thomas; his brother-in-law Home; and Lord Lindsay. The Scots crossed the river Tweed at Coldstream, stormed Wark Castle, bombarded Norham Castle into surrender with the great cannon 'Mon's Meg', seized Etal Castle and burnt down Ford Castle, but only after the king spent several days with Lady Heron of Ford. This was said to have been a deliberate ploy by Lady Heron, as keeping the king in her bed allowed the English time to assemble their forces at Alnwick. The Scots made camp nearby on Flodden Hill and Angus, not liking the position, suggested the army should either advance further or withdraw altogether. The king accused Angus of weakness and said he should leave if he were too old to fight. Angus left in fury, leaving his two sons to fight. The Scottish position was very strong, but the

Earl of Surrey led the English forces in a sweep behind James's army and cut off his path of retreat.

The Scots had a substantial advantage over the English in both men and artillery and they fought with long pikes whereas the English used the shorter bill hook. James gave lords Home, Huntly, Argyll, Erroll and Bothwell commands over divisions of his army which thus lacked an effective command structure. The Scottish guns could not make use of their advantage as they had to fire downhill and were unable to concentrate their fire on the massed English troops. James decided to rally his soldiers by dismounting and fighting on foot and many of his nobles joined him but his tactics were disastrous and his army was massacred with over 10,000 killed against only 500 English soldiers. James was killed, as were Yester, William and George Douglas, William Hay of Talla, the earls of Erroll and Bothwell and eight other earls and 300 nobles. No Hay survived the battle and 87 lairds and gentlemen of that name were killed. In truth was it said that 'the Flowers of the Forest are all wede away'. Angus died shortly afterwards, consumed by grief, and he was succeeded by his grandson Archibald, the son of the dead George Douglas, Master of Angus.

John Hay succeeded his father as 3rd Lord Yester aged 23. He had three brothers: George of Oliver Castle, William and Thomas, who was preceptor of St. Leonard's Hospital in Peebles. Yester's first wife was Elizabeth Douglas, the sister of Archibald, 6th Earl of Angus, who he had married when he was nineteen and they had one child in 1509, his heir John. However Elizabeth died just after the birth, and Yester then married the daughter of John Dickson of Smithfield, from whom he received a large estate and by whom he had five more children. His sister Christian married William Stewart of Traquair, and his other sister Elizabeth married the 5th Lord Saltoun.

James V was only eighteen months old when his father was killed. His mother Margaret Tudor was made Regent, but she married the 24-year-old 6th Earl of Angus within a year of being widowed and the Scottish magnates replaced her as Regent with John Stewart, Duke of Albany. He was the young king's great uncle and had lived all his 35 years in France. Angus soon tired of Margaret and he went to his estates in Forfarshire where he had fallen in love with Jane, the daughter of the Laird of Traquair, with whom he had a daughter. It may well have been Yester's sister Christian who introduced them as she had married Jane's brother. Margaret revenged herself on Angus by refusing to support his ambition to become Regent and she was joined by a number of nobles, including Yester, who signed a letter to Henry VIII in 1516 refusing his request that Albany be replaced as Regent. Yester thus followed the pro-monarchy policy of his grandfather John, but it must have been a painful decision given that Angus was his brother-in-law. His choice to support the monarchy rather than to pursue the narrower ambitions of self or family was one that all his descendants would follow until the reign of Charles I.

He made the right choice because Angus and Home lead a revolt against Albany which was easily defeated. Angus was pardoned but Home was executed, one of the charges being that he had been responsible for the death of James IV. Yester was one of the signatories to the peace treaty with England signed in 1517 and Albany returned to France, where he stayed for four years as King Louis wanted to keep good relations with England. In Albany's absence, Scotland was ruled by a Council consisting of Angus, Arran, Huntly and his brother-in-law, Argyll.

Kings Louis and Henry also made peace and Louis therefore no longer needed Scotland as an ally. Albany returned to Scotland in 1521 as Regent and Margaret renewed her support for him. The rivalries between the magnates to take control of the king re-emerged in 1526 when Lennox moved against Arran, denying the legitimacy of Arran's heir, James. This was because of the dispute over Arran's first wife Elizabeth's marriage with

Thomas Hay who, Lennox claimed, had married Kathryn Borthwick, sister of Lord Borthwick in 1489, but had been 'slayne by the theves of Asedale in 1491'. Lennox's claim was dismissed but he refused to back down and, supported by Margaret and Cardinal Beaton, he raised an army of 10,000 men and tried to capture the young king. Arran defeated him at the battle of Linlithgow Bridge and Lennox surrendered, only to be later murdered by an illegitimate son of Arran.

Angus now took full control of the king and kept him in Falkland Palace under the care of his brother, Sir George Douglas. Angus was made Chancellor in 1527 but he became increasingly unpopular because of his pro-English policy. King James escaped in 1528 and fled to his mother in Stirling Castle from where he summoned the Privy Council to meet him at Edinburgh. Angus and his allies were forfeited of their lands and titles and he and his brother, Sir George, fled to England. James's and Margaret's hatred of Angus influenced the early policy of his reign which was described by Andrew Lang in his *History of Scotland* (1900): 'James became implacable to the whole Douglas name... but to shake off the Douglases was to turn away from England... from Protestantism, to court France, and to choose the doomed cause of Catholicism... These dull and squalid intrigues of a selfish, sensual termagant [Margaret] and her unscrupulously ambitious husband Angus, determined the fate of the Stuart line. They were to lean on France, and were to lose three crowns for a mass.'

James's first priority was to secure his domestic position, which was weakened by the lawlessness which swept Scotland, especially in the Borders. He targeted the family and associates of Angus and imprisoned some of the most prominent magnates, notably Lords Bothwell, Home, Maxwell, Ker, Argyll and Scott. Angus's brother-in-law, the Master of Forbes, was executed and Angus's sister, Lady Glamis, was burned at the stake, both for conspiring against the king. He stripped Yester of his Sheriffdom of Peebles on the pretext that he had let a border raider escape from prison, but Yester appealed to the Privy Council and he was reinstated on the grounds that the king had acted arbitrarily. This was remarkable as it showed both how limited was the authority of the king and how important a figure Yester was becoming.

James appointed as Chancellor his tutor, the pro-French Archbishop of Glasgow, Gavin Dunbar and they continued the policy of prosecuting nobles, often for no other reason than to seize their lands. This, coupled with papal-approved taxation of the Church, greatly increased the king's wealth; however he increasingly alienated the nobles, leading one contemporary to lament 'so sore a dread king and so ill beloved of his subjects, was never in that land; every man that hath any substance fearing to have a quarrel.'

Patrick Hamilton, the grandson of James II, became one of the first Scottish Protestant martyrs when he was burned in 1528 for heresy at Saint Andrews and further religious prosecutions and executions followed over the next two decades. James was thus pursuing political and religious policies that risked serious confrontation with England. In 1537 he compounded this by marrying Madeleine, daughter of King Francis of France, but she died within a few weeks of landing in Scotland; he then married another strong Catholic, Mary of Guise. James continued to disregard both King Henry's overtures of friendship and his request that James follow his example and break with the Catholic Church and Henry retaliated by burning the towns of Roxburgh and Kelso. Seeking revenge, James proposed to invade England in 1542, but the magnates refused to support him. Ignoring them, he ordered Lord Maxwell to take an army through Liddesdale to invade England. Maxwell refused to fight the English at Solway Moss and Oliver Sinclair, a favorite of James, took over command, but most of the nobles refused to fight under him and the Scottish army was crushed by the English. James's two sons and his mother had both died in 1541 and this defeat broke him completely. He withdrew to Falkland Palace and died there in 1542, a few days after the birth of his daughter, now Queen Mary, in Linlithgow Palace.

Mary of Guise was passed over and the heir presumptive, James Hamilton, who had become the 2nd Earl of Arran in 1536, became Regent. He formed a government which supported an English alliance against the background of growing support for Reformation in Scotland. King Henry wanted his son Edward to marry the infant Queen Mary and force the Scots to accept the Protestant religion so he restored Angus's estates, made him a Privy Councillor and sent him to Scotland to negotiate the marriage, which was finalised by the Treaty of Greenwich in 1543.

Yester died that year and his son John inherited aged 33 as 4th Lord Yester. He had married Margaret Livingston in 1533 and her uncle, Alexander, the 5th Lord Livingston, was appointed Guardian to Queen Mary. Yester's sister Elizabeth had married the 5th Lord Seton in 1531 and Yester gave Seton lands near Gifford as part of her dowry. Seton was the son of Joanna Hepburn, daughter of the Earl of Bothwell, who lived near Yester at Hailes Castle. Seton also lived close to Yester at Seton Palace, his grand house near Prestonpans. There he was given custody of Cardinal Beaton, the Papal Legate in Scotland, who opposed the English marriage, but he allowed him to escape. Sir Richard Maitland, who was the descendant of the Robert Maitland of Thirlestane who had bought Lethington from the Giffards, was the Seton family's legal adviser and the history of the Hays of Yester was to be increasingly dominated over the next 150 years by their relationship with the Maitlands and the Setons.

Arran, who wanted his son, James Hamilton, to marry Queen Mary, became a Catholic and reneged on his support for the English marriage in December. The Scottish Parliament also decided to reject Henry's overtures and instead renewed the alliance with France so Henry declared war in what became known as the 'Rough Wooing'. He ordered the Earl of Hertford to devastate southern Scotland, which he did in two expeditions in 1544, burning Edinburgh, Leith and many other towns, and the great Abbeys of Jedburgh, Kelso, Melrose and Dryburgh, as well as laying waste Seton Palace and the estates of Angus, Yester, Scott of Buccleuch and other Lothian lords. Angus and his brother George plotted to replace Arran as Regent with Mary of Guise but they were arrested and imprisoned but Arran later released them and restored their estates in return for their support for his new plan to marry Queen Mary to the French Dauphin.

Yester was made a Privy Councillor in 1545 and he was a signatory to the treaty with France against England after the English continued their attacks on Scotland. The Scots raised an army of 5,000 men under Angus and a similar number of troops from Fife under the Earl of Rothes. These were joined by soldiers supplied by Yester and Scott of Buccleuch and they confronted the English near Jedburgh where the English army of 3,000 German and Spanish mercenaries, and 1,500 English borderers, were led by Sir Brian Layton. The Scots had the advantage of surprise and, in a rare victory, they defeated the English who lost their commander and 800 of his soldiers.

A year later, Cardinal Beaton raised religious tension in Scotland and with England by executing George Wishart, the leading Calvinist preacher. In retaliation, and with the probable encouragement of King Henry, a group of rebels seized Beaton at his castle at Saint Andrews and murdered him. These 'Castelians' were then joined by John Knox and held out until 1547, when they were forced to surrender to a French squadron and were sent to the galleys. The English again invaded Scotland and a small detachment attacked Yester Castle, which Yester defended strongly, forcing the English to abandon their attack and retire to their main army at Pinkie, near Musselborough, where was fought the last pitched battle between English and Scottish armies. The Lord Protector, Edward Seymour, led the English forces, which also included German and Italian mercenaries, and Arran led the Scottish forces, which Yester had now joined. Despite the example of Flodden, the Scots sought to maintain the medieval chivalric code and on the eve of the battle Home led out the Scottish cavalry and challenged an equal number of English cavalry to combat. The English won easily and the Scots fled the field and played no further part in the battle. Despite this, on the next morning Arran challenged Somerset to single combat. When this was rejected, he suggested combat between twenty chosen champions from each side. This was again rejected and the two sides entered into full battle. Pinkie stands on an estuary and the English had warships offshore whose guns raked the Scots, as did the arquebusses of the foreign mercenaries. The Scots were outgunned and outmanoeuvred and soon broke and, with no cavalry to protect them, they were swiftly overrun. William Patten wrote in 1548 'Bodies lay as thick as men may note cattle grazing... the river ran all red with blood so that in the same place were counted about 14,000 dead.' However there were few noble casualties, perhaps because the cavalry played no part in the actual battle.

Yester was captured and held at Berwick. His cousin Sir George Douglas asked the English commander, Lord Grey of Wilton, to release him but Wilton instead sent troops to seize Sir George who escaped, leaving his wife and son to be captured. Grey released her on her promise she would convert her husband to the English cause and she seems to have succeeded, as Grey later wrote to Somerset: 'Sir George Douglas desires his kinsman, Lord Hay of Yester, be loosened home on sureties,' but this had no effect, as Somerset ordered Yester to be sent immediately into the custody of Sir Roger Lascelles in Yorkshire, where he stayed until peace was concluded in 1550.

After Pinkie, the English wanted to establish a strong base in the region by taking all the main castles into their hands and they built a castle at Haddington to 'insult over and annoy the whole

Kingdom'. Yester Castle was captured and placed under the responsibility of Sir George Douglas but it was later recaptured by William Hay, Yester's eldest son. Lord Grey later wrote of 'the house of Yester kept by Spaniards, which I have not seen, but mean to before I depart,' and he later ordered it to be 'razed if not soon fortified'. These instructions seem not to have been carried out, but the castle had been badly damaged.

Queen Mary was smuggled to France in 1548 by Yester's brother-in-law Livingston because the Scots had secured her betrothal to the French Dauphin, the future Francis II. Mary of Guise became Regent in 1554 and Arran was rewarded for his loyalty by being given the title of Duke du Châtellerault; no clearer sign was needed to demonstrate to England that Henry's strategy had completely failed and that French influence over Scottish policy was now dominant. Yester opposed Mary's Regency but he was clearly a man whose support Arran wanted as he was made Warden of the Middle March and a Privy Councillor in 1554 and a year later he was elected Provost of Peebles. In the same year, Mary appointed Yester's neighbour, William Maitland of Lethington, Richard Maitland's eldest son, as her Secretary of State.

Angus died in 1557, leaving as his final legacy his daughter Margaret by Margaret Tudor. She married the Earl of Lennox and their son was Lord Darnley, who was to marry Queen Mary. Yester died aged 47 in the same year as Angus, and thus ended the extraordinary period of the relationship between the Hays and the Douglases. As the power of the latter waned, so that of the Hays began to rise, less controversially and certainly with more loyalty to the interests of the Stuarts. William Hay inherited as 5th Lord Yester, aged twenty. His brother Thomas was Minister of the Cross Kirk in Peebles and his two sisters had both married Lauders, who owned the Bass Rock off Dunbar, which was used as a fortress and as a prison for enemies of the crown.

Yester inherited against a background of increasing unrest in

Scotland caused by anti-French and anti-Catholic feeling, which was fuelled by the increasing success of the Reformation in both Scotland and England. The Church in Scotland was extremely wealthy, enjoying an annual income of £18 million compared with the Crown's income of £1 million. This disparity became increasingly uncomfortable as the monarchy's need for finance increased. The head of the Church was Archbishop Hamilton, Arran's half-brother, but the reputation of the higher clergy was not good. Cardinal Beaton had eight children and he had endowed an illegitimate child with a dowry that no earl could have matched. The anti-Church movement became official in 1557 when the first Covenant was signed by the Lairds of Kincardineshire binding the 'Congregation of Christ' to resist the 'Congregation of Satan'.

Queen Mary married Francis in 1558 and he succeeded as King of France a year later. Mary's heart was in France rather than in Scotland and she signed secret documents which effectively ceded Scotland to France if she died childless. The accession of Elizabeth in England in 1558 had given fresh hope to the reformers in Scotland and John Knox returned in 1559 and inspired reformers to sack churches in Perth. A group of Protestant lords, known as the Lords of the Congregation, drew up another Covenant to 'maintain, set forth, and establish the most blessed Word of God and his Congregation,' although the main purpose of the document was not religious, but to secure Scotland from the threat of France. The Lords were led by Sir William Kirkcaldy and were supported by William Maitland, who abandoned Mary of Guise and secured the backing of Queen Elizabeth. Mary marched against the Lords at Perth with an army led by the Earl of Argyll and Lord James Stewart, the illegitimate son of James V, but when she garrisoned French mercenaries in Perth they abandoned her and she was forced to begin negotiations. The Lords were now joined by many nobles including the earls of Marischal, Atholl, Morton and Glencairn but Yester did not join them as he was willing to support changes in the administration of religion but not in his fundamental Catholic faith. Edinburgh fell to the Lords in July and in October Mary was deposed as Regent and she retreated to Dunbar. Châtelleraut had been reluctant to do anything as long as his son was held hostage in France, but in 1559 he escaped and Châtelleraut now joined the Lords as their leader. He was appointed President of a new Council of the Realm and Mary stripped him of his ducal title.

She was sent fresh French troops and in November they drove the Lords back to Stirling. An English fleet arrived in the Firth of Forth in January 1560 in support of the Lords and Mary retreated to Berwick. In February Yester was a signatory to the Treaty of Berwick, negotiated by William Maitland, whereby England agreed to help the Scots against the French. Mary died in June and the Treaty of Edinburgh secured the withdrawal of both French and English troops from Scotland, leaving power in the hands of the Lords.

Yester attended the Parliament in Edinburgh in July, which consisted of 14 earls, 6 bishops, 19 lords, 21 abbots, 22 burgh commissioners and over 100 lairds. The Committee of the Articles recommended the condemnation of transubstantiation, indulgences, purgatory and papal authority and the redistribution of the wealth of the Church to the ministers, the schools and the poor. Yester was clearly beginning to soften his stance on religious reform as he was one of the nobles who signed The *Book of Discipline* in 1561, which sought to establish the Kirk and the whole nation in accordance with the Will of God by placing ministers throughout Scotland, backed by a system of national education and poor relief. This was not accepted by Parliament as the finance for it would have had to come from the revenues of the Kirk itself, much of which was controlled by the nobles.

Parliament did approve, however, a Reformed Confession of Faith and passed three Acts abolishing the historical practices of the Church. Under these, all previous acts not in conformity with the Reformed Confession were annulled, the celebration of the Mass was made punishable by death and papal jurisdiction in Scotland was removed. However, the clerical estate remained legally intact and, more importantly, in possession of the revenues. Formal decision on all this was, however, delayed, as King Francis had died in December and Queen Mary was returning to Scotland.

Arran still wanted his son James to be Mary's husband, and he was supported by those who did not wish to advance too swiftly towards Protestantism. However, many had no desire to see the Hamiltons increase their influence and Mary's ship was diverted and met by moderates led by James Stewart, her half-brother, and by William Maitland, who believed that Scotland's destiny lay in a union with England and that Mary should be Elizabeth's heir. Mary accepted their arguments, created Stewart Earl of Moray and made him her Chief Adviser.

In 1560 Yester married Margaret Kerr, the daughter of Sir John Kerr of Ferniehirst, Warden of the Middle Marches, who was famous for his ferocity. When he recaptured Ferniehirst Castle from the English in 1549 he had brutally massacred all those English troops taken prisoner and three years later he had been party to the murder of Lord Buccleuch. Yester was a strong supporter of Mary, as was his kinsman the 7th Earl of Erroll, but he did not want Arran to control her. He entertained her at Neidpath Castle in 1563 and signed an address by a number of nobles asking Elizabeth to marry Arran's son. Mary married Lord Darnley, the son of the Earl of Lennox, in 1565. He was next in line to the throne after Mary and the marriage was extremely unpopular with many of the nobles, especially with Morton, Lennox's old enemy Arran and with Secretary Maitland. Yester was reported as saying that he would oppose Darnley and 'hang with the Douglases', meaning Morton, but he nevertheless led her army alongside Darnley opposing Moray and Arran, who had raised an army against the marriage. Yester triumphed, Moray and Arran both fled to England and Arran only returned to Scotland in 1569, when he was imprisoned until 1573. His son was declared insane in 1562 and he lived until 1609, dying alone and forgotten as the man who could have married either the Queen of Scotland or the Queen of England.

Mary gave birth to Prince James in 1566 and he was baptised a Catholic. Darnley was murdered a year later and Mary quickly married the Earl of Bothwell, much against the wishes of many of the nobles, especially Maitland, who considered him responsible for Darnley's death. They raised an army in June and forced Mary and Bothwell to withdraw at Carberry Hill near Musselborough. Yester was again with Mary's forces and it was reported that 'Yester and Borthwick were horsed in the field, and came away when they saw all was lost'. Mary and Bothwell spent a last night together at the rebuilt Seton Palace then Bothwell fled to Norway, where he died after eighteen years of imprisonment and madness. Mary was imprisoned in Loch Leven Castle and deposed and Moray was appointed Regent for the young King James VI.

Mary escaped in 1568 and Yester again joined her supporters and was one of the signatories to a bond calling for her restitution, signed by eight earls, nine bishops, eighteen lords, twelve abbots and nearly one hundred barons. At the battle of Langside in May 1568, Yester and Argyll led Mary's army against forces led by Moray and Morton but they were defeated and Mary fled to England, never to return. Despite this, Yester remained loyal to her and he joined a group of nobles who wrote to Queen Elizabeth in 1570 asking for Mary to be released from captivity. He was named that year as being 'head of Mary's party' and he was punished for this and declared forfeit by Parliament, which granted Francis Stewart, a grandson of James V of Scotland, lands owned by Yester and by Bothwell, whose title of Earl he was also given. The charter authorising this was signed, amongst others, by John Maitland, William's younger brother, but Moray later suspended Yester's forfeiture at the request of Elizabeth.

Moray was killed in 1570 by a Hamilton who shot him from a window in Edinburgh in the first recorded assassination of a political leader by a firearm, and Lennox, Darnley's father, succeeded him as Regent. This angered many nobles and civil war again erupted. William Maitland and his brother John led Queen Mary's supporters which included Yester in a rare example of cooperation between the two neighbouring families. Elizabeth decided to intervene and she sent the Earl of Sussex north with an army, and he seized Lethington. The Maitland brothers were dismissed from office and took refuge in Edinburgh Castle, with one of Yester's sons. The English forced the surrender of the castle and William Maitland was found dead in his room. His brother John was held in Tantallon Castle for a year and then allowed to live with Lord Somerville at his castle in the Pentland hills on surety of £175,000.

Lennox was killed in 1571 and Morton became Regent. Yester had become a Presbyterian, realising that his loyalty to Mary no longer made sense and he gave his support to Morton who made him Commissioner of Muster in 1574. Two years later Yester was one of the signatories of the Bond of Roxburgh, by which the nobles pledged their allegiance to King James VI. The importance of Yester's conversion is shown by comparing the fortunes of his descendants with those of his kinsmen, the Earls of Erroll, who largely remained fervent Catholics.

The Reformation greatly complicated the position of the king. John Knox considered that the godly had a duty to revolt against an ungodly monarch, and this theme was also taken up by the political writer and tutor to James, George Buchanan. When Knox died in 1572, Andrew Melville took over as leader of the Kirk and pressed for Episcopacy to be abolished and for Presbyterianism to be established in Scotland. Melville made his position clear to

James: 'There is two kings and two kingdoms in Scotland. There is Christ Jesus the King, and his kingdom the Kirk, whose subject King James the Sixth is, and of whose kingdom not a king, nor a lord, nor a head, but a member.'

Melville was, however, overconfident about his ability to control the king as the Reformation had deeper consequences for the balance of power in Scotland than he realised, especially in regards to Scotland's ability to truly remain an independent nation. The defeat of the pro-French and pro-Catholic Queen Mary had only been achieved with help from Protestant England, with which Scotland was now at peace and this meant that the monarchy did not have to rely so heavily on the magnates for support. The Scottish Reformation would never have succeeded without their leadership and they immediately benefitted as their clerical rivals for power had been removed and this provided them with a new source of wealth; but they retained great ambitions for power and the king's patronage remained important. The lairds, however, also benefitted from the Reformation and they emerged over time as competitors to the magnates. The Englishman Sir Henry Killigrew wrote perceptively in 1572 'Methinks I see the noblemen's great credit decay in this country and the barons, burghs and such-like take more upon them.'

Yester wanted to be closer to Morton and government and Neidpath was far from Edinburgh so he decided to return to East Lothian. He had seven children and his damaged Yester Castle was not suitable for such a large family. Scotland was now at peace so there was little need for a castle so he decided to build a new house on a site a mile from Yester Castle, close to St Cuthbert's and the village of Bothans. The new house was finished in 1582, which date was inscribed on a fireplace lintel still preserved in the servants' hall of the current house. It was a traditional L-shaped building with a four-storey tower, but it had the aspect of a country house rather than a fortified house like Neidpath, where his eldest son, William, continued to live.

Despite his position in government, and his increasing domesticity, Yester seemed at times unable to control his natural hotheadedness, for in 1578 he was declared a rebel for attacking the officers who had been sent to seize his assets, but he was soon restored to favour. His champion, Morton, was, however, overthrown in 1580 and executed in a coup inspired by James's cousin and favourite Esme Stewart, who was made Duke of Lennox. Lennox was hated by the nobles because of his character, his religion and his influence over the king, but Yester seemed to have hedged his bets as he declared in the Parliament of 1580 that he was 'neutral as to Lennox'. Lennox was supported by James Stewart, who was made Earl of Arran, and James put him and Lennox in charge of his government.

Yester did not stay long in his new house, however, as he changed his mind about Lennox and in 1582 joined a group of Presbyterian nobles led by the Earl of Gowrie in the Raid of Ruthven, where they abducted the sixteen-year-old king from Gowrie's castle in Perthshire. Gowrie was made Lord High Treasurer and he led a strict Presbyterian government and Lennox was exiled to France where he died a year later. Arran led a group of Catholic nobles who helped James escape in 1583 and the Ruthven Raiders were convicted of treason and exiled and Yester went with Lords Boyd and Wemyss to the Low Countries. James now imposed his authority and had Parliament pass the 'Black Acts' which gave him authority over 'all persons and causes in his kingdom'. They confirmed the authority of the bishops but ensured that the Kirk was subordinate to the State.

Queen Elizabeth needed to know that Scotland would not support Spain against her. She distrusted Arran and his government, which was full of Catholics and supporters of Mary, including John Maitland who had been restored to favour. She wanted to restore the exiled lords, so she sent Edward Wotton, a cousin of

Walsingham's to Scotland in 1584 to meet John Maitland to negotiate their return as part of a more general agreement with England, which would include confirmation of James's right to succeed her to the English throne, the prize he valued most highly of all. At the same time, Elizabeth had instigated a plot against Arran in which Yester's nephew, Sir Thomas Kerr, was unwittingly to play a major role. Kerr had a meeting with his opposite English Warden of the Middle March, Sir John Forster, to deal with the increasing problems in the borders but there was a fight at this meeting and Lord Russell was killed. Kerr was a Catholic and Arran's appointee and Wotton used this to accuse Arran of instigating the murder to break the relationship between Scotland and England.

Yester and the other exiled lords landed at Kelso in October where they were joined by other nobles and marched on Stirling, where the king and Arran were. Arran fled and the lords formed a new government with John Maitland appointed as Secretary of State. Arran lost his earldom and all the properties he had accumulated whilst in power but he and his supporters were treated leniently; but he was later murdered by Sir James Douglas, Morton's nephew.

The Scotland James ruled over was still quasi-medieval with a poor, mainly agrarian, economy, which produced little taxation revenue for the king. He had no standing army and no trained bureaucracy, and his patronage was limited as many important offices were hereditary and held by nobles who ruled over their estates like monarchs, with tenants and kinsmen giving them their service and paying them their dues. The strength of the monarchy still depended on the personal strength of each monarch, and no monarch had ascended the throne except as a minor in the last 200 years. This gave the nobles every opportunity to assert their individual ambitions for power, as James had seen several times already.

James was well advised by Maitland, who increasingly took control of the machinery of his government. The king appointed the members of the Privy Council, which was responsible for the day-to-day administration of government and which controlled the Committee of the Articles. The members of this were also chosen by the king and it was the only channel by which Acts could be brought before Parliament. James could call a Convention of Estates as an alternative to a formal Parliament, but only to vote on taxes and to modify Acts of Parliament. He did not have the same control over the judiciary, since the office of Justice General was the hereditary possession of the earls of Argyll and the members of the civil court, the Court of Session, were appointed for life. However, its fifteen senators were appointed by the monarch who could also appoint Extraordinary Lords of Session.

James wrote in his *Basilikon Doron* of 1599: 'The greatest hindrance to the execution of our laws... are these heritable sheriff-doms and regalities, which being in the hands of great men, do wrack the whole country: for which I know no present remedy.' Such regalities also included the Wardens of the Marches, which were tightly held by a few noble families. Between 1558 and 1603, five members of the Ker family were Wardens of the West March, as were six members of the Home family for the East March and there were nineteen separate Wardens of the West Marches, principally from the Maxwell and Johnstone families.

James's priority was to prevent the union of magnates and Kirk that had brought down his mother. He wrote in his *Basilikon Doron* of the nobles' 'feckless arrogant conceit of their greatness and power (which) arose from the fact that for forty years or more they had only for governors in this kingdom women, little children and traitrous and avaricious regents... little by little he would have them in good order.'

He decided to build a new cadre of men from amongst the lairds, the lawyers, and the younger sons of the magnates, who would thus depend on him for their position and remain loyal. The lairds had benefited from feu farms, which appeared in the middle of the 14th century but were not widely used until the middle of the 16th century. These gave security of possession to their leaseholders who were thus less dependent on the magnates. It was through these lairds that James ran his government and the magnates were increasingly isolated and the treaty of peace with England in 1585 meant that they could no longer use England as a base of support for their personal ambitions. The English Ambassador wrote that 'the greatest strength of Scotland consisteth in the gentlemen which they here call lairds, and the boroughs which are almost all well reflected in religion; therefore the king with these may easily bridle the earls.' Some lairds, like Douglas of Lochleven and Scott of Buccleuch, became as powerful as the magnates. Yester's family benefitted from this new policy as he was a Lord of Parliament and, although this was essentially a courtesy title, he identified himself with the strong emerging class of lairds rather than being in thrall to the now less relevant magnates.

The Parliament of 1587 was the defining one of James's reign. Two key acts were passed with the first being the Annexation of the Temporalities of Benefices to the Crown. Since the 1470s the highest offices in the Church had become the monopoly of the magnates, as members of their families became bishops, abbots or commendators of monasteries. After the Reformation these were confirmed in their positions, but one third of their income now had to be paid to the Crown. The Act now gave James the power to decide who should be the holders of such offices and those he appointed were called Lords of Erection. The second key Act allowed the lairds to enter Parliament.

Yester did not enjoy his new house for long as he died in 1586 aged only 49, a year after his return from exile, leaving five daughters and two sons, both of whom succeeded him as Lord Yester. Three of his daughters married into the Lothian families of Borthwick, Swinton and Ker; and one married her cousin, Sir James Hay of Barra, one of the Hays of Linplum.

William Hay inherited aged 25 as 6th Lord Yester. He had inherited his father's hot headedness and his absence overseas had allowed him the freedom to exercise it. Southern Scotland was experiencing a general breakdown in law and order as the absence of war meant that many were seeking alternative ways to enrich themselves, or just avoid tedium. The Borders were filled with thieves and freebooters but the fights were as often between the lairds themselves as between them and the vagabonds. William took it upon himself to impose discipline, acting in his role as the son of the Sheriff of Peebles. He rode through the countryside with 50 men, taking the law into his own hands and hanging without trial many of the criminals he caught.

He married Elizabeth Maxwell, the daughter of Lord Herries, the Warden of the Western March, and they had one son and six daughters. In 1584 King James had revoked a charter that had been drawn up in William's minority whereby William, then Master of Yester, had confirmed the lands and barony of Snaid in Dunfries and of Meggett and Oliver Castle in Peebles to himself and his wife Elizabeth Maxwell and their male heirs and, failing those, the male heirs designated by Yester himself. William's only son had died aged only eleven and someone had challenged this charter on behalf of his six daughters. The revocation found 'great iniquitie therein, in respect of the manifest hurt and prejudice which it should carie to the heirs of line, be the laws of God and nature, ought to succeed to their said father's heritage'.

He was arraigned for the murder of the laird of Westrawis's servant in 1585 and in the same year a complaint was made against him before the Privy Council by John Livingstone of Belstane regarding a violent attack William had made on him. Livingstone said he had left his home before sunrise when suddenly he had been attacked by about 40 heavily armed men. They were led by William and consisted of sons of other nobles accompanied by men at arms who Livingstone accused of trying to kill him. He fled to his house, which they then surrounded, firing at him continuously for over three hours. The attackers were denounced as rebels by the Privy Council, but it seemed reluctant to impose any sentence.

The next year William was again brought before the Council on a complaint made by Sir John Stewart of Traquair and his brother, James. The Traquairs' house stood on the bank of the Tweed near Neidpath Castle and they had been strong supporters of Mary and had often given refuge to Catholic priests. They complained that William had unlawfully taken on his father's responsibilities as Sheriff and had arranged numerous illegal wappenshaws, which were musters of men under arms, thereby gathering arms illegally. The Council summoned both William and his father to answer the charges, but only William attended, as his father was too sick to travel and William was ordered to stop his attacks on the Traquairs for one year or until judgement was brought.

The king was hunting in the Borders in 1587 and he stayed at Neidpath Castle with William, now Lord Yester. James summoned the Traquairs to meet him there to resolve the dispute and he arranged for letters of affirmance to be drawn up between them, but Yester refused to sign. James threatened to denounce him as a rebel and ordered him to enter into ward north of the Tay and to stay there until released by his command. Yester refused and he was imprisoned in Edinburgh Castle, from where the Keeper, his father's friend, Sir James Hume, allowed him to escape.

❧

Walsingham had revealed Queen Mary's involvement in the Babington Plot in 1586, and it was also revealed that she had planned to disinherit James and exile him to Spain. The Giffards played a small role in this as Queen Elizabeth often stayed with Sir John Giffard of Chillington, the High Sheriff of Staffordshire. Gilbert, one of his sons, had gone to Paris where he was asked by Walsingham to intercept letters from Queen Mary. He was entrusted by an English exile in Paris to carry a letter from Mary to Thomas Morgan, her most trusted agent in Paris, and he did so without revealing the letter to Walsingham. Morgan was arrested in August 1586, and Gilbert confessed his role and betrayed his co-conspirators. The French threw him into gaol, the English refused to help him and he died there in 1590. Sir Edward Stafford, the English Ambassador in Paris, wrote of him: 'He has shown himself the most notable treble villain that has ever lived, for he has played upon all the hands in the world.'

James was chiefly concerned that Mary's crimes might negate his rights of succession and he showed little remorse when she was executed in 1587. There was, however, great anger in Scotland which Arran tried to take advantage of by accusing all his enemies, especially Maitland, of being accessories to her death, but he found little support. James showed his confidence in Maitland by giving him the lordship of Musselburgh and by appointing him Chancellor, the first that century who was neither a bishop nor a magnate.

James was determined to stop the feuding between the nobles so in 1587 he summoned them all to Edinburgh to resolve their differences and to unite in support of him. After a banquet at Holyrood, they processed hand-in-hand to the Cross of Edinburgh and there, before a great crowd of onlookers, James made them pledge their friendship and support. Yester alone refused and he was again committed to Edinburgh Castle where, after a few months' imprisonment, he at last repented and was released.

He was forgiven by James and was appointed to the Privy Council in 1589 but he died two years later, aged only 30. Just before he died he had made a charter creating a new lordship and barony of Yester to his heir, his brother James, who then inherited as 7th Lord Yester aged 26. William had obviously learned from the revocation of the earlier charter as the new one contained a clause stating 'for the exoneration of our conscience and the conscience of the said William, Lord Hay of Yester' that, for excluding his daughters from their inheritance of lands, the eldest daughter should be left £100,000, the next £65,000 and the remaining four £50,000 each. The charter was dated 1591 but it had not been officially approved when Yester died. John Maitland, who was living nearby at Lethington, saw his chance to add to his family's estates and, as the price for granting the charter, he demanded that the new Lord Yester cede him the lands of Lethington and Haystoun and Yester had to agree.

Maitland perhaps felt guilty at his coup, because a year later he arranged the marriage of Yester to Margaret Kerr, daughter of the Earl of Lothian. He also acted as ward to William's six daughters, successfully arranging marriages for two of them, which led to later additions to the estates of the Hays. Jean was married to Tweedie, the laird of Drumelzier, which lay near Neidpath Castle, and Maria was married to Alexander, Laird of Horseburgh, who was killed in France fighting under Sir James Douglas and whose estate was left to Yester's eldest son, John.

It was during the life of James, Lord Yester that the fortunes of the Hays of Erroll rapidly declined whilst those of the Hays of Yester continued their slow but strong ascent. A crucial cause of the relative changes was that the Errolls remained Catholics whereas the Hays of Yester were Presbyterians. Their disparate fortunes also reflected the last great attempt by magnates to subjugate a King of Scotland by arms. Both main branches of the Hays were involved in this through their respective support of the Catholic Earl of Huntly in the north and the Presbyterian Earl of Bothwell in the south. The Earl of Bothwell had received his title in 1570 after Queen Mary's husband was forfeited and he had also been given his lands of Morham and those in the parish of Yester. He married the daughter of the Earl of Angus and was made the hereditary keeper of Liddesdale and Lord High Admiral of Scotland in 1588.

Francis Hay, the 9th Earl of Erroll, had a difficult upbringing. His two brothers were declared insane as children and his mother died when he was still a boy. Francis married Margaret, the daughter of the Earl of Moray, in 1584 and a year later both Margaret and Francis's father died. He married Mary, the daughter of the Earl of Atholl, in 1586 but she died two years later. Finally he married Elizabeth, the daughter of the Earl of Morton in 1590, by whom he had five sons and eight daughters. One of these, Mary, married the Earl of Buccleuch and she gave birth to a daughter, Jean, who would become the wife of Yester's son, John Hay, the 1st Earl of Tweeddale.

The next five years of James's reign were dominated by the plots of the Catholic earls and of Bothwell, who were united only in their hatred of Maitland. Huntly and Errol entered into a plot with Philip II of Spain in 1589 to land troops in Scotland and then invade England. Elizabeth demanded their punishment but James treated them with leniency but later that year the two earls were joined by Bothwell and they rose against the king. They surrendered to him at Aberdeen and were convicted of treason, but he freed them after only a few months imprisonment.

James attended in 1591 the trial at North Berwick in East Lothian of a group of people accused of witchcraft. James was fascinated by witches and he had even written a treatise on them saying they should be burnt. He interrogated the accused himself and he learned that some of their spells had been directed against him. John Fion, one of the accused, admitted that he had been engaged by Bothwell in such witchery and he was sentenced to be burnt at the stake at Edinburgh. When James heard that Barbara Napier, another witch, had been saved from death because of her supposed pregnancy, he instructed Maitland: 'Try by the mediciners' oaths if Barbara Napier be with bairn or not. Take no delaying answer. If you find she be not, to the fire with her presently, and cause her (disem)bowel her publicly.' She did not pass the test and she also was burnt at Edinburgh.

James arrested Bothwell and ordered his exile, but he escaped and fled to Hermitage Castle. Although he seemed to be able to move freely from there about Scotland, James's authority over the magnates was clearly growing as in 1591 both Atholl and Marischal were warded for giving support to Bothwell and the Lord Treasurer, the Earl of Glamis, who was an enemy of Maitland, was also censured. Nobles in the Western Marches were warned not to give Bothwell refuge and two Catholics, the laird of Fentry and the Master of Angus, had their property seized and were exiled for doing so. Huntly, however, told James that Bothwell was in Leith but he escaped before the king could capture him.

Yester was torn between his loyalty to James and his hatred of Maitland but he decided that Bothwell was driven by his own hatred of Maitland rather than from any disloyalty to the king. He also considered that Bothwell was the only southern lord capable of challenging Maitland's influence; hence he gave him his support, though never openly enough for him to be censured. In December, Bothwell failed to seize the king and Maitland at Holyrood and Lennox, Angus, Morton and Mar were all accused of complicity in the raid. They denied it but did say to James 'they were as the rest of the nobility, in word and deed contrary to the chancellor, who, they said, abused His Grace, the nobility, and common weal'.

Huntly brutally murdered the young Earl of Moray in 1592, but James showed little concern, even when Moray's mother brought her son's body to him and vowed it would not be buried until his death had been avenged. However James and Maitland's refusal to arrest Huntly turned public opinion against them leading

Robert Bowes, the English ambassador to Scotland, to report: 'The grudge of Moray's slaughter so works in the heart of most men... that they will not give their endeavours to touch Bothwell.'

Queen Anne disliked Maitland and was sympathetic to Bothwell but James declared him a traitor and forfeited him and he responded by attacking the king at Falkland Palace. James ordered Maitland to stay at Lethington, although he remained as Chancellor, and in his absence Lennox, the son of James's favourite Esme, became the dominant figure at court. Elizabeth wrote to James encouraging him to pardon Bothwell, who she allowed to travel freely in the north of England. As James did not do as she asked she stopped his pension payments. This was not good for James as his finances were never healthy and he relied on the pension of £800,000 a year Elizabeth paid him.

George Ker was seized in December carrying letters of various Scottish Catholics to their friends on the Continent. These included a number of blank letters bearing the seals of Huntly, Erroll and Angus, which Ker admitted were to be used in a plot involving the landing of 30,000 Spanish soldiers in Scotland. Queen Anne told James to take immediate action against the Catholic earls and she sent an envoy to Bothwell asking for his help. James set up a commission, headed by Maitland, to decide what to do with the catholic earls, while he focussed on dealing with Bothwell. Anne was now pregnant and this had the added benefit of easing the rivalry between Lennox and Lord John Hamilton as to who would inherit when James died.

The Convention of Estates passed the Act of Abolition in November 1593, requiring everyone in Scotland to either embrace the true religion by February 1st or to go into exile and it also declared that anyone choosing exile would receive immunity for all crimes except murder. The earls were given until January 1st to announce their decision. Maitland seemed, however, to be hedging his bets, for the English ambassador, Lord Zouche, wrote: 'I am told for certain that the Lord Chancellor works underhand for the earls and receives great sums of money to that end.'

Bothwell raided Leith in April 1594 and James led a force to oppose him but he soon 'came riding in to Edinburgh at the full gallop, with little honor.' There he promised: 'If the Lord gives me victory over Bothwell, I shall never rest till I pass upon Huntly and the rest of the excommunicated lords.'

Parliament declared in May that the earls were guilty of treason and voted an increase in supply to finance the army needed to confront them. Elizabeth sent James £2.5 million and told Bothwell not to attack the king whilst he confronted the earls. Despite this, James wrote to Maitland saying that he did not have enough to meet his household bills, pleading 'Help me now, or never.'

James had succeeded in breaking Bothwell's support in the Borders so he was forced to once again cast his lot with the earls and helped them defeat Argyll at the battle of Glenlivet where Erroll was severely wounded and Huntly's chief military adviser killed. James razed Erroll's Slains Castle and Huntly's castle at Strathbogie, they were exiled and their property forfeited to Lennox, who elegantly returned it to their wives. Angus was also exiled and his property was forfeited, but this time Lennox kept it. For Bothwell there was no mercy: his property was shared between Home, Buccleuch and Ker, he was excommunicated and his brother executed. He eventually left Scotland in 1595 and he died impoverished in Naples in 1631.

In October 1595 John Maitland, lay ill at Lethington and was asked what advice he should give the king. He replied: 'It is too late, my thoughts are upon another world' and he died that night. James composed a sonnet that was carved on his tomb in St Margaret's Church in Haddington. Huntly and Erroll returned to Scotland secretly in 1596 and abjured Roman Catholicism; Huntly was created a Marquis and made Lieutenant of the North, but he never abandoned Catholicism and he died out of favour. Erroll was appointed a commissioner to negotiate Union with England in 1602 but, like Huntly, his conversion was suspect and in May 1608 he was declared an obstinate papist, excommunicated, deprived of his estate and imprisoned for three years. James, however, always seemed to like him and released him and he died peacefully at Slains in 1631. 'He was,' said Sir Robert Douglas, 'a truly noble man, of a great and courageous spirit, who had great troubles in his time, which he stoutly and honourably carried; and now in favour, died in peace with God and man, and a loyal subject to the King, to the great grief of his friends.'

Thus ended the last rebellion by magnates against a Scottish king; driven by the toxic combination of religion and the thirst for power. Yester watched as his kinsman, Erroll, and his most powerful Lothian lord and neighbour, Bothwell, destroyed their reputations, their positions and, ultimately, their lives. The Hays of Yester had seen many such examples of men ruined by ambition over the years and the examples of the Douglases and of the Catholic Earls showed what their fate could be if driven by greed and disloyalty to their monarch.

Yester, however, remained rebellious, albeit for very local and personal reasons. He was summoned in 1594 for seizing Broun of Froisthill and taking him to Neidpath Castle, where 'he put he in the pit thereof, and detained him as captive, he being his majesty's free subject... having committit nae crime nor offence, and the said lord having nae power nor commission to tak him.' The king ordered Yester to liberate Broun but was ignored; Yester refused to attend the court and officers were ordered to again denounce him a rebel. As nothing happened, he must have decided to behave and perhaps he had also learnt a lesson from the fate of his kinsman Erroll.

Yester was involved in the last trial by combat in Scotland's history. He had a page called George Hepburn and a Master of

Horse called John Brown, who also worked for Yester's kinsman, Hay of Smithfield. Brown said to Hepburn: 'Your father has a good knowledge of physic, I think you should have some also, you might have great advantage of something.' Hepburn asked him what he meant. Brown said that as Lord Yester had lost his first son, Hay of Smithfield was therefore his heir, and 'if you could give him some poison you should be nobly rewarded.' Hepburn told Yester about this but, when challenged, Brown denied saying it and it was decided that the dispute should be settled by combat.

This was held in public at Edstonhaugh on the banks of the Tweed near Neidpath and the Laird of Buccleuch acted as judge for Brown and the Laird of Cessford for Hepburn. The two combatants fought on horseback with spears and swords; Brown was thrown from his horse and Hepburn stood over him challenging him to tell the truth. Brown tried to continue the fight but had no real strength and Hepburn felled him with the flat of the sword. Hepburn was declared the victor but Brown never recanted.

Yester decided to concentrate his estates on East Lothian so he sold various lands in Peeblesshire and bought the estate of Linplum, which lay close to Gifford. He was sued for neglecting his role as Sheriff of Peebles in 1599, and he died in 1609, aged 45. He left four children: John, who inherited as 8th Lord Yester, aged sixteen; Robert, who died young; William, who inherited the estate of Linplum; and Margaret, who married Alexander Seton, the fourth son of the 7th Lord Seton, as his third wife. Yester's widow, Margaret, married Sir Andrew Kerr, Master of Jedburgh, and she built the Lady Yester church in Edinburgh, where services are still held.

Whilst Maitland lived, James was prepared to support his policy of conciliation with the Kirk and in 1592 the Golden Act had legalised the Presbyterian courts. James also recognised the preeminence of the General Assembly and in return the ministers agreed to recognize the office of bishop. However, in his *Basilikon*

Doron, James revealed his true feelings about the ministers, saying they preached 'that all Kings and Princes were naturally enemies to the liberty of the Church... [they were] very pests in the Church and Commonwealth, whom no deserts can oblige, neither oaths nor promises bind, breathing nothing but seditions and calumnies.'

The Kirk was now at the peak of its powers and this inspired Andrew Melville, to make his speech outlining his view of the two Kingdoms of Church and State where he spoke of 'two kings and two Kingdoms in Scotland' and of James as 'God's sillie vassal'. There was a riot in Edinburgh in 1596 after James threatened to punish the minister of Saint Andrews who, in a sermon, had called all kings 'children of the devil' and had accused Queen Elizabeth of atheism. The riot collapsed under James's threat of force and he moved to establish an episcopal system similar to the one in England. He replaced Maitland's office with an eight man Commission, lead by Alexander Seton, who was appointed President of the Court of Session in 1596 and he told the General Assembly in 1597 that he would never hold another one if they did not accept his right to summon it.

He now felt secure and he challenged Melville's doctrine of the Two Kingdoms in his own book titled *Trew Law of Free Monarchies* of 1598, where he set out his own doctrine of the divine right of kings: a good king should always rule justly and in accordance with the law, but his position as king depends neither on the law nor on the goodwill of his subjects, he is accountable only to God. James proposed that ministers of the Kirk should be able to vote in Parliament, that the commissioners be elected for life and that they should attend Parliament. The General Assembly of 1600 rejected his proposals but he went ahead anyway and made three appointments as bishops.

Chapter 6 – James, King of Scotland and England

Elizabeth died in 1603 and James became King of England, Ireland and Scotland. He appointed Alexander Seton as Lord Chancellor of Scotland in 1604 and he held that post till his death in 1622. Seton married three times, each time to a teenager. His last wife was Margaret Hay, the new Lord Yester's sister, by whom he had his son and heir, Charles. Seton lived at Pinkie House in Musselburgh, and it was there that he looked after Prince Charles when Queen Anne took her eldest son, Prince Henry, to England in 1603. Pinkie was an L-plan tower house built in the 16th century by the Abbots of Dunfermline; Seton bought it in 1597 and, when he married Margaret in 1607, he added a long south wing which included a magnificent 96-foot painted gallery with an inscription in Latin: 'Alexander Seton has planted, raised and decorated a country house... he has brought together everything that might afford decent pleasures of heart and mind.'

Prince Charles was a sickly child, suffering from rickets and there was at Yester a picture of him as a young man walking with a stick because of this. Seton's first wife, Grizel, took great care of the young prince, for which he was ever grateful. She was the half-sister of John Leslie, Earl of Rothes, whose family was to be heavily involved with the Hays over the next hundred years.

James was confident that governmental union would swiftly follow his accession and Seton was appointed a commissioner to this end but he was the only senior member of James's ministry who did not go with the king to London. James was so pleased with his work that he created him Earl of Dunfermline in 1605. Seton was, however, a Catholic but he had taken the oath of office as Lord of Session in 1588; he later told a Jesuit priest 'I have to live in Scotland, and I must give way to circumstances. When the opportunity presents itself, and there is any hope of success, I shall not be sparing of my goods, my blood, or my life, for the restoration of the Catholic religion.'

A number of Yester's kinsmen were given appointments by James and the one who gained greatest prominence was James Hay of Kingask who the king called his 'prime favourite.' He was knighted and made a Gentleman of the Bedchamber and later Comptroller of the Treasury He was made a baron, a Knight of the Order of the Bath and, in 1615, he was given the English title of Lord Hay of Sawley. In the same year he was sent to France to negotiate the marriage of Prince Charles to Princess Christina, though without success. He married Lady Lucy Percy in 1617 and he helped Lord Holland negotiate Prince Charles's marriage with Henrietta Maria. He was created Earl of Carlisle and granted the right over all the Caribbean Islands and he died in March 1636. Clarendon wrote that he left a reputation as 'a very fine gentleman and a most accomplished courtier, and after having spent in a very jovial life he left not a house or acre of land to be remembered by'. At his death the peerage became extinct in the Hay family.

Carlisle had brought with him to England his cousin, George Hay of Megginch, who was with James when he was almost murdered by the Gowries in 1600 and who was to become one of his most important ministers. Alexander Hay of Fosterseat was appointed to the Court of Session and later made a Privy Councillor and Lord Clerk Register of Scotland whilst Alexander Hay of

Whitburgh was appointed Secretary of State for Scottish Affairs.

These Hays proved the exception as, apart from Lord Balmerino, who was made Secretary of State for Scotland, few Scots reached positions of power as James retained most of Elizabeth's officials, including Cecil as Secretary of State. These served him so well that he could write of Scotland in 1607: 'Here I sit and govern it with my pen... by a Clerk of the Council I govern Scotland, which others could not do by the Sword.' James did, however, appoint many of his favourite nobles to his Household, including Sir George Home as Master of the Wardrobe, Lord Kinross Master of the Rolls and he appointed twelve nobles to the English Privy Council. Many of these received generous pensions which by 1608 amounted to £2.4 million annually. The Venetian agent wrote in 1603: 'No Englishman, be his rank what it may, can enter the Presence Chamber without being summoned whereas the Scottish lords have free *entrée* of the privy chamber, and more especially at the *toilette*.'

James made Sir George Home Earl of Dunbar in 1606 and was ordered to end the lawlessness in the borders. Dunfermline had become unpopular and James replaced him with Dunbar, but James asked him to serve as Dunbar's second in command. Archbishop Spottiswoode was made President of the Exchequer Commission, the first churchman to hold that post. Dunbar reduced the Privy Council from 90 to 36 members by removing the judges and Balmerino, a Catholic, was convicted of treason and removed from office. On Dunbar's death in 1611, Dunfermline again became James's principal minister in Scotland and he effectively took control as governing England was taking up most of James's time, especially after Salisbury had died in 1612.

Yester was sent abroad in 1611 aged eighteen 'for the better exercysing of himself in all such virtues, comelie and worthie exercises as becometh one of his rank and qualitie'. He was appointed a Commissioner for the middle shires of Tweeddale in 1619 and was made a Justice of the Peace four years later. It was said of him that he had 'great industry and sagacity in business'. In 1624 he married Jean Seton, who was Dunfermline's daughter by his second wife, Grizel; hence Dunfermline became both his father-, and brother-, in-law. Yester described his bride as 'a comely wench and may be a wife to the best in the kingdom'. However she tragically died in 1626, only eight days after giving birth to his heir, John. Yester was distraught and asked his sister, the Countess of Dunfermline, to look after the boy. This she did till he turned six, when he was sent to school in Haddington, before going on to Edinburgh College.

George Hay of Megginch was knighted in 1612 and succeeded Alexander Hay as Lord Clerk Register, one of the oldest offices of state in Scotland, dating from the 13th century. Between 1577, when Sir Alexander Hay of Easter Kennet had held the post, and 1641, the office was almost hereditary for members of Clan Hay. Sir George had interests in glass and iron and he shared the monopoly for whale fishing and he was one of the first businessmen to hold high office in a Scottish Government.

James visited Scotland in 1617, the only time he was to do so after his succession in 1603. He presided over a meeting of the Privy Council where his new favourite, the Earl of Buckingham, was the first Englishman to become a member. He then went hunting for two weeks and returned to attend the Whitsun service in Edinburgh where Argyll, Dunfermline, Sir George Hay and all the bishops took communion kneeling, in the Catholic fashion. James was eager to bring the Scottish Church closer to the Episcopalian Church of England and he proposed an Act of Parliament that would allow the king, after consultations with the bishops and ministers, to make binding decisions on 'all matters decent for the external policy of the Kirk'. This referred to the Catholic-influenced Five Articles of Perth which James forced the General Assembly to accept in 1618.

The Marquis of Hamilton was appointed High Commissioner to Parliament and the Act was passed in 1621, with Yester in the dissenting minority. Archbishop Spottiswoode celebrated, saying 'The king is Pope now, and so shall be.' However, passing the Act was one thing; getting everyone to accept it was another, and many senior clergy and ordinary people chose not to attend services rather than follow the Articles. By then James's focus had turned to more immediate concerns as the Thirty Years War had begun and he needed financial support from Scotland. Hamilton succeeded in getting increased Supply voted and Sir George Hay raised this through a tax on annual rents, which represented the first time tax had been raised from the middle class, showing how Scotland's economic prosperity was growing. Sir George replaced Dunfermline after his death in 1622 and Hamilton's brother was made Lord Clerk Register. Hay's officials came mostly from the rank of the lairds, lawyers and the younger sons of the magnates.

James died in 1625 and Charles succeeded, knowing little of, and perhaps caring even less about, his native land. Scotland had suffered from crop failure and famine for three years, but Charles did nothing to help. He sought instead 'the aggrandisement of the crown in wealth and influence, the emancipation of lesser men from the power of the magnates and the material well-being of the church'. He relied on the advice of two London-based Scots, the Earl of Nithsdale, a Catholic who was 'arrogant, stupid, deeply in debt and much disliked by the ruling triumvirate', and the poet, Sir William Alexander, who had been the principal proposer of a scheme to colonise Nova Scotia, to be financed by the sale of baronies.

Without consulting even these advisers, Charles announced his intention to issue an Act of Revocation over all the gifts of land which had belonged to either the Crown or the Kirk, as well as all grants of hereditary offices, made since 1540. This was a step that was traditionally allowed to Scottish kings on their succession to protect them from the consequences of any misgovernment during their minority but he was the first king since Robert III in 1390 to succeed as an adult and thus the the Revocation was considered inappropriate. Charles's intent was to increase both clerical stipends and royal revenues but, as this would affect every landowner in Scotland, their reaction was very negative. The amount of such property involved was significant as lands held by the Kirk, and former Kirk property now held by laymen, accounted for half of all the tax raised. Sir James Balfour wrote in 1824 that this Act 'in effect was the ground stone of all the mischief that followed after'.

Charles believed he had the right to impose anything he liked as long as it was within the law and he sought to increase his authority further by separating the Privy Council and the Court of Session and ordering that the nobles, privy councillors and judges should no longer sit on the Court. This again was a direct attack on the historic privileges and power of the nobility.

Melrose was President of the Court of Session and he led the challenges to many of Charles's proposed changes. Charles summoned him, Rothes and John Campbell, Earl of Loudon to London in January 1626 where they presented their case for a fortnight after which they returned north 'defeated and resentful'.

Charles could not understand their concerns, even when they pointed out that if this Act were passed then no Scottish landlord could be sure of his property now or in the future. Even Sir George Hay told Charles that those who had advised him to issue the Revocation had 'made shipwreck of their own estates, and would now fish in drumlie waters by shaking all things loose that they may get some part to themselves; some of them having no wit at all, some of them half witted, and neither of them of great honesty.' Charles did, however, agree to set up a Commission to oversee the structuring and implementation of the Revocation but this was, in reality, just for appearances, as he did not want to debate policy; he just wanted to be obeyed.

The new Scottish Ministry was announced in March 1626 with Montrose as President of the Privy Council and Archbishop Spottiswoode as President of the Exchequer Commission. Hay remained Lord Chancellor but his power was eclipsed and he was compensated by being made Viscount Dupplin and later Earl of Kinnoul. Charles soon complained that the Council acted with too great independence and that it would not have defied his father's orders as they had his. Mar gently summed up the difference between the approach of Charles and his father:

> 'Alas Sir, a hundred times your worthy father has sent down directions unto us which we have stayed, and he has given us thanks for it when we have informed him of the truth.'

For the first four years of his reign Charles was at war; first with Spain, in support of his sister and her husband, Frederick, the deposed Protestant Elector; then with France. This had a profound effect on Scotland as it sent 4,000 troops and suffered from the increase in taxes to pay for them, but the greatest cost was that trade with France was forbidden. Both wars were a failure and their proponent, Buckingham, was assassinated in 1628. The English Parliament then presented Charles with the Petition of Right, which declared that taxation without parliamentary consent was illegal. Charles dissolved it in 1629 and it did not sit again for eleven years.

Charles made his first visit to Scotland as king in 1633 and, while he was staying with the Setons, he met Yester's heir, the six-year-old John Hay who later wrote that Charles had kissed him and said 'God make you a better man than your father', a reference to Yester's voting in Parliament against the Five Articles. Charles was more supportive of Yester's kinsman, George, 10th Earl of Erroll, and made him a Privy Councillor. Erroll was the first of his line to be brought up a Protestant but 'he lived in so extravagant fashion that he was compelled to dispose of his ancient family lordship of Erroll,' and he died only three years later in 1636.

Charles, like his father, was intent on getting the Kirk to accept the practices of the Church of England and he appointed a number of Englishmen, including Bishop Laud, to the Scottish Privy Council. Charles created the new position of Bishop of Edinburgh against the wishes of the Burgh and one critic wrote: 'By means of the statute the king proposes to introduce the whole of the English ecclesiastical ritual into Scotland.' Charles appointed the Clerk Register, Sir John Hay of Barra, a descendant of Sir Edmund Hay of Linplum, to advise him on tax collection and Hay ordered a substantial tax increase. Hay was, in the words of Sir James Balfour, 'a man altogether corrupt, full of wickedness and villainy, and a sworn enemy to the peace of his country'. One sufferer wrote of 'the avarice of the officers and favourites of the prince, who are brought foolishly to believe that by tearing off the skins of the flock they shall turn the shepherd rich'.

Charles left Scotland after only one month, leaving behind great resentment, not least from the magnates who felt ignored and powerless and further away from influence at court than ever. They felt that Charles was wholly an English king and that Scotland was increasingly neglected. This seemed justified when Charles increased the power of churchmen by appointing Spottiswoode Lord Chancellor, following Kinnoul's death in 1634, and by appointing eight bishops to the Privy Council. In addition, Laud was made Archbishop of Canterbury and, two years later, Bishop Juxon became Lord Treasurer of England. Charles, under Laud's influence, then sought to increase the income of the bishops. In this he was supported by Sir John Hay, whose son was appointed to a commission to decide on the payment of teinds. Hay recommended that all lords who did not willingly surrender their abbey lands should be prosecuted, as Charles wanted the bishops to be the new owners. In addition, Charles proposed that as many as 50 new abbots be appointed, who would not only receive land, but who would also sit in Parliament, thus ensuring a majority for the king. Such was the uproar against this measure that Charles abandoned it but he had destroyed any remaining trust held in him.

The Earl of Traquair was made Treasurer in Scotland in 1636 and became effective head of the administration in Scotland. Baillie wrote that he 'now guides our Scots affairs with the most absolute sovereignty that any subject among us these forty years did' but his thirst for power increasingly led him to make misjudgements. He was determined to prevent the increase in the influence of the bishops and he also failed to prevent what became one of the defining moments in Scottish history, Laud's attempt to impose the new Prayer Book in St Giles's Cathedral in July 1637. Professor Lee writes that this was 'bound to arouse... every existing fear among all the groups who counted in Scotland: fear of Popery, of clerical rule, of alien rule, of the destruction of the influence of the landed classes... of the ends of Scots law... of Scotland as an independent entity.' As soon as the Dean of Edinburgh began to read from the Prayer Book there was uproar in the cathedral, stools were thrown at him and he 'was almost trampled underfoot and... almost stoned to dead'.

Yester joined the protestors: he had been a strong supporter of the Kirk against the efforts of both James and Charles to move it closer to the Church of England. He had voted against the Five Articles and the 1633 Act regulating the apparel of ecclesiastics and he joined those opponents of the Prayer Book who met in Edinburgh in September. Sir John Hay had been made Provost of Edinburgh but he was unable to prevent the burgh council presenting a petition against the Prayer Book, and this provoked similar moves by most of the other burghs. Charles ordered the Privy Council to leave Edinburgh and this led the protestors to appoint an executive body called The Tables, headed by Balmerino, Montrose, Rothes and Loudon. They drew up a petition to the king condemning the imposition of the Prayer Book and the increase in the power of the bishops.

Traquair wrote to Hamilton: 'The king is not pleased to allow any of us to come and inform him. I am in all these things left alone and, God is my witness, never so perplexed what to do. Shall I give way to this people's fury, which, without force and the strong hand, cannot be opposed.' In November he and the Earl of Lauderdale met the petitioners in Edinburgh and told them to present the petition to the Privy Council directly. Lauderdale was the son of James's Chancellor, John Maitland, and he had married Lady Isobel Seton, Dunfermline's daughter by his first wife, Lillias Drummond. As such he and Yester shared the same father-in-law, though Lauderdale was twenty years older.

The Tables presented Charles in February 1638 an address 're-newing the old Covenant for religion'. This referred to the Confession of Faith signed by James VI in 1581, wherein the signatories had bound themselves to uphold the true religion of the Church of Scotland. The National Covenant was then signed in Greyfriars Church on 28th February by the nobles, including Yester, the lairds, 300 ministers, the Commissioners of the burghs and the people of Edinburgh. Drawn up by Alexander Henderson, a minister from Fife, and Archibald Johnston of Warriston, its main declaration was that there should be no innovations in church or state that had not been approved by the General Assembly or by Parliament.

Charles's policies had thus produced the same alliance of nobles and the Kirk which had destroyed his grandmother but, unlike her, he had also alienated the general population. He was seen as English, arrogant and distant, who imposed punitive taxes and a religion increasingly seen as Popish. The signatories were, however, not yet anti-monarchy and they swore to 'stand to the defence of our dread Soveraigne... in the defence and preservation of the foresaid true Religion, Liberties and lawes of the Kingdome.'

It was not until June that Charles sent Hamilton as his High

Commissioner to try to reach a settlement. He had fought for the Protestant cause in Europe and was the only Scottish magnate at the English court trusted by the Covenanters. However they were not convinced by the concessions he offered and proposed instead that a General Assembly and a Parliament be summoned.

Charles ordered him not to agree to a Parliament unless the Covenant was first renounced and Hamilton advised the king to speed up his plans to invade Scotland and that he should not declare the Covenanters traitors until his invasion fleet had sailed. Charles's plan was for the Earl of Antrim to lead his Irish forces against the west of Scotland whilst the English army landed in the east, capturing Edinburgh. However Charles found that raising the army was more difficult than he had anticipated. Hamilton ordered a meeting of the General Assembly in Glasgow for November and a Parliament for May 1639. Hamilton could not get the Assembly to agree to any of his proposals and he dissolved it writing to the king: 'So unfortunate I have been in this unlucky country... for I have missed my end in not being able... to curb the insolency of this rebellious nation, without assistance from England, and greater charge to your Majesty, than this miserable country is worth... next Hell I hate this place.' He ordered the Privy Council to leave Glasgow but most councillors ignored him. The Assembly also continued to sit and declared that the six Assemblies that had met between 1606 and 1618 were unlawful, and that Episcopacy and the Five Articles should be abjured. In December it deposed all the archbishops and bishops and declared that no churchman could again hold civil office.

The Tables sent a letter around the country in January 1639 saying that Scotland was under threat and that this must be resisted by all lawful means. Committees of war were set up in each shire and Scotland was divided into four areas, each of which was ordered to raise an army, to be led by General Leslie. Charles announced he was raising an army to resist a Scottish invasion but the Covenanters responded by affirming their loyalty to him and asked that their case should be judged by the English Parliament. They held that they were two nations in one island 'now happily reconciled and tied together by the most strict Bonds, which we desire rather to increase than diminish'.

This had no effect and the The First Bishops' War began when Montrose and Leslie took Aberdeen. Yester was appointed to the command of the East Lothian Regiment and the Covenanters occupied every castle in the borders. Traquair fled to England and Charles reached York in March, naming Hamilton as the commander of his forces in Scotland. Hamilton arrived in the Firth of Forth in May only to be confronted by his mother, who threatened to shoot him. He wrote to the king saying there was no hope of the Covenanters submitting peacefully and this was soon confirmed at the Battle of Kelso in June, when the Scots defeated Charles's army of 3,000 men, forcing him to begin negotiations.

The Scottish Parliament, consisting of 50 nobles, 48 barons and 52 burgesses, met at the end of August with Traquair as High Commissioner. The Committee of the Articles included Argyll, Rothes, Montrose and Lauderdale, and only two nobles who were not Covenanters; the barons and burgesses were all Covenanters. The Commissioners of the shires demanded that each estate should choose its own representatives to sit on the Articles, which should now answer to Parliament and not to the king. They also proposed that the shire Commissioners fill the estate left vacant by the clergy. The measures were passed but Traquair did not approve them and he prorogued Parliament until June 1640. Charles created a Committee for Scottish Affairs, which included Hamilton as the only Scot and began preparation to restart the war. His determination was strengthened by the discovery of a letter to Louis XIII asking for his support signed by Leslie, Mar, Rothes, Montrose and Loudon. However the English Parliament would not support his plans so Charles dissolved it in May.

CHAPTER 7 – CIVIL WAR

The Scottish Parliament met in June 1640, defying Charles's orders that it remain prorogued and it passed several revolutionary Acts: that it should meet at least every three years, whether the king was present or not; that all matters and grievances were to be debated; that the Articles be chosen by the king but that they could only deliberate on matters brought to them by Parliament; and that each Estate should chose its representatives to sit on the Articles. A Committee of Estates was set up consisting of twelve from each of the three estates of nobles, lairds and burgesses, plus three ordinary Lords of Session, with full powers to rule Scotland. Argyll was given the task of defeating the royalists in the North and, by the end of July, Leslie's main Covenant army was at Duns where Yester joined it. His loyalty to the monarchy made him refuse to accept any command but he marched with it into England, starting the Second Bishops' War. Yester was present at the surrender of Newcastle, Charles proposed a meeting of a Council of Peers in York and negotiations began at Ripon in October. The Scots sent eight Commissioners comprising two members of each Estate, including Rothes, Baillie, Warriston, Loudon and Yester's cousin, Charles Dunfermline, and the English sent 16 peers. The English offered to pay the Scots £170,000 a day and it was agreed that each army was to retain its position during the negotiations of a formal peace treaty to be held later in London.

The Scottish Commissioners arrived there in November. Rothes took with him his 14-year old great-nephew, John Hay, as Yester feared for his safety in Scotland if the English did invade. Baillie wrote that the Puritans gave the Commissioners a great welcome, telling them that they were responsible for the summoning of Parliament and the protection of England's religion and liberties. Charles attended the first meeting but Rothes refused to negotiate with him, so Charles withdrew and played no further part in the negotiations, but he accepted all the Acts that had been voted by the Scottish Parliament in June.

The Scots now demanded uniformity in church government between England and Scotland, which essentially meant that Episcopacy would be abolished in England. This was too much for the English to accept immediately and it was agreed that Parliament would consider the matter at a later date. The Scots also sought civil and economic unity but again found little enthusiasm for these in England. The Treaty of London was signed in August, the Scottish army was disbanded and left Newcastle four days later and the king announced his intention to visit Scotland.

The Scottish Parliament had met again in July, with the Earl of Wemyss acting as High Commissioner, and approved an oath for signature by all members 'to maintain the king's person, honour and estate as is exprest in our national covenant,' and to do all they could to preserve the peace between the two nations. They then focused on dealing with those they considered their enemies, which included Traquair and Sir John Hay. Charles attended Parliament in August and he was forced to accept that it was responsible for choosing Ministers of State. Parliament proposed Argyll as Chancellor, Charles proposed Morton, and Loudon was accepted in compromise. Charles was forced to remove a number of royalists from the Privy Council and most of the leading

Covenanters were rewarded with pensions. Argyll was made a marquis, Leslie an earl and Loudon and Crawford were restored their earldoms. Yester was made a Privy Councillor and acted as Commissioner to the General Assembly of the Church of Scotland in 1642. Of the Covenanters' enemies, only Traquair was tried and found guilty, but he was not punished.

Yester, now 48, married Lady Margaret Montgomerie in 1641. She was the eldest daughter of the Earl of Eglinton, and, at 24, only nine years older than Yester's son John. She bore Yester four sons and three daughters, all of whom died in childhood, except William, who was to inherit the estate of Drumelzier, which Yester had bought in 1633. He had taken advantage of the financial problems of his cousin Tweedie to buy his barony and estate, which lay close to Neidpath Castle. It had been held by the Tweedies since 1320 and tradition held that it was where Morgan le Fay had imprisoned Merlin and where he was later buried. Yester's son John and his cousin John Maitland, the Earl of Lauderdale's son, were expelled from Parliament in 1641; they had sat as observers, along with all other eldest sons of noblemen and their removal was as a result of a vote in Parliament proposed by the lairds and the burgesses.

In October the Irish rose in rebellion and the English Parliament denied Charles the command of the army needed to suppress them because they could not trust him not to use it against themselves. The English were happy, however, for the Scots to send an army to defeat the Irish and proposed that 10,000 men be raised. By January 1642 this had been reduced to 2,500 but, by then, relations between the king and Parliament had deteriorated further. Charles ordered the Scottish Privy Council to declare their support for him, which they declined to do, so Charles again sent Hamilton to Scotland to rally support. He failed and in August the General Assembly appointed a Commission to pursue religious unity with England. Charles raised his standard in

Nottingham and the Civil War began. John Hay was at Nottingham with his uncle Dunfermline, who had been appointed a Gentleman of the King's Bedchamber, and they accompanied Charles to Shrewsbury. Yester was only too aware of how events could evolve so he went to Shrewsbury and took his son back to Scotland, where he persuaded him to become a Covenanter.

The English Parliament asked the Scots for military aid, citing the 1641 treaty whereby each country was obliged to help the other in suppressing 'the common enemy of the Religion and Liberty of both nations'. When Charles heard of this he wrote to the Scottish Privy Council claiming that the English Parliament had ignored all his proposals for peace and that he, Charles, had only taken up arms to maintain the Protestant religion and the liberties of England. Both Parliament's letter and Charles's letter were considered by the Council in December. Lauderdale argued for publishing both letters; Argyll, Yester, Loudon and Balmerino said neither should be published immediately; Balcarres voted that only Parliament's letter be printed. The last possibility, that only the king's letter be printed, was proposed by Hamilton and his brother Lanark and it was carried by eleven votes to nine, with Yester voting against.

This vote greatly worried the Covenanters and they decided to govern instead through a Committee of Estates, appointed by Parliament. They offered to mediate on behalf of both king and Parliament as long as Episcopacy was abolished in England, but Charles rejected their offer. However he saw that the Covenanters were increasingly split between the hardliners, lead by Argyll, and including Yester, who wanted to send troops to England, and the moderators, lead by Hamilton, who Charles had made a duke, and who wished to keep Scotland out of the war entirely. A third group of extreme royalists, led by Montrose and Huntly, were preparing to rise against the Covenanters in Scotland.

Argyll called a Convention of Estate which Hamilton did not

oppose as he felt he could control it. However the Scots captured the Earl of Antrim, Montrose's plot was revealed and Argyll had no problem securing the votes to support the English Parliament against the king. Most nobles supported Hamilton but those, like Yester, who were Covenanters joined the lairds and burgesses in giving Argyll almost unanimous support. The English sent Sir Henry Vane as the head of a group of Commissioners to the Committee to propose a civil union, as the Parliamentarians had agreed to put aside religious differences until the king had been defeated. The Scots, however, insisted they also wanted a religious union.

John Hay was not enjoying being at Yester, not least because he did not get on with his stepmother. He wrote in his *Autobiography* that he had told his father he 'wanted to go on his travels but not being able to prevail with his father, and all his friends especially his mother's relations using their outmost endeavours to have him settle at home, and marry he then being seventeen years of age'. However, there were some reasons why staying in Scotland had attractions. He admitted he was 'somewhat engaged in affection to Lady Jean Scott [sister of Francis, Earl of Buccleuch],' who he had first seen 'in the Abbey Church [of Holyrood] when the king was last seen in Scotland... but never having spoke to her...and could find none so proper as to engage with her brother [as] so many of the nobles were engaged to serve in this war.' As John was six when the king was last in Scotland it seems unlikely that he fell in love with Jean then, but there was no doubting that she had induced a *coup de foudre* at some early stage in his life.

The Committee agreed the Solemn League and Covenant with the English Parliament in August 1643. This contained: a promise to: preserve the reformed religion in the church of Scotland and the reformation of religion in the church of England; to remove popery; to preserve the king's authority in the defence of the true religion, and of the rights of the Parliaments of both kingdoms; and to preserve the peace and union between their two kingdoms. Everyone was ordered to sign and Hamilton fled to England where Charles had him imprisoned because he considered he had betrayed him.

The Committee agreed to raise an army of 20,000 men, for which England would pay some money monthly and the rest when the war ended. John Hay took over the command of the East Lothian Regiment from his father, who had become ill, but he confessed in his *Autobiography* that he only soldiered to impress Lady Jean. The English Parliament set up the Committee of Both Kingdoms which was given authority to coordinate the war effort against Charles. All the Scottish Commissioners sat on this body, as did fourteen English MPs and seven peers. Lauderdale's son, John Maitland, played the leading role from the Scottish side.

Alexander Leslie, now Earl of Leven, led the army south in January 1644 and there remained only a small army in Scotland to prevent any royalist uprising there. Hay's regiment took the fort at Southshields near Newcastle and defended it against the attempt of the Marquis of Newcastle to retake it. Hay's soldiers skirmished in this area for some weeks in atrocious weather and they had to march to the coast to pick up provisions from Scottish ships because that was the only way they could be victualled. Newcastle withdrew to York and Hay's regiment followed him but again the Scots marched randomly and fought a few skirmishes. Hay and some of his fellow officers soon grew tired of this increasingly pointless activity, especially in such terrible conditions, as they realised they could never take York; so Hay 'resolved to leave the army, and pursue the design of his amour'.

Leven failed to take Newcastle and camped in Northumberland, sending a request to the Committee for more soldiers. He then laid siege to York, where the parliamentary army joined him. In London, Baillie, one of the Scottish commissioners, found that the progress of the Scottish army had not impressed the English.

He wrote: 'We are exceeding sad, and ashamed that our army, so much talked of, has done as yet nothing at all. What can be the reason of it, we cannot guesse, only we think, that God, to humble our pride... he's not yet pleased to assist them... the best of the English have a very ill will to employ our aid.' Problems also developed in Scotland as Charles encouraged Montrose and Huntly to start an uprising in the Highlands, promising them the support of Antrim with 2,000 Irishmen.

Argyll crushed Huntly's uprising and the Earl of Callendar, the overall commander in Scotland, soon forced Montrose to retreat to England. Callendar was Yester's brother-in-law as Yester's sister Margaret had married him after the death of her husband, Dunfermline. There was another Hay connection, as Callendar's mother was the sister of the 9th Earl of Erroll. Callendar was ordered to attack Montrose in the north of England and then to join forces with Leven. Hay joined Callendar's army and marched with him in June to England where they laid siege once again to Newcastle. Hay did not stay long with Callendar and returned to Scotland in July, where his engagement to Jean Scott was announced. They married in October when he was eighteen and she fifteen. She brought him a dowry of £450,000 and, in return, renounced any claims she might have on the estates of her father, Walter, 1st Earl of Buccleuch. John and Jean began their married life at Neidpath Castle, which Yester had made over to them whilst he lived in Yester House. Hay was asked by the burgh of Peebles to stand as its representative in Parliament and he was encouraged to do so by Lauderdale and by Lanark but Archibald Johnston, now Lord Warriston, told him not to accept 'as no nobleman's son had ever served in parliament in place of a baron, except Lord Kinnoul's son'. Hay agreed not to stand for a Parliament where, in his words, 'so many delinquents were to appear, and many of them likely to suffer death'.

Meanwhile, his regiment had fought at the battle of Marston

Moor in July, where Prince Rupert's army was defeated and York taken, but the Scottish army performed poorly at the battle and Callendar did not take Newcastle until October. The political situation in England was becoming more complicated as the Parliamentarians were split between the Presbyterian and the Independent parties. The Scots favoured the Presbyterian Party and suggested putting Cromwell on trial and opened negotiations with the king in November. Negotiations with him predictably failed and in June 1645 Cromwell routed the royalist forces at Naseby. The Scottish army played no part in this as Leven had refused to march south because of the danger raised by Montrose's victories in Scotland.

His army consisted of only 2,500 men but they were fierce fighters, principally Catholics, and united in their hatred of the Campbells whose chief, Argyll, was sent to oppose them. Montrose was supported by the 4th Earl of Kinnoul and his kinsman Sir William Hay of Delgatie. They took Perth in August, then Aberdeen, and over the next twelve months won seven battles, with the last being a major victory at Kilsyth near Perth in August 1645. The Committee ordered Sir David Leslie to attack Montrose. John Hay and his brother-in-law, Buccleuch, who had raised a force of 300 cavalry, joined Leslie, who had marched with his army of 6,000 men from Nottingham and in September they attacked Montrose at Philiphaugh and defeated him. After the battle, Buccleuch stayed with his sister and Hay at Neidpath, where Hay's son and heir, John, had just been born.

The Scots reached agreement with the English Presbyterians on peace proposals which were taken to Paris by Sir Robert Moray, who was related to both Maitland and Hay through his marriage to Lady Sophia Lindsay, daughter of the Earl of Balcarres. As a young man, Moray had joined the *Garde Écossaise*, a regiment that had fought in the army of Louis XIII, and he became a favourite of Cardinal Richlieu. He had joined the Covenanters army in Edinburgh in 1638, was appointed Quartermaster General for the invasion of England and was knighted in 1643. He became a prisoner-of-war in Germany in 1645 and he was released on the payment of a £200,000 ransom by Crawford, Lauderdale and Cassillis. Maitland lent him £100,000 three years later and Moray thanked him, writing 'My dearest Friend, you may easily guess there is no place in all the earth I would more gladly be in, than where you are'. He was also to become one of John Hay's closest friends and later his partner in governing Scotland.

Moray's mission came to nothing as Charles continued his duplicity, entering into simultaneous discussions with the Independents, to whom he revealed the Scottish discussions with the French, and admitting he would never impose Presbyterianism in England as he believed 'the nature of Presbyterian government is to steal or force the crown from the king's head. For their chief maxim is... that all kings must submit to Christ's the 1st kingdom, of which they are the sole governors.' As Charles distanced himself from the Scots, so too did the Independents who passed an ordinance stating that all church courts should be subordinate to Parliament.

Charles left Oxford in May 1646 and, disguised as a servant, went to Newark to the house of Jean de Montereul, the French diplomat with whom the Scottish Commissioners had been negotiating but when Lothian, representing the Committee of Estates, arrived to demand Charles's surrender, he told Charles that he had no knowledge of the terms agreed with Montereul. Charles became the prisoner of the Scottish army and was taken by them to Newcastle, as they feared that the New Model Army would move between them and Scotland. Argyll visited Charles and told him if he signed the Covenant and agreed to establish Presbyterianism in England, he would be assured of his support, but Charles refused.

John Hay also visited Charles at Newcastle in May and found a number of his kinsmen with the king. Sir James Hay of Smithfield, a descendant of the 2nd Lord Yester, had been made Baron Smithfield and Squire of the Body. He had fallen into debt with a cousin, Archibald Hay, Surgeon to the King, who was also in attendance and this resulted in John Hay receiving a charter of the lands of Smithfield from Charles. Another relation was John's first cousin, Sir James Hay of Linplum, who was serving as Cup Bearer. John and Charles spoke often and he relayed to the king the discussions in the General Assembly, leading Charles to refer to him as the 'ruling Elder'. Yester then joined his son in Newcastle and paid court to the king. Charles told John he wanted to make him an earl but he replied, 'It might be to his prejudice, his father having married a proud wife and it being more acceptable to the son that the father had it.' So Yester was made Earl of Tweeddale and John was given in compensation the patronage of Peebles, which he considered the 'best benefice in Scotland'.

The Scottish army realised how their capture of the king had increased their vulnerability and they accepted the English Propositions of Newcastle that required the king to sign the Covenant and agree to it being imposed on his subjects. Religion in England and Ireland would be reformed as set out in the Covenant and the move to uniformity with Scotland would be advanced. Charles asked for time to consider the proposals but the more he vacillated, the greater the Scots' discomfort grew and in December they accepted an English proposal to pay them £80 million, half immediately and half later, to withdraw their army from England and to abandon Charles to his fate.

Hamilton was released by the English and he returned to Scotland, where his supporters and those of Argyll constituted the two principal political factions with the nobility supporting Hamilton and the lairds and burgesses Argyll. In England, the departure of the Scottish army meant that the Presbyterian Party gained support and now controlled both Houses of Parliament. Charles accepted the English Parliament's proposal of Presbyterian government for three years and his giving up of the militia for ten years and the Scottish Commissioners, led by John Maitland, now Earl Lauderdale, supported this. Parliament tried to disband the New Model Army but failed and the army then made its move. Charles was arrested in June by Cornet Joyce and taken to Fairfax's headquarters at Cambridge, and in July the army took control of London. The Committee of Estates now made its own proposals to Charles, offering a weak form of Episcopacy with strict limitations on the king's power and Charles accepted this in September. However, nothing came of this as the Committee was split between the two factions, as was shown by Hamilton's vote to disband the army, which Argyll opposed, winning by only one vote out of the 61 cast.

Charles's immediate destiny lay in the hands of Lanark, Hamilton's brother Loudon and Lauderdale, who met Charles at Hampton Court in October and encouraged him to flee to Scotland. Charles did flee, but only to Carisbrooke Castle on the Isle of Wight, from where he continued to make proposals to both the Scots and to the English Parliament, seemingly uncaring about his obvious duplicity and insincerity. The Papal Nuncio wrote: 'I am alarmed by the general opinion of his Majesty's inconstancy and bad faith, which creates a doubt that whatever concessions he may make he will never ratify them unless it pleases him.'

Charles signed the Engagement with the three Scottish emissaries in December 1647, making the decision that was to seal his fate. He agreed he would accept military support to restore him to government in England in return for his making the concessions he had offered to Parliament in May, namely Presbyterian government for three years and his giving up control of the militia for ten years. He agreed to confirm the Covenant in the English Parliament but neither he nor his subjects would be compelled to accept it and he agreed to 'endeavour a complete union of the kingdoms'. In addition, he seperately promised

Hamilton that Westmoreland, Cumberland and Northumberland would be incorporated into Scotland. The emissaries agreed to all this as Charles had threatened otherwise to sign an agreement with the English, and leave the Scots with nothing. The Committee approved the Engagement, but the Commission of the Church did not, arguing there was no justification for war. The Scottish Parliament met in March 1648 and overwhelmingly supported the Engagement but Tweeddale voted against, at odds with his son John, who voted in favour.

Parliament authorised the levy of an army of 30,000, Leven was replaced by Hamilton and Middleton was appointed as Lieutenant General. Such was the fervour of the Engagers that they refused to consider the answers the English Parliament gave to their demands, which included a number of concessions. Because of this, Loudon broke with the Engagers and he and Argyll withdrew to their homes to observe events.

John Hay was made Colonel of the East Lothian Regiment of Foot, which had 1,300 men and was raised at Haddington, with Sir James Hay of Linplum as his Lieutenant Colonel. Gilbert, the 11th Earl of Erroll, also served in the army, as Colonel of the Horse. They marched in April and Hay's regiment joined the main army in taking Carlisle, but he played no further part in this campaign as he left the regiment at Selkirk for Neidpath as Jean was about to give birth. This was her third confinement as the year before she had had a daughter, who had died at birth. Mindful of this and of his mother's death so soon after his own birth, Hay wanted to be with his wife. Their son, Francis, was born in August and Rothes, Buccleuch and Crawford-Lindsay attended his christening.

Hamilton's army was riven by dispute amongst its generals and it marched slowly south with no real resolve or purpose, and received no support from the English. Callendar and Middleton were in charge of the cavalry at Wigan, whilst Hamilton and the foot soldiers were twenty miles north, near Preston. On August

17th Cromwell attacked and, in separate engagements over the next three days, inflicted heavy casualties on the Scots, killing 2,000 and capturing 9,000, leading Hamilton to surrender a week later. He was imprisoned, and beheaded the following year.

The Committee fled Edinburgh but were soon captured by Monck. Cromwell entered Edinburgh in October and forced the Committee to agree that no Engagers could hold public office, after which Cromwell and his army returned to England. The Committee appointed 80 new members, of whom only eight were nobles, and the subsequent administration was known as the rule of the Kirk Party. Argyll was its head, Loudon was Chancellor and Leven was reinstated as head of the army.

The Independents seized Charles in December, purged Parliament, put the king on trial and executed him on January 30th 1649. The Scottish Parliament proclaimed Charles's son as King of Scotland, but also of England and Ireland. Royalist attacks continued in the north and Inverness was taken, which led to the execution of Huntly, who had been imprisoned under sentence of death since 1646. Montrose landed in Scotland again in March 1650 with 1,200 men under instructions from the king to force the Kirk Party to change the conditions they demanded of him before they allowed him to return to Scotland. Montrose's army was destroyed by Sir David Leslie and he was captured and executed with Sir William Hay of Dalgety. John Hay realised how vulnerable he was so he put a garrison in Neidpath Castle and took his wife and young son north to Dundee, where he joined his brother-in-law Francis.

Lauderdale was sent to contact Charles II and found him with a small fleet off the east coast of England and it was from this meeting that the great friendship between the two developed. Charles landed in Scotland in June, but not until he had been forced to sign the Covenant. The radical minister James Guthrie was 'passionate against the proclaiming of the king, till his qualifications for government had first been tried and allowed' and the Government forced him to live at Falkland Palace, where none of his friends were allowed to stay with him. However Hay, who was staying nearby with his uncle Charles at Dunfermline, managed to meet the king on several occasions.

Charles Dunfermline had been as a young man 'much inclined to all sorts of gaming, and careless of his business.' Sir John Scott of Scotstarvit wrote that he lost his fortune 'in a few years after his majority by playing and other inordinate spending... and when he was debarred by promise to play no game, he devised a new way to elude his oath by wagering with any who was in his company who should draw the longest straw out of a stack with the most grains therein.' He had accumulated large debts and his uncle Tweeddale agreed to guarantee these, which seem to have reached £3.5 million by 1659 and Callendar agreed to underwrite half of these for as long as Tweeddale lived. Tweeddale also asked Hugh Montgomorie, his new brother-in-law, to underwrite part of his own guarantee and he promised Montgomerie's father, Eglinton, that his son would not suffer any liability from this. Dunfermline's debts were to haunt Tweeddale and his family for many years and had ramifications far beyond those financial.

Cromwell and his army crossed the Tweed in July and he used Pinkie House as his headquarters, probably under the invitation of Tweeddale who held it as surety for Dunfermline's debts. King Charles visited the army that was defending Edinburgh and he received such a strong reception that the Committee forced him to leave and purged it of 80 officers and 3,000 men, leaving it much weakened. Charles was further humiliated by being forced to sign a declaration regretting his past failings as well as those of his father and mother, and he was made to endure a day of public atonement for his ancestors' opposition to the Reformation and for the changes to religious practice forced through by his father and grandfather.

Cromwell had withdrawn to Dunbar with his army because it

had been weakened by illness. The Scottish army, commanded by Leslie, now left Edinburgh and moved south to block Cromwell's passage to England. Leslie had 22,000 men to Cromwell's 11,000 and Cromwell wrote on September 2nd: 'We are upon an engagement very difficult. The enemy have blocked up our way... through which we cannot get almost without a miracle.' He decided to attack and did so at four in the morning of September 3rd, catching the Scots by surprise and destroying them, killing 4,000 and capturing 10,000.

The Committee made one last attempt at resistance and sent Chiesly to command the army of the Western Association which was comprised of burgesses and lairds and had no officers above the rank of colonel. Meanwhile Argyll was lobbying the king in Perth, who agreed to make him a duke and a Knight of the Garter, whenever he thought fit. Charles was rather better than his father in the practice of duplicity and was happy to promise Argyll whatever he wanted, as long as Charles needed him. His revenge for Argyll's traitorous behaviour would come later, as would Guthrie's, who had inspired one remonstrance condemning the Committee for supporting the king; and another demanding he be excluded from power. The Committee rejected these, Guthrie was accused of making divisions, and he resigned his ministry.

The Western Association was routed by General Lambert and Cromwell concentrated his forces on capturing those castles still held by the Scots in the south. Neidpath was the last to fall but its commander, Captain John Brown, negotiated a deal with Lambert whereby his men were allowed to withdraw, leaving the castle's contents secure and yielding only its arms and ammunition. The defeat at Dunbar created further divisions among the Scots and the more extreme Covenanters blamed it on the ungodliness of those in command, and they raised a remonstrance against Charles. The moderates, however, realised they had to relax their ban and recommended that royalists be re-admitted to the army.

CHAPTER 8 – THE RESORATION OF CHARLES II

Charles was crowned at Scone on January 1st 1651. John Hay officiated and 'carried Charles's pale from the house to the Church'. Cromwell's army remained inactive, weakened both by illness and shortage of supply, and it was unable to take over the area which the Kirk Party still controlled. The Scottish army was also weak, poorly armed and provisioned, but in June the Committee repealed the Act of Classes, which had prevented royalists from holding office, as long as they performed public penance. This Guthrie made Lauderdale, Hamilton and Middleton do, forcing them to wear sackcloth in church; they were also forced to 'express and declare their sense of the sinfullness of the Engagement... craving pardon of God for it and promising in his strength never again to own that or the like course'. Argyll had lost all credibility and it was said of him: 'He is gone down the wind; nobody takes any notice of him.'

Cromwell's army grew stronger during the summer and it took Perth so the Scottish army now had two choices: to remain in Stirling and be starved into submission or to invade England through Carlisle. Charles chose the latter but his leaders had no illusions. Lanark, now Duke of Hamilton, wrote: 'We must either starve, disband, or go with a handful of Men into England. This last seems to be the least ill, yet it appears very desperate to me.'

In another letter he wrote that Lauderdale and others 'are now all laughing at the ridiculousness of our condition. We have quit Scotland, being scarce able to maintain it; and yet we grasp at all, and nothing but all will satisfy us, or to lose all. I confess I cannot tell you whether our hopes or our fears are greatest; but we have one stout argument, despair; for we must now either stoutly fight it, or die.'

The East Lothian Regiment was not part of the Scottish army, probably because Cromwell's occupation of East Lothian had prevented it from being mustered. Neither was Hay, for he had not rejoined the army. He was no coward, but he must have seen little reason to risk his life for what must have seemed a hopeless cause. What prospects would his young wife and children have if he were killed?

The Scots had high hopes for support from the English Presbyterians, but only the Earl of Derby provided any meaningful number of men. In addition, Cromwell had anticipated Charles's plans and his army of 30,000 men attacked the 12,000 Scots at Worcester on September 3rd. The Scots fought hard but they were routed. Hamilton, as he had prophesied, was one of the 2,000 killed and 8,000 were captured including Lauderdale, Rothes, Derby, Crawford-Lindsay and Middleton, but only Derby was executed. Cromwell issued an edict against Lauderdale that he 'be made an example of justice', but he was spared thanks to Lady Tollemache, whom he was later to marry, and who persuaded Cromwell to spare him.

Charles escaped and was escorted by Charles Gifford to his cousin Walter's Boscobel House, where he famously stayed the night in an oak tree. Cromwell's soldiers came to the house and asked Walter if he had seen the king, telling him he would be killed if he lied. Gifford 'was too loyal and too much a gentleman to be frightened into any infidelity and resolutely denied knowing anything'. The soldiers left, but not before they had hanged

Francis Yates, one of Gifford's servants. Charles later awarded both Giffords annuities of £17,000 for life as members of the Knights of the Royal Oak. Charles then went to France where, when he was asked if he wanted to return to Scotland, he replied that he would rather be hanged.

General Monck captured most of the Committee and the General Commission of the Kirk at Alyth near Dundee, which he took brutally three days later, killing over 800 of its inhabitants. This was the last major engagement of the war in Scotland, just as Worcester was the last in England. Hay had left Dundee before Monck attacked and he joined Buccleuch in Aberdeen. He was now fearful of being arrested as an Engager and moved frequently about the Highlands. His wife, however, remained in Dundee, where their son Francis died, aged only three.

Argyll finally made peace in August 1652 and a year later the Instrument of Government determined how Scotland would be united with England, allowing Scotland 30 MPs to sit in the Barebone's Parliament. A nine-man Council of State was set up in Edinburgh; its President was an Irish peer, Lord Broghill and only two Scots were members. Those nobles who had been Engagers were forfeited but their tenants and vassals were pardoned. The revenues gained thereby were used to pay for the administration but the cost of the garrisons in Scotland was very great, which resulted in heavy taxation. The General Assembly was forbidden to meet but allowed to continue its religious practices. Bishop Burnet wrote: 'We always reckon those eight years of usurpation a time of great peace and prosperity... but it was at a cost, the pride and independence of Scotland was broken, its nobles cowed and its king a refugee.' Another wrote 'As for the Union of Scotland with England, it will be as when a poor bird is embodied in the hawk that has eaten it up.'

Tweeddale was able to secure a pass allowing John and Jean to return to Neidpath Castle but he himself was being pursued by

Dunfermline's creditors. Dunfermline and Callendar were both in Holland and Eglington was in prison in England, so Tweeddale was the only guarantor in Scotland. He was owed a great deal of money by Sir William Dick, who had given substantial sums to Charles and Montrose, but he had died in a debtors' prison. Tweeddale was unable to satisfy his creditors and his estates were seized. John had to redeem them and satisfy the creditors so he borrowed £500,000 from Jean's brother, Francis Buccleuch, at 6% interest a year and, by 'stretching his credit as far as it would go, and mortgaging his lands... satisfied all the creditors'. Dunfermline's debts, however, remained large and continued to grow as the interest rolled up remorselessly. Buccleuch then died very shortly after agreeing the loan, aged only 24.

Tweeddale made over all his estates to John and left Yester House in 1654 for Berwick, perhaps with the intention of fleeing the country, but he died there soon after and John inherited as 2nd Earl, aged 28. His situation was not good: he was classified as an Engager, he was heavily in debt and he had little prospect of making anything of his life. His debts had also increased because his stepmother had married the Earl of Glencairn, to whom he had to pay a large lump sum as a dowry, as well as an annuity. He now asked his father's fellow guarantors to pay their share and when they refused, he sued them. Eglinton reminded him that John's father had guaranteed Montgomerie would not suffer any loss so John and Callendar took possession of Dunfermline's estates, with John taking two thirds.

He raised some money by selling the baronies of Swed and Arthearmoor in Dumfries but he felt not unduly concerned about his long-term financial position as he had high hopes for his wife's financial prospects. She was a member of the richest family in Scotland, with an estate yielding £1 million per year. Her brother, Francis, had drawn up an entail in 1650 leaving his estate to his surviving children, Mary, born in August 1647, and Anna, born in February 1651, the year Francis died. There were conditions precedent to their inheriting, one of which was that they could not seek to change the entail in any way. If both daughters died, or if the surviving child tried to change the entail, then Francis's sibling, Jean Tweeddale, would inherit. However, the uncertainty surrounding this entail was to cause very great problems for Tweeddale over the coming years.

He was also due to inherit money from the Dunfermline estate, both from the Dowager Countess of Dunfermline, his aunt, who had brought him up, but also from Charles Dunfermline's wife, Mary Douglas, daughter of the 7th Earl of Morton. Both ladies were, however, in robust health and were unlikely to die soon. He thus realised that his only hope was to improve his relationship with the new regime, which, given his history with it, seemed an insurmountable challenge. However, in 1656 he was chosen as the Parliamentary representative for East Lothian, which he served for four years as one of only 14 Scots chosen for the 30 Scottish seats in the Commons and, in his *Autobiography*, he claimed he had stood 'to alleviate the hardships faced by Scotland'. He was also appointed to the Commission that tried those accused of treason against Cromwell. He claimed that, because of his and the other Scottish Commissioners' efforts, the proportion of the expenditure borne by Scotland 'was brought from [£1.5 million] a month to [£650,000] per month and a free trade settled in all three dominions with one another... so that the Scots had the same freedom in England and in their plantations as the English themselves had.'

His concern to maintain his relationship with Cromwell is shown by a letter which appeared in the Public Intelligence, a newspaper published in England. It refers to a pamphlet that was published mentioning Tweeddale's name entitled *A Short Discovery of his Highness the Lord Protector's intentions touching the Anabaptists in the Army*. Tweeddale defended himself, writing:

May it please your Highness, Amongst the bad accidents of my life (as who will excuse himself) I count it not a small one, that my name is used to a Forgery, wherein many bitter expressions is cast upon your Highness, and the present Government; and though God has raised your thoughts above the considerations of such, that possibly it neither has nor should come to your knowledge, but for my boldness in the way I take to vindicate myself, and bear testimony against such an untruth as is contained in a printed paper relating to a discourse of your Highness to me, the falsehood of the thing being sufficiently known to your Highness. All I say for myself is, that if I had been a person to whom your Highness had communicated any purpose of importance in reference to the Government, I would not have been so unworthy of your favour as to have divulged it without your Highness' order of license, much less to the prejudice of the peace and quiet of the people, or fomenting the jealousies of any. I beseech your Highness to give this charity to my discretion; a good consciense I desire to keep towards all men, and likewise excuse the presumption of Your Highness' most dutiful and humble servant, Tweeddale.

Jean Tweeddale's sister-in-law, Margaret Buccleuch, married the Earl of Wemyss in 1653. This was the third marriage for both partners and between them they had 28 children, 20 of whom died in infancy. Ten tutors were named to oversee her remaining children, and these included Tweeddale, her brother Rothes and Eglinton. She and her children moved to Wemyss Castle in Fife as Monck had occupied the Buccleuch's Dalkeith Castle, from which he governed Scotland, continuing to punish those who had been Engagers. Some, like Lauderdale, were imprisoned and had their estates confiscated, others were financially penalised. Erroll was fined £250,000 and the Buccleuch estate £1,650,000, almost double the annual income of the estate and it had to be paid by the end of the year, otherwise the estate would be forfeited. The tutors turned to Tweeddale to help them; they had earlier loaned him £35,000 to help him pay off his creditors and they believed his relationship with the Government would enable him to have the fine reduced. Gideon Scott of Haychesters, another of the tutors, went with him to London but Tweeddale met Cromwell alone and pleaded for the fine to be reduced. Haychesters was furious at his exclusion and wrote to the tutors in September making a formal complaint against Tweeddale. He also wrote to Lady Wemyss saying that Tweeddale wanted to blacken her name with the English and to use her two daughters for his own purposes. He also said that Tweeddale was accusing Lord Wemyss of betraying Francis to the English, thus causing the fine in the first place. Above all, Haychesters was certain that Tweeddale wanted his 12- year-old son, John, Master of Yester, to marry Jean's young niece Mary and thus make certain of the Buccleuch inheritance. Margaret believed Haychesters and turned against Tweeddale which suited Haychesters very well as he also had a young son of his own whom he wanted Mary to marry.

The Buccleuch fine was cut by 60% to £990,000 as part of the general Act of Pardon and Grace in 1655 and the tutors paid up. Margaret sent her husband to petition Cromwell that she be allowed to continue to raise her children until they reached the age of twelve as Tweeddale had made 'a strong endeavor to remove them from her... for certain ends of his own'. Cromwell wrote that her request was reasonable and instructed the tutors to agree to them; they invited Tweeddale to a meeting but he declined, 'knowing how little my presence with you at this time could signify... to the good of any of the affairs of that family I choose not to occasion unprofitable debate, being resolved to submit in my judgement to wiser, and in my will, to higher powers.'

In 1657 Tweeddale suggested that Yester should marry the ten-year-old Mary, but Margaret wrote to Jean saying it was too early to discuss any marriage. Cromwell died the following year and in January 1659 Margaret and Haychesters agreed that his son should marry Mary. Five of the tutors supported the proposal and the Kirk agreed to dispense with the reading of the banns. The marriage was held in February and Haychesters's 14-year-old son was made Earl of Buccleuch and granted a large income.

Tweeddale, supported by his fellow tutors Scotstarvit and Erroll petitioned Monck that both girls should be taken away from Margaret's custody and that the marriage be annulled. A parliamentary commission ordered Mary to be sent to Edinburgh and be put in care but Margaret argued that she should be sent to Dalkeith under Monck's care, and she stayed with her there until September. Wemyss joined her and together they worked hard to persuade Monck to support the restoration of King Charles.

Tweeddale was elected to Parliament again in 1659, becoming, in the words of one historian, a 'collaborator'. He was only one of eleven Scots elected, whose number included Argyll. Extensive legal petitioning by both sides about the Buccleuch marriage continued until May, when Richard Cromwell resigned. The Protectorate dissolved, the Union with England ended and Monck restored the Rump Parliament, which was sympathetic to their former Prebyterian allies. Tweeddale immediately left for London and petitioned Parliament to annul Mary's marriage. He was closely followed by Haychesters with his own petition.

Argyll suggested that Yester should marry Mary's younger sister, Anna, then aged eight. Margaret wrote to Haychesters: 'I think Tweeddale's interest in her is none at all, nor never shall, so far as I can have power over [the] ungrateful, false man.' She also said that Tweeddale should pay Mary the money he owed from the original Buccleuch loan. His position regarding this was improving as the Dowager Countess Dunfermline had died in 1659 and he had inherited Pinkie House and various other lands and titles. He visited these to determine their value and soon realised that the rents he would receive from them would barely pay half of the interest on his debts; so he raised £20,000 by selling some of the land and put Pinkie up for sale. The poor political and economic climate meant there were no buyers for such a large house and so he had to sell more land to the Earl of Oxfuird for £50,000.

That same year Tweeddale's cousin Lauderdale wrote to him from Windsor Castle, where he had been imprisoned for six years, asking him to use his influence with Parliament to secure his release. Tweeddale could only obtain a proposal of banishment from Lambert which Lauderdale considered in a long letter to him, writing: 'It is true to be banished is much more desireable than to be put to the severe and ugly want I am in prison... nor indeed am I very free to be the carver to myself of a punishment which in all ages hath been looked on as next to death.' He joked that to obtain his release the Governor should certify his crime 'as original Sin, for I told him seriously nothing can be charged against me but I was born in Scotland and obeyed the laws and Supreme authority whence I only owe my allegiance'. When he was released in 1660 the king wrote to him from Breda: 'I am very glad you are at liberty. I believe you as entirely my own, as any man and that no other men's passions can work upon you.'

The Restoration of Charles II was widely celebrated in Scotland, with the nobility especially glad to see him crowned. David Stevenson writes: 'Socially and politically the experience of 1637–51 inclined the upper ranks of society to reactionary conservatism. The nobility in particular concluded that resistance to the king and the establishment of Presbyterian Church government was socially subversive and politically disastrous. Undermining the king undermined the nobility; Presbyterianism threatened social hierarchy and deference.'

The Scottish nation was also glad to be rid of English rule and anticipated a significant reduction in taxation. The Kirk was comforted by a letter written by Charles saying: 'We do also resolve to protect and preserve the Government of the Church of Scotland, as it is settled by law, without violation.' However, Charles had no liking for Scotland or its people and he never visited Scotland after his Restoration.

Tweeddale, like the rest of the Scottish nobility, had high hopes of preferment from Charles and of restoring their fortunes and influence. He was particularly eager as Dunfermline had been forced to flee the country when Charles was executed and he was declared bankrupt soon after his return. His total debt now amounted to £3.5 million and Tweeddale's liability was set at £785,000. The value of assets secured against this, however, was substantial, with Pinkie House alone valued at £1.2 million, whilst producing an income of £190,000 a year. However Tweeddale's debt to the Buccleuch estate now stood at £623,000.

He was one of the first Scottish nobles to journey south and he was greatly concerned that his 'collaboration' with Cromwell would do him harm, but he hoped his earlier friendship with both Charles and his father would be remembered and that he would be forgiven. His charm must have been considerable, and Charles's generosity great, for Charles pardoned him, made him a Privy Councillor and also ruled that the greatest part of his estate should be changed from ward to blench, which reduced substantially the amount of annual rent he had to pay the crown.

He may well have been helped by Lauderdale, who had been released and who remained very close to Charles. The king was most supportive of those Scots who had fought at Worcester, who had spent years as prisoners and who had suffered loss of family and land in his support. Lauderdale was one of these and, as soon as he had been released from prison, he had visited Charles in the Netherlands who said he would 'venture Lauderdale with any man in Europe for prudence and courage'.

Clarendon, the Lord Chancellor, considered Lauderdale to be a man of considerable intellect, but thought him 'flattering and dissembling... with no impediment of honour to restrain him from doing anything that might gratify any of his passions'. He added: 'All his discourses were as such as pleased all the company, who commonly believed all he said, and concurred with him.' Burnett who, like so many of Lauderdale's contemporaries, started as a friend and ended up greatly disliking him, wrote:

He was the coldest friend and the violentest enemy I ever knew... His great experience in affairs, his ready compliance with every thing that he thought would please the king, and his bold offering at the most desperate of counsels, gained him such an interest in the king, that no attempt against him, nor complaint of him, could ever shake it, till a decay of strength and understanding forced him to let go his hold. He was in his principles much against popery and arbitrary government; and yet, by a fatal train of passions and interests, he made way for the former, and had almost established the latter.

Lauderdale found, however, support amongst his original Covenanting friends, one of whom wrote: 'He was truly a man of a great spirit, great parts, great wit, a most daring man... a man very national, and truly the honor of our Scots nation.' Clarendon suggested that he be made Lord Chancellor of Scotland, as that would keep him out of England, but Charles made him Secretary of State for Scotland, which gave Lauderdale the base in London that he wanted. He was also made a Gentleman of the Bedchamber, being the only Scot who held that position. Lauderdale was, above all, a practical man and his philosophy throughout his time in office was succinctly expressed to his wife in 1663: 'My reso-

lution is to prefer the King's interests [over] all others on earth…
whatever the king commands shall be punctually done.'

Charles chose Middleton as his first High Commissioner of
Scotland and made him an Earl. He told Clarendon: 'Middleton
had the least in him of any infirmities most incident to the nation
that he knew, and… he would find him a man of great honour
and integrity.' The Earl of Glencairn, who was married to
Tweeddale's stepmother Margaret, was appointed Lord Chancellor, Rothes was appointed President of the Privy Council and
Crawford-Lindsay became Treasurer.

The Scottish Parliament was called in 1661 and passed a wide
range of Acts covering tax, trade, manufacturing and debt collection. The matter of religion, however, was not specifically addressed. The most comprehensive piece of legislation was the
Act of Rescissory, which declared illegal all the Acts of Parliament passed since 1633. One result of this was that Charles could
now decide what religion Scotland should follow which, in effect,
meant the imposition of Episcopalianism. Lauderdale argued
against this, saying in a letter to the Chancellor: 'If you now ex-
punge all those acts at one breath, farewell to that unity in Scotland which is so useful to his Majesty.' These words were to be
shown to be very prophetic. Lauderdale also criticised Middleton's religious policies to Charles directly and suggested that a
General Assembly be summoned. This made him unpopular
with Middleton who called him 'wholly Presbyterian [and] the
great agent of my Lord Argyll.'

Charles was not vengeful and very few of those he considered
traitors were punished. One whom he could not forgive, however, was Argyll who had rushed south to greet Charles in 1660
only to be arrested, tried and executed. Charles had waited long
for his revenge and he relished its realisation. The leading religious Covenant leaders were also targeted. The Assembly asked
Guthrie to make an address to the king on his Restoration but it

was an odd choice, as Guthrie had been so critical of Charles in 1650. He had also been given the task by the Commission of forcing Middleton and Lauderdale to make penance when the Act of Classes was abolished. Guthrie prayed for the safety of the king and asked him to conserve the reformed religion of Scotland, but reminded him that he had sworn to uphold the Covenant. The king immediately had him arrested and Guthrie was sentenced to death and hanged. Tweeddale was the only Member of Parliament who opposed the sentence.

Parliament was adjourned in July 1661 and the focus of decision-making shifted back to London, where the Scottish Council was responsible for directing Scottish affairs. There were two immediate areas of focus: the future of the English garrisons in Scotland and the timing of the restoration of the bishops. Charles was not in favour of military rule; it was, he told Lauderdale and Tweeddale, 'next to the people... the worst government'. Clarendon was more concerned with keeping the garrisons but Lauderdale overruled him and they were withdrawn in 1662.

Charles declared that Presbyterianism was not compatible with the dignity of the monarch and that Episcopacy would be restored. Middleton and Rothes strongly supported this but Lauderdale was not eager to see the early restoration of the bishops. Only Tweeddale and Alexander Bruce, the Earl of Kincardine, spoke openly against this policy, suggesting instead that the king summon the General Assembly. Middleton, who considered Tweeddale a lackey of Lauderdale, inspired Charles to order Tweeddale's arrest in September on the basis that his opposition to Guthrie's sentence amounted to treason. Tweeddale later wrote that he was 'thunderstruck... having used greater freedom of speech than was agreeable to the Commissioner he did upon his return to court represent him so unfavourably to the King that an order was given to the council to send him to the Castle... despite the Earl had invited the Commissioner and most of the nobility to a splendid entertainment at Pinkie and that they had parted in great friendship.'

Tweeddale was imprisoned in Edinburgh Castle and he wrote to the king: 'Your Majesty's displeasure was to me the messenger of death.' He said that he did not doubt Guthrie's guilt but that he did not vote for Guthrie's death because he wanted Charles to mitigate the penalty. He pleaded to the king and many others that he be released and allowed to return to Yester House, as his wife was in a late stage of pregnancy. After two weeks he was allowed to go home but he had to pay a surety of £10,000 and he had to stay at his house for six months until May 1662, after which he was allowed to attend meetings of the Privy Council.

Whilst under house arrest, Tweeddale began thinking about improving Yester House. Rothes, Kincardine and Lauderdale were all building fine houses and Tweeddale wanted to keep up with them. However, his position was in no state to allow him to start anything and he had first to focus on restoring his status in Scotland and in rebuilding his finances. He had to, however, re-roof the house and he bought 'the finest blue slate of stobo hill' from Peebleshire.

Maurice Lee argues persuasively that another motive lay behind his imprisonment. Margaret Wemyss's brother, Rothes, had taken advantage of the absence of his sister from Dalkeith Castle to gain the support of Monck to further his own political and financial ambitions. Burnet wrote of him: 'He was a sincere but weak man, passionate and indiscreet... a zealous Presbyterian. He had no advantage of education, no sort of literature; nor had he travelled abroad... all in him was mere nature. But it was a nature very much depraved... he delivered himself to all the pleasures of wine and women... he had but one maxim... that he was to do everything, nor deny himself nothing, that might maintain his gratness, or gratify his appetites. He was unhappily made for drunkenness... so that he was either sick or drunk.'

Rothes had, however, fought at Worcester and had been held in the Tower for a year. He had been one of the first to visit Charles at Breda in 1650 and he was made Colonel of the Fife Regiment of Horse. His political standing was much better than his financial position: he had carried the Sword of State at Charles's coronation but he depended on his sister's support to live. He had lobbied Monck to support the Restoration and he presided over a group of Scottish nobles and burghers who prepared a loyal address to the king, which he gave himself at Breda in 1659. There he was rewarded with the honorary post of the President of the Council but, more importantly, he was made responsible for the wardship and marriage of his two Scott nieces. After Margaret remarried, Rothes did not want to undermine his new position, so he agreed with his sister that he would share the wardship of the two girls with Lord Wemyss and the two worked together to pursue their respective objectives.

Mary Scott turned twelve in September 1659, her marriage was ratified before witnesses who included Monck and her young husband was allowed to consummate the marriage immediately. Mary asked Haychesters to petition Parliament to keep her sister Anna safe from Tweeddale. However, it was Mary who was most vulnerable. She was probably suffering from bone cancer, for which her mother had tried several cures unsuccessfully, and she now tried one final and seemingly desperate cure. Mary wrote to her young husband: 'We think the virtue of his Majesty's touch is like to cause the fresh bone cast out the rotten.' Her mother took her to London in June 1660 and asked the king to effect a cure, but this was not Margaret's only motive for approaching him.

Mary's visit predictably produced no cure and she returned to Dalkeith in September. There her uncle Rothes encouraged her to make a new will, cutting out her husband entirely and naming himself and Wemyss as co-executors. This would be worth £800,000 to each of them, and loans made by the family to

Rothes were forgiven, which also meant that Anna's inheritance was greatly reduced. When Margaret complained to the king he told her: 'I am confident you will not mislike it when you consider it is for the advantage of the family you are come of, and for a person I have so great kindness for.'

One month later Mary was dead. Anna, the sole survivor, was only ten and the curators were convened to decide her future. Their numbers showed how the domestic situation had changed: Scotstarvit, Gorrenberry and Thirlestane, all supporters of Tweeddale, were members and Haychesters and his supporters were discarded. Margaret was convinced that Rothes would sell Anna to Tweeddale. Her fears may have been justified as Tweeddale was no innocent party; he had already asked his East Lothian neighbour, the lawyer Sir John Nisbet, if the terms of Francis's will, which spoke of the 'heir female', could be interpreted to mean that Lady Tweeddale could be the heir to Mary, bypassing Anna entirely. He was told no, and that he could not challenge Anna's inheritance until 1676, when she became 25.

Margaret proved a match for both her brother and Tweeddale and she executed her masterstroke in May 1661 when she offered Anna as the bride to Charles's twelve-year-old illegitimate son, James, by his former mistress Lucy Walter. Charles was delighted and immediately accepted. Rothes knew he had been outsmarted and wrote to Charles: 'I shall not meddle as to the disposal of my niece without your Majesty's commands' and Charles allowed him to act as sole ward to Anna. The marriage could not take place until 1663, when the bride and groom would reach the legally required ages of twelve and fourteen respectively. Professor Lee considers that Charles deliberately sent Tweeddale to prison in 1661 as a warning to him not to try any repetition of his opposition to Mary's wedding.

Charles began negotiating the marriage contract and received advice as to its legality and the possible consequences of it triggering the entail clause, which would result in Lady Tweeddale inheriting the estate. Charles's choices were not easy and of particular importance was his son James's illegitimacy. If James's heirs could not inherit because of this, then Lady Tweeddale would eventually inherit. However, if James was made legitimate then the Duke of York would be denied his inheritance. Sir John Gilmour, the President of the Court of Session, was summoned to give his opinion. He could find no case of any King of Scotland having legitimised any of his bastards but he advised that a bastard could make a will and that his heirs, if legitimate, could inherit. Charles was delighted but he made two additional points: if Anna predeceased James and had no children, James should inherit. In addition, if Anna predeceased James and James then died with no children, it should be James's heirs who would inherit. This in effect meant that it would be Charles and his heirs who would inherit. This clearly broke Francis's entail, and Margaret was so advised by her lawyers. In addition, Anna's curators, who had signed the marriage contract, were very vulnerable as they could be pursued for the total value of the estate if such events occured.

Charles carried on with the marriage plans regardless and, ignoring Clarendon's advice, made James Duke of Monmouth, an English peerage ranking below only the Duke of York. Gilmour, as President of Scotland's highest court and the man who had drawn up Francis's entail, was in a very difficult position and he hedged his bets with wonderful evasion by giving a negative ruling but refused to sign it. The young couple married in April 1663 when Anna was twelve and James fourteen but, unlike her sister, Anna had to wait two years before the marriage was consummated. Charles rewarded Margaret Wemyss by raising the Earldom of Buccleuch to a Dukedom.

Charles asked Lauderdale in July to confirm the marriage contract by Act of Parliament. This seemingly innocuous request held significant implications for the nobility of Scotland generally, as the contract violated Scottish law and meant, if approved, that no Scot could be sure he could pass on his estates to whoever he chose. A wider point was that no Scottish contract was now safe from an arbitrary Act of the English Parliament. Gilmour was again consulted and he passed the decision to the Court of Session. That court's verdict was unanimous: 'Such an act could not pass in Parliament to make void entails, as to be excepted out of the act *Salvo juris cuius libet* which is the security of subjects in cases of ratifications of private rights.' The Act *Salvo* was always passed at the end of every session of Parliament and it held that none of the private Acts passed during the session could prejudice the legal rights of others. The judges said that Charles's Act 'was most unfit to be pressed by his Majesty'. Charles accepted the verdict since he had been driven to make the request by the relentless Margaret Wemyss. She, however, would not give up and she pressed Monmouth to lobby his father, which he succeeded in doing. Charles wrote angrily to Chancellor Glencairn, blaming him and Gilmour for the impasse: 'Since I see that the exception of the act *Salvo jure* is passed in some cases... therefore I do expect it in this.' Glencairn was very worried about his position and sought to reassure Charles that there was a solution. Gilmour, however, remained adamant, as passing the Act would 'altogether revert the fundamental law of the kingdom'.

Lauderdale and Rothes tried very hard to change Charles's mind but Lauderdale wrote a typically feline letter to Charles: 'We durst not move what was so positively illegal without a clear order, but if it be your will you shall see we know no law but obedience.' Sir Robert Moray, who was now a member of the Scottish Commission and who had been appointed to the Scottish Privy Council, set out the case against Charles's intended course of action but his English officials ignored him and advised the king to present the Act to the Scottish Parliament. It was a typically honest move by Moray who had been given an apartment by Charles in Whitehall with a pension of £38,000 a year.

It was now clear to Tweeddale that only he could oppose the Act and ask Parliament to support him. Moray wrote to Lauderdale that Tweeddale should support the Act if 'he could find it in his heart to do it… a more handsome sacrifice than the Roman did (I have forgot his name) that saved Rome by leaping into the Gap.' Tweeddale was in an impossible position. He was 38, with six children and with debts to the Buccleuch family alone of just over £844,000, which were rising by 6% a year, and he had borrowed money to buy more land, including the baronies of Linton and Newlands in Peebleshire. He had no immediate prospect of paying off these debts but he was at the beginning of what promised to be a great career in Scotland. He was the member of various parliamentary committees including the key committee overseeing the Mint. If he opposed Charles he would never again hold office; and for what purpose, as Parliament was certain to pass the Act? The memory of his recent imprisonment must have pressed heavy on him.

However it was clear that the law was on his side and Lauderdale supported that view but told him the wishes of the king were impossible to ignore. In earlier times, as we have seen, men who were not 'cautious and fearful', men who showed no regard to the king's interests and who wished to pursue their own, ventured as far as regicide to achieve their ends. After the Restoration, times had clearly changed. The behaviour of the Scottish nobles were often driven by unprincipled self-interest, dressed up in a cloak of religious or political ideology, but usually they supported the monarchy as there was no other route to preferment.

Tweeddale thus had two options: to vote for the Act, which would have been an open betrayal of his wife and children's rights; or to do nothing. He may have considered, as Charles's Act was plainly illegal that, on Charles's death, he could always go to the courts to seek restitution. On the day of the vote in October, he left the procession of MPs on its way to Parliament and visited the house of a goldsmith, Alexander Reid, where he made sure there were witnesses to see him. The Act was passed in his absence and his wife's rights removed. In his *Autobiography* he wrote bitterly: 'The Act *Salvo* ... was burthened with an act, and Ratification, past in favours of the Duke and Dutchess of Balcleugh their contract of marriage which was a manifest breach of the entail in favours of the Countess of Tweeddale and her children, which is declared to be no ways comprehended therein, and then the parliament was dissolved.'

It was not easy for Tweeddale but he had made the right choice. Burnet wrote: 'His compliance... brought a great cloud upon him... though his children were... by this robbed of their right he had given way to it so frank a manner that the king was enough inclined both to oblige and to trust him.' Charles summoned Tweeddale to London, where he was given a very warm welcome. Later Charles changed the entail to confirm that if the Monmouths both died without issue, then Lady Tweeddale would inherit. Charles also appointed Tweeddale as one of Monmouth's curators.

❧

The ecclesiastical settlement of 1661 returned Scotland to the Episcopalian state that had existed during the reigns of James I and Charles I. All ministers, who had previously been appointed by their congregations, now had to agree to serve under the bishops or be ejected. Lauderdale did not agree with this policy but, as Charles and Clarendon were set on it, he gave it his support but advised against its immediate imposition as he felt it would cause Presbyterian ill feeling towards the king. Middleton's policy had an instant effect as 300 ministers, one third of the total, either resigned or were ejected from their parishes. More importantly, the percentage of those in the southwest who left their parishes was very high and this was to cause severe political problems in Scotland for the next three decades. Tweeddale joined Lauderdale in supporting ejected ministers and, in nearby Haddington, a Presbyterian minister shared the pulpit with an Episcopalian minister and the congregation was allowed to choose which one to support.

Middleton persuaded the king that Lauderdale was out of touch and that the people wanted to be rid of the Presbyterians. Parliament was summoned in May 1662 and its first order of business was to admit bishops to its benches and to restore their powers over the Kirk. An Act of Indemnity was passed, as was an Act that revoked any action taken by Charles or his father since 1637, meaning any oaths they had made to uphold the Covenant were abrogated. Parliament voted to extend this by requiring all officials to swear that all such oaths had been illegal. Crawford-Lindsay refused to so swear and resigned as Treasurer but Lauderdale, who was Middleton's chief target, 'laughed at this contrivance and told them he would sign a cartful of such oaths before he would lose his place'. Middleton now tried another tactic to use against him and advised Charles that Parliament wanted to exempt some individuals from the Act of Indemnity and ban twelve people from public office through a secret process known as billeting. He later told Parliament that the king had authorised such legislation and that this would also result in fines totalling £800,000 being collected, which would be used to defray taxation. Lauderdale, Tweeddale, Rothes, Moray, Crawford-Lindsay, Cassillis and Loudon were all billeted but Lauderdale found out through his Edinburgh-based associate, William Sharp, brother of the Archbishop of Saint Andrews, before the list was given to the king. Lauderdale complained about the underhand process to Charles, who was furious with Middleton and replaced him with Rothes in 1663.

Rothes was only 32 and cannot have expected this appointment.

Because of the situation with his nieces, he was no friend of Tweeddale. He had written a number of letters to Lauderdale saying that Tweeddale had favoured freedom for the great Covenanter Warriston, who had been captured and hanged earlier that year, and that Tweeddale had been criticising Lauderdale, saying: 'I believe that he will prove to those that trust him another Argyll.' Rothes was however, when sober, a clever operator. 'The subtlety of his wit obliged all to court his friendship,' wrote Mackenzie of Rosehaugh and Rothes swiftly replaced his father-in-law as Treasurer, thus becoming a potential rival to Lauderdale.

Lauderdale reacted to this by building his own power base in Scotland. He asked his good friend Sir Robert Moray to be his secretary-depute in Edinburgh but Moray was reluctant to leave London. He was close to the king, who had appointed him a Privy Councillor, and he shared Charles's passion for science, being one of the founders of the Royal Society and serving as its first President. Charles praised him as 'a companion fit for any king in Christendom,' and Burnet described him as 'the sincerest, the generousest, the friendliest and best natured man I ever knew'. Moray agreed to take the post, in part because he wanted revenge on Middleton for billeting him. He was also obliged to Lauderdale, who had lent him £100,000 in 1648. He was also close to Tweeddale as he and Lady Sophia Lindsay, his wife of two years, were staying in Tweeddale's Edinburgh house when she died in childbirth in 1653.

Tweeddale wanted to strengthen his relationship with Lauderdale, who had always appreciated the efforts Tweeddale had made in his attempt to secure his own release in 1659. He had also been grateful to Tweeddale for not challenging Charles's behaviour over the Buccleuch entail as Charles had expressed his own great gratitude to Lauderdale for ensuring the Monmouth marriage had been made legal. He saw that Tweeddale could be a very useful ally, so he asked him to join Moray in his administration in Scotland. Lauderdale now had his own men in Scotland, both of whom were related to him and with whom he had a strong and trusted relationship.

Lauderdale visited Scotland, for the first time since 1651, to attend Parliament in June 1663. One of the first matters considered was the billetting affair and Lauderdale headed a committee to examine it. This reported in July, Middleton was censured and Rothes recommended that he should lose his position as Commander-in-Chief, probably because he wanted the job himself. Lauderdale also focused on tackling the growing problem of religious disorder, especially in the southwest. Parliament passed an Act against conventicles, which were public religious meetings not held in churches, and Lauderdale told Charles it was 'the most effectual Act for the settlement of the church, which has yet been made'. Parliament also decreed that all public officials had to sign a declaration denouncing the Covenant and it repealed an Act of 1662, which had limited the king's power to pardon the descendants of traitors. One of the biggest beneficiaries of this was Lauderdale's nephew Lord Lorne, the son of the executed Marquis of Argyll, who had earlier been condemned to death and had been awaiting execution for over a year. He now had his titles and estates restored to him.

The south front of Yester House.

The north front of Yester House.

St. Cuthbert's.

Goblin Ha', Yester Castle.

Lennoxlove.

Charles Seton, 2nd Earl of Dunfermline,
painted by Sir Anthony van Dyck.

Neidpath Castle.

Yester House c.1690 attr James de Witt.

John Hay, 1st Earl of Tweeddale.

John Hay, 1st Marquis of Tweeddale, painted by Sir Henry Raeburn, Scottish National Portrait Gallery.

John Leslie, 1st Duke of Rothes, painted by L. Schuneman, Scottish National Portrait Gallery.

John Hay, 1st Marquis of Tweeddale with his wife Jane and their children and in-laws.

John Maitland, 1st Duke of Lauderdale and his wife, Elizabeth.

John Hay, 2nd Marquis of Tweeddale, painted by Gerard Soest, Glasgow Museums
www.scran.co.uk.

James Hamilton, 4th Duke of Hamilton, painted by Ferdinand Voet C. Glasgow Museums www.scran.ac.uk.

John Hay, 4th Marquis of Tweeddale, painted by William Aikman, Scottish National Portrait Gallery.

George Hay, 7th Marquis of Tweeddale, painted by Alexander Naysmith.

James Douglas, 2nd Duke of Queensberry, painted by Sir John Baptiste de Medina, Scottish National Portrait Gallery.

Charles Hay, 14th Marquis of Tweeddale.

George Hay, 8th Marquis of Tweeddale, painted by Sir Henry Raeburn, Scottish National Portrait Gallery.

The Saloon.

The Saloon.

The Saloon.

CHAPTER 9 – TWEEDDALE IN GOVERNMENT

Tweeddale became Lauderdale's closest ally in Scotland and Lauderdale helped him develop his relationships in London, especially with the king, who soon appointed him an Extraordinary Lord of Session. He was also asked to help negotiate the marriage of Lauderdale's daughter Mary, but this did not progress and, if it had, both Tweeddale's and Yester's lives would have been very different.

Gilbert Burnet was made Archbishop of Glasgow in 1663 and he thanked his 'two grand supporters the Earls of Argyll and Tweeddale'. When Chancellor Glencairn died in 1664 Tweeddale was considered as his successor, but he was strongly opposed by Archbishop Sharp. Burnet agreed, paying no heed to Tweeddale's role in his own appointment, writing to Sharp that 'if one of the late professing converts' got the job, the church would be ruined. Sharp concurred: 'There is an effectual design laid to crush the interest of the clergy and encourage that faction which looks for a reviving of the covenant.' Instead, Rothes was made Chancellor, a position he did not want and he was replaced as Lord Treasurer by a five-man Commission, of which he was President, with the four others being Tweeddale, Moray and lords Bellenden and Cochrane, which Tweeddale effectively controlled. Rothes's mood was lightened by his being appointed Commander-in-Chief, the position he had always wanted. Sir John Nisbet, Tweeddale's lawyer, was appointed Lord Advocate and Lauderdale's brother, Charles Maitland of Halton, became a Privy Councillor. Tweeddale was made President of the Privy Council and sat on various parliamentary committees, most importantly on the committee overseeing the Mint. He and Lauderdale were now in regular correspondence, addressing each other as 'Dearest Brother'.

Tweeddale's initial focus was on border control and religious issues. He and Moray also looked after Lauderdale's estates in Scotland, which consisted principally of Thirlestane Castle in Midlothian and Lethington, and his role as curator to the Monmouths took up an increasing amount of his time. Rothes had submitted his enormous fee of £1.25 million for his consent to Anna's marriage, which the curators said had to be paid over twelve years because of the debts of £2.5 million the young couple had inherited. Rothes was also due a sum of money for handling Mary Scott's will. As Lauderdale and Tweeddale were responsible as curators for advising Charles on what Rothes should be paid, Rothes was careful not to alienate them.

As Rothes was Chancellor, Commissioner and Commander-in-Chief, he was the source of great patronage and Tweeddale warned Lauderdale: 'I fear few or none will acknowledge you to have any share.' He also warned Lauderdale that, if Rothes remained Commissioner, 'little discovery will be made of the evils the country groans under... whereas a truer prospect will be had of the condition of affairs in one month after this curtain is drawn, than a whole year's sufferings will make appear'. Rothes was now drinking heavily and was often seen drunk in public, so Tweeddale lobbied Lauderdale to have his responsibilities reduced. Moray supported Tweeddale and wrote to Lauderdale: 'I am deadly afraid we shall discover more horrid things in the management of the king's rents than would ever have entered in your heart to think of.'

The Dutch war started in 1665 and proved ruinous for Scotland. Trade with the Continent collapsed and taxation was increased because Charles insisted that the Scots raise and pay their own army in case of a Dutch invasion. This meant Scotland would have a standing army for the first time in her history. Tweeddale said the country was so impoverished by the fall in trade that no tax should be levied unless an invasion was imminent. That this was true was shown by Rothes, who had to borrow money on his own surety in order to build the fortifications he considered necessary for defence.

Charles was unsurprisingly intransigent and in April insisted that the tax be raised. Tweeddale wrote to Moray, who was in London, expressing his concern that all was not well in Scotland and he added 'but I am so apprehensive of worse that I desire no change'. Tweeddale was prescient, for the very next month fifteen Dutch warships sailed up the Forth and bombarded the coast. Matters were also not helped as the fiercly Episcopal Archbishop Sharp had been appointed Primate of Scotland but Lauderdale guessed that he would be his own worst enemy. He was soon proved right as the combination of Sharp's policies and the economic hardship caused by the war produced a revolt in the southwest and Lauderdale warned Charles that he should be careful about accelerating Episcopacy, but fighting between religious factions continued for many years in different parts of Scotland, especially in the southwest. Tweeddale wrote despairingly to Lauderdale: 'It will appear neither the establishment nor the good and peace of the country is sought, but men's own interests and ends by upholding an unlimited power backed by the sword over a poor nation that I dare not say would fayne live in quiet if free of extremity of arbitrairiness and oppression.'

Tweeddale was very involved with determining the level of military presence needed in Scotland and he was very suspicious of the generals. He thought they only wanted 'an unlimited power backed by the sword over a poor nation that would... live in quiet...

free of arbitrariness and oppression and if a remedy be not found will be rendered miserable'. He wrote to Lauderdale setting out what he wanted when peace came: 'Endeavour... to put us in the condition the parliament left us in when you were last in Scotland... a well-ordered militia, for better the country be all in arms than ruined by a few that are not sufficient to defend it if invaded.'

Tweeddale's own position with the Buccleuch estate remained acute as his debt to it now stood at over £950,000. His father had made a claim against the estate, which had had a favourable ruling from the Court of Session in 1633 but he had not pursued it. Lauderdale recommended that Tweeddale write to the king about it 'as short as you can, and written in a fair hand'. The sums involved were very large and the claims were very complicated. One involved a claim on an estate in Roxburghshire which dated from 1468, and another a claim for rents that had not been paid since 1629, and which had accumulated to a total of £1.4 million. In addition, Jean Tweeddale's brother, David, had died intestate and Tweeddale thought that she could make a claim of £870,000 on half of the estate. Thus the Tweeddales felt that these claims would more than satisfy the debt they owed.

Lauderdale recommended that Tweeddale come to London since 'without your own presence it will run great risk to miscarry, and your friends cannot help you in your absence as they can in your presence'. Tweeddale replied that he would prefer for the lawyers to meet first and set out the whole case before the king. In August 1667 the court ruled that Jean's claim was valid and this enabled Tweeddale to achieve a complete settlement: Jean was to be paid £762,000 but Tweeddale only £194,000. His debt to the Buccleuchs was calculated at £1.25 million, so he owed £244,000. The king endorsed this and promised that the Monmouths would ratify it when they reached their majority. Tweeddale now felt that all his inherited problems were behind him and he could now concentrate on helping Scotland recover and prosper.

Tweeddale was becoming closer to Lauderdale for another reason. In 1666 he spoke with his son, Yester 'who was verrie desirous of it to go abroad as he had studied the french language so well at home... and by his private studies had acquired in his father's house (never having been at school) the perfect understand of the Latin, Greek and Hebrew'. Both Lauderdale and Moray advised him not to go as the French were putting English ships in quarantine because of the plague, so he went to London instead and stayed with Lauderdale at his house in Highgate. While there, Lauderdale encouraged him to pay court to his only child, Mary, his daughter by his wife Lady Anne Home. Tweeddale was cautious but Moray encouraged him to let matters take their course.

Mary Maitland was not the bride he had wanted for his son, but his failure to secure a Buccleuch heiress made him more amenable to her. She was ten years older than Yester and she had been rejected by a number of other prospective partners as she was not very attractive. The Tweeddales were later to write: 'her other defects would be small inducement to engage a young man's affection,' and they even considered that her physical problems might prevent her having children. Yester was, however, easy to influence and Moray and Lauderdale pushed him to be 'more ambitious than amorous,' and he wrote optimistically to his father about his prospects and the pleasures of court life.

They were married in 1666 and Charles gave away the bride. A guest at the wedding described her as 'very homely and like a monkey,' and remarked that Yester 'seemeth to deserve such a wife and no more'. Lauderdale said that he was so satisfied at gaining Yester as his son-in-law that the loss of his own son at birth was fully compensated for. As part of the marriage settlement, it was agreed that, if there were only one son of the marriage, then that son would inherit the titles of both Tweeddale and Lauderdale. If two sons were born, then the second would take Lauderdale's titles and he would be paid a dowry of £480,000 over the next decade. Lauderdale insisted that a clause be inserted allowing him to change his mind about these clauses on the payment of a rose noble, in which event he would pay his daughter and any of her children £900,000 on his death.

Charles's credibility was weakened when the Dutch raided Chatham in June, destroying three warships and capturing the flagship whilst, it was rumoured, he was enjoying the pleasure of his mistress Barbara Villiers. This was not an isolated incident as Pepys wrote that it was generally agreed that Charles was governed by wine, women and rogues. Peace was made with the Dutch in 1667, Clarendon was forced to resign as Chancellor and Lauderdale was appointed to the five-man Cabal that replaced him. Clarendon's fall also meant the end of the Scottish Council and from now on Lauderdale himself would decide policy in consultation with the king. He wrote to Tweeddale: 'Oh, it would do your heart good to see what a new world is here and how bravely all the king's business goes on... now the king is the king himself.'

Because of Lauderdale's increased responsibilities and because Moray was still in London, Tweeddale was now effectively running Scotland. Moray wrote to him: 'All mists are now cleared up. Nobody can make the king suspect your loyalty, your integrity, your affection to him, nor the candour of your professions as to the things ecclesiastical as well as civil.' Burnet wrote of him: 'His great experience in affairs, his ready compliance with every thing that he thought would please the king... gained him such an interest in the king, that no attempt against him... could ever shake it' and the Covenanter Roger North wrote of him: 'He was truly a man of great spirit... a man very national, and truly the honor of our Scots nation.'

Tweeddale set out his agenda: 'The army disbanded, the country settled, the peace secured, the customs and excise well farmed' and he sent Lauderdale his plans to keep the western region quiet; local nobles should be relied on, amnesty should be granted for good behaviour and the people should be encouraged to attend church. He recommended a militia be raised, as this would weaken the power of the generals, and recommended cutting the troops' wages significantly as too much money 'doth but debauch them'. This angered the Duke of Hamilton, as he was still owed £1.6 million by the Crown and he wanted to keep his troops to control the west but Tweeddale insisted that this was the responsibility of the militia. A standing army of 1,200 was retained and Atholl was given the responsibility of controlling the Highlands. Moray congratulated Lauderdale saying that he and Tweeddale had 'the king's service and the welfare of the church and state in our hearts'. Lauderdale replied: 'For the Lord's sake be sure you have taken your measures aright... if the Devil should again possess our foolish fanatics I hope you will consider... who will bear the blame... they must destroy us or we them... for my part I will never trust them, they are mad men... God forgive you all if it be not kept peaceable.'

Tweeddale and Moray again pushed for Rothes to be removed as Commissioner but Lauderdale was in no hurry to ask Charles to do this. Tweeddale was frustrated and wrote protesting that the Commissioner 'had stood in the way of all attempts whatsoever at recovery and at this hour does so more than ever... Let not all our hopes be shipwrecked in the harbour. We cannot answer for the peace... after my lord commissioner is gone in that capacity to England.' Lauderdale was convinced and Charles removed Rothes both as Commissioner and as Commander-in-Chief but allowed him to remain as Chancellor, despite Rothes hating the post and despite Tweeddale's advice that he be replaced by Moray. Lauderdale was appointed High Commissioner which prompted Pepys to write 'Lauderdale hath got the whole power of Scotland into his hand... is never far from the king's ear nor council... he is a most cunning fellow.'

Tweeddale was desperate to have Moray in Scotland, both because he was a trusted friend but also because he was finding the burden of office very heavy. Hamilton was very upset by Rothes's loss of office as he had been his constant drinking companion and had plotted with him to prevent Tweeddale's changes to the military but he began to dine regularly with Tweeddale, who was celebrating the birth of his first grandchild. Moray at last arrived in Edinburgh in June 1667 and worked well with Tweeddale, focusing initially on the perennial problem of finance. The Treasury Commission controlled all the Crown's revenues and payments and was thus the most important arm of government. Lauderdale preferred to deal with it as it included his strongest supporters, unlike the Privy Council, which included too many independent nobles. Tweeddale was promoted President of both the Treasury Commission and the Exchequer and his workload became increasingly demanding as the Commission had to consider not only finance but also a wide area of other matters including the army and militia, trade, preventing another western rebellion and ongoing religious problems.

The Commission met four days a week and Tweeddale soon found that he and Moray had to undertake most of the work as both Cochrane and Bellenden suffered from ill health and Rothes was not interested. Lauderdale's man in Edinburgh, William Sharp, the Archbishop's brother, was appointed cash keeper and he took care of most of the everyday duties, controlling all receipts and disbursements. Tweeddale ran a very efficient operation. One historian wrote: 'Expenditure was, in most instances, tightly controlled by the treasury commission. It never exceeded income to any significant degree.' Maurice Lee comments: 'Tweeddale, once he had made up his mind, showed a stubborn, single-minded determination, verging on inflexibility, which was often to characterise his behaviour in his years in power.'

Tweeddale told Lauderdale that people were pleased that the

government now stood 'upon the old foundations of law and administration'. How to maximise revenue was the prime consideration and a debate began between the two methods of collecting it, tax farming or direct collection, and it was decided that farming was preferable. The customs and excise tack had historically been auctioned on an annual basis and Sir Walter Seaton had won the auction in both 1664 and 1665, bidding £2.2 million. Tweeddale considered that Seaton was corrupt and Moray and Lauderdale's brother, Halton, organised a seperate bidding group which outbid Seaton in 1666, offering £3.67 million to Seaton's £3.6 million. The actual sum collected was £3.28 million so Halton's syndicate was well out of pocket and Tweeddale wrote to Charles hoping he would not 'suffer the gentlemen to be losers when cheats have gained so much by embezzling and bringing his revenues as good as nothing'. This experience convinced Tweeddale that direct collection of taxes was preferable to farming and this was to cause him significant problems in the future.

Tweeddale removed Bellenden from the Commission and replaced him with Halton, giving him the opportunity of advancement, which he seized eagerly. Lauderdale asked Tweeddale to 'be kind and frank to him and I hope he will mend his faults'. The Commission was tough on disbursements, and pensions were cut by half. Rothes had been entitled to £400,000 a year as Commissioner and this was cut entirely. On the other hand, the Commission increased revenues for the king from Crown lands, which greatly pleased Charles. Paying for the army was the most difficult challenge but this was removed when Charles gave the order for its disbandment, although this was challenged by both Hamilton and Burnet as they saw the army as the only way to control the western religious dissidents. The bishops, led by Burnet, were increasingly critical of Tweeddale and Moray, who wrote to Lauderdale that the bishops should 'presume that your Lordship's ends and ours are the same, and if there happens any difference about the means conducing thereunto, we shall not stick to our opinion, but in submission and paying all becoming deference to your Lordship's great judgement and experience'. Privately Moray and Tweeddale were more forthright. Moray, who was known as 'the great Scotch Presbyterian', but who supported episcopacy, told Tweedddale 'these people are unfit, or indeed unable, to manage matters aright,' and Tweeddale said: 'We laughed until we were weary [at a letter] of this silly company of people.'

Lauderdale was very pleased with how his cousins were running Scotland and wrote to Tweeddale in September of his letters 'The more I get the more I desire. He [the king] is fully satisfied with your whole carriage (I mean both you and MR for I don't separate you). Moray had invented codes for them: Lauderdale was JR (John Red), Tweeddale was SS (Sir Simon) and Moray was MR. Moray now wanted to pay off his debt to Lauderdale who wrote to Tweeddale 'Be sure to take no more than the first principal of [£100,000], for I will have no more of the interest till he be richer'. Tweeddale expressed his frustrations in a letter to Lauderdale in September 1667, complaining about Burnet's attacks on the government generally and on his accusation in particular that he intended to undermine Episcopacy itself. Lauderdale, who nicknamed Burnet 'Long Face', agreed and removed Burnet from the Court of Session. Archbishop Sharp warned Tweeddale that conventicles were increasing in the west and spreading eastwards. Tweeddale wrote to Lauderdale: 'The whole outed ministers have a design to set up and preach again in private houses... in the time of divine worship when there is none in the parish, and after sermons where churches are planted... from a despair they have even the soberest of them ever to be admitted to churches... They think it well enough if they gather not people to the fields as the mad fellows do... Be thinking of it and consider how we are to provide from danger.' He then suggested 'the dangers of what I wrote in my last concerning the outed ministers is not so great but that it may be prevented if any of the soberest were settled somewhere in churches where there is no danger from them'. Lauderdale adopted this suggestion and offered moderate ministers churches 'in convenient places where they may be connived at', but he later wrote 'If the Devil should again possess our foolish fanatics...they must destroy us or we them...I never trust them...they are mad men'.

Religious disturbances and the holding of conventicles had significantly increased by 1668 and Charles ordered that a militia of 20,000 foot and 2,000 horse be raised, but that they should only be quartered in 'reliable districts'; he did not want them used against his own government. This was an expensive commitment as a soldier cost £12,000 a year and a cavalryman three times that. Only those who took the oath and signed a declaration against the Covenant were allowed to bear arms. The king said that soldiers should not have to pay their debts but Tweeddale persuaded him to change his mind and he also advised that people should be persuaded to go to church, rather than be forced to, as Archbishop Burnet wanted.

The conflict persisted between England's need for revenue and Scotland's difficulty in satisfying that need, often caused by situations of England's own making. One of these had been the renewal in 1663 of the Navigation Acts, which effectively treated Scotland as a foreign country, forbidding any trade being carried on Scottish ships between the two countries and with England's colonies. Lauderdale had tried to ease these as soon as he was appointed Secretary but had been unable to do so and the Dutch War had made matters much worse. Rothes complained that 'money does grow daily scarcer so as in a short time there will I believe be none' and when the French raised tariffs on Scotland Tweeddale led the demand for a trade commission with England saying it was 'now or never'. His greater ambition was, however, for political union and he later wrote: 'This business of trade...

will I hope fairly introduce the consideration of a union.'

He understood probably better than any man in Scotland the logic for union. His experience during the Cromwellian union and his own experience of trade gleaned from the tax he raised from the port of Dunbar had persuaded him that union was far more important than agreements on trade. He knew, however, that without concessions on trade, the Scots would not even consider union, but he was sceptical as to the prospects of it being achieved.

When the Dutch war ended, a commission was set up to examine the state of trade between England and Scotland. In the debate before choosing the English commissioners, Sir Thomas Clifford referred to Scotland disparagingly as 'our Indies', since it provided England with raw materials and bought its finished goods. The Scottish commissioners were lead by Lauderdale and included Tweeddale, Moray, Dunfermline, Kincardine and Rothes. In January 1668 they met the English commission led by the Earl of Buckingham, Lord Bridgeman and Sir George Downing, the Anglo-Irish Lord Treasurer, who was no friend of the Scots. He had been the driving force behind the restitution of the Navigation Acts and wanted nothing to alter the current balance of trade, as that would reduce the revenue to the Treasury. The Scots laid out their main grievances: import duties on cattle, linen, salt and beer; English export duties on horses and grain; the prohibition of export of wool and hides; and the insistence that all goods sent to Scotland passed through Berwick or Carlisle. The resulting discussion seemed endless, no chairs were provided, the rooms were unheated and some of the commissioners showed little interest in the proceedings. Dunfermline behaved true to form 'who would not leave play at Hampton Court for so small a matter,' and Buckingham killed his mistress's husband in a duel only a few days after the meetings began. Lauderdale told Tweeddale he should return to Scotland and he did so with alacrity.

Lauderdale announced his plan to visit Scotland; he had not

been for five years and he wanted Parliament's approval for trade negotiations to proceed. He also wanted to see how the improvements to Thirlestane were going, which Moray had told him would make it the best house in Scotland. He told Moray that he would have to go to England in his absence. Tweeddale was not happy and wrote to Lauderdale: 'I will not think of it but when I resolve to flee out of Scotland for alone I will not stay in it.' Lauderdale ignored him and Moray left for London in June. A week later, Charles told Lauderdale he should not go to Scotland until the spring of 1669, and also told Moray he had to stay in England for the rest of the year. He had clearly missed his company and the science they explored together. Tweeddale wrote an anguished letter to Lauderdale, setting out the long list of what needed to be done, and he concluded: 'You may apprehend me near dotage for I am sure I shall not hold long out at this rate of business. Mortal man must have some ease and relief.' On top of everything, Jean Tweeddale was having a difficult pregnancy, but she successfully gave birth to their sixth son, Gilbert, in November. Lauderdale was not wholly sympathetic and told Kincardine: 'The king hath now twice declared his pleasure, and yet [Tweeddale] gives not over grumbling.' He wrote to Tweeddale, focussing on his own problems: 'There is nothing but toil and little pleasure for me in this world. I received my doom, that I must not this year enjoy the satisfaction of seeing fair Scotland and my friends in it which I have so longed for.'

Yester moved to London in January and Tweeddale asked Moray to look after him as he needed training in the art of the politics of Court and of Parliament: 'Instruct him in the way of Monarchs... he is by succession your disciple.' Moray did as he was asked but never returned to government in Scotland as his life was soon irrevocably changed. Earlier that year he had written of 'his indifference to the world and things in it'; he then visited Lady Balcares, his late wife's sister, who had been recently widowed and who was living at Balcares Castle with her son and her two daughters, Henrietta and Sophia. Sophia was eighteen and her formal title was Lady Sophia Lindsay, the same as Moray's late wife. She was a troubled girl who suffered from fits but spoke of great religious visions that came to her during them. Burnet was asked to visit her and found her 'a young woman of fine parts and very devout... a moderate share of beauty and not much discretion'. He and Moray encouraged her to go to Yester House to recover and also advised her former suitor, Sir Francis Scott, to renew his interest. However, as Burnet reported, 'she was so smitten by [Moray] that she fell desperately in love, tho he was old and a coarse sort of man, yet he was not insensible'.

Moray had also fallen for her and he wrote to Lauderdale: 'She is an admirable child, worthy to be the wife of a prince... in a word so like my Aunt [an interesting slip of the pen; he meant *her* Aunt, i.e. his late wife] that I cannot but have all the kindness for her... she is genuinely kind to me as if I were her father.' She was advised by the doctors to take the waters in Bath and Moray took her to London in July where Charles encouraged him to stay and they never visited Bath. Moray's behaviour prompted Lauderdale to write to Tweeddale: 'What you have done with him in Scotland I know not but truly he is much changed... He minds nothing but his niece and his alchemy... the bewitching chemistry (on which our dearest Master spends at least 2 to 3 hours every day) are like to be too hard for you and me both.'

Charles had recently set up his own laboratory in Whitehall where he, Buckingham and Moray spent an increasing amount of time. Rumours began to circulate about Moray's fixation with Sophia with one writing 'Lewd men thought very ill of it, others were sorry to see so great a Philosopher dote so in his old age'. Tweeddale wrote to Moray berating him for spending more time with Sophia than he did with his own wife. He also warned Lauderdale about his workload: 'All our endeavours... without more hands and more force will be disproportioned to the difficulties we meet with and which I do forsee will occur.' Lauderdale promised Tweeddale he would soon send Moray back 'in spite of alchemy and monstrous love'. But he later wrote: 'You do well to say no more of MR he will do you no good this year, and himself neither hurt nor good here.' However, it was Sophia who was sent back to her mother and Moray never saw her again. After his death, she wrote to Tweeddale that Moray 'in his mortal state had been not only to me the best of fathers but my most exemplary guide towards the glory that succeeded it'.

Tweeddale was still full of hope about trade and the prospects for union and he had written to Lauderdale in April: 'I am joyed the king and the duke have so good an opinion of Scotland and confidence in it, and hope they shall not be disappointed, for it may be turned into a citadel for his majesty's service in time.' In June he wrote hoping Lauderdale would bring with him to Scotland 'a good issue of the business of trade, which will make way for the union proposed'. In London the talks about trade and union took on a more serious nature. Lauderdale told Lord Bridgeman 'this discourse of the union will, I am confident, advance and not retard the matter of trade,' which was the opposite of Tweeddale's view. He was becoming sceptical about the intentions of the English and wrote to Lauderdale in September: 'I have small hope of the trade with England, and I apprehend the matter of union was proposed to divert it.' Lauderdale must have given him comfort for he later wrote: 'Oh if the king would mind it as it is of importance, and all we do or can is but fending over to put off an evil time that must come unless that be done... I am glad to hear the union looks so hopeful, for then the trade needs not trouble you much.'

Tweeddale's 'fending' focused on the cattle trade, because the success of it totally depended on England. In July 1668 he had ordered the English custom farmers to explain why they had been charging duty on Scottish cattle and Charles ordered that no such duty should henceforward be charged. This was almost the Scots' only victory, they had not negotiated well but they felt the English had never intended to show any flexibility. Lauderdale told Tweeddale that Downing 'would ruin the treaty if he can,' and Tweeddale, in a rare moment of *realpolitik*, suggested to Lauderdale that bribery might ease matters: 'Sir George Downing barks for a bone, he has been accustomed to get money from Scotsmen.'

Charles was determined not to be controlled by Parliament and he wanted union as his financial problems were acute; his principal purpose was to inject Scottish members into the English Parliament in order to give him control over it. Lauderdale reported in October that Charles had ordered a proposal for union to be prepared and he sent Tweeddale a draft letter outlining the plan, which he suggested should be circulated to a few key people. Tweeddale showed it to Argyll first and, based on his input over the nobility's proposed representation of only ten peers in the merged Parliaments, Tweeddale told Lauderdale: 'You must either prevail for a greater number or get some assurance of calling more speedily.' He added that, unless he were to receive some assurance on this, there was no point discussing it with anyone else. Charles then prorogued the English Parliament and no further work on union took place for six months.

In Scotland, religious matters still had to be settled. Discussions continued with Archbishop Sharp about allowing moderate nonconformist ministers to enter vacant parishes. Both Sharp and the leading nonconformist minister, Robert Douglas, were hesitant and wanted the matter resolved by the Court of Session and in July 1669 Sharp survived an assassination attempt. Tweeddale was shocked but the reaction of the people was probably best summed up by a Presbyterian minister who wrote: 'The cry arose, a man was killed. The people's answer was, it's but a bishop: and so there was no more noise.'

Tweeddale wrote Lauderdale a long analysis of the religious situation saying that the current state was in accord with neither 'the genius of the nation nor the interest of the magistrate': the bishops were very unpopular; Sharp had to be told by Charles to stay out of politics; and the Nonconformists should be allowed to preach, but this permission could not be made official. He confessed: 'I must tell you, I was never so put to it to know what is best for neither leniency will work with these people nor severity be suffered by them; and without they be divided there is no ordering them, for god's sake therefore think of all ways to do it.' He asked for and was given £60,000 a year to pay informers for news about the spread of conventicles. Lauderdale was supportive, agreeing that 'the beasts we have to deal with are furious unnatural irrational brutes, and so the king understands them right'.

Charles recognised the problems Tweeddale was facing and the strain he was under as Moray had told the king that governing Scotland was worse than governing France. Charles made Tweeddale a member of the Privy Council of England when he came to England in June to see his first grandchild, named, perhaps tactfully, Charles. During that visit he learnt about Lauderdale who was seeing a great deal of someone he described as 'our friend at Ham'. This was Elizabeth Murray, Countess of Dysart, who Lauderdale believed had persuaded Cromwell to spare his life after Worcester. The countess was a red-headed beauty and a formidable operator. Although she was a close friend of Cromwell, and was even rumoured to have had a son by him, she joined the secret Royalist organisation, the Sealed Knot, and visited Charles in Breda several times. She had tried to persuade Cromwell to let him return to England and Charles rewarded her with a pension of £90,000 a year at his Restoration. She was Moray's second cousin and he had been at one time selected by her father as a suitor to her, but in 1648 she had married Sir Lionel Tollemache and had eleven children, six of whom had died in infancy. Tollemache became very ill and spent much time in France seeking a cure; Catherine was a passionate lady of 43 and she needed company and she turned to Lauderdale who eagerly responded and spent much of his time at her home, Ham House in Richmond, neglecting his own sick wife. Dunfermline and Yester frequently visited Ham House and Yester told his father that his health was drunk at every meal. Tweeddale was uncomfortable about the rumours and drafted a letter to Lauderdale suggesting his 'choosing another place and company for diversion than was your custom,' and confessed that it was 'all riddles to me', but he seems, wisely, not to have sent it.

He was less sensitive about his dealings with the bishops generally, and with Burnet in particular, who continued to fight openly about the grant of Indulgence to the Nonconformists. Tweeddale was very critical of Burnet, who promised 'absolute submission' but he soon reneged on this and was summoned to appear before the Privy Council. Moray considered Burnet's behaviour to be 'the greatest ignominy that ever Episcopal government fell under since the reformation,' and Charles gave Lauderdale full freedom to handle Burnet as he thought fit. Tweeddale had other problems to deal with, one of which was the increasing lawlessness in the Highlands. This was caused by clan leaders such as Cameron of Lochiel wanting to seize his neighbours' lands, and by rustlers who preyed on the lucrative cattle trade.

Argyll was desperate to both reduce his debts and increase his influence. He was angry that the commission to keep the peace in the Highlands had been given to his rival, Atholl, and he blamed Tweeddale for this and for a whole series of other matters. He had been recently widowed and this may have made him more than usually difficult, possibly causing Tweeddale to be gentle with him. He refused, however, to have any discussions with Tweeddale, who decided to deal with him when Lauderdale, who was Argyll's uncle, came to Scotland. Tweeddale appointed James Campbell of

Lawers as the new peacekeeper for the Highlands and he accelerated the creation of the militia, advising Charles: 'I am confident it will prove as good as any standing army ever was in Scotland.' Parliament passed the Act of Creation in 1669 which allowed Charles to use the militia anywhere. 'In effect,' wrote Tweeddale to Moray, this created 'a standing army with less burden to the country and less charge to the king.' Despite this, Charles was not prepared to pay for it. Almost immediately the militia was used against the conventicles in the west, as well as to collect taxes in the north. Yester was appointed commander of the Haddingtonshire militia, which was paid for by the 'heritors', the feudal landholders, of the parish but Tweeddale was reluctant to raise a militia in the Highlands until he felt comfortable with who would lead it.

Finance remained the perennial problem for Scotland as well as for England. In Scotland, the cost of the militia escalated as did pensions, which more than doubled in a year to £3.2 million; Tweeddale himself was paid £100,000. Charles approved the process of direct tax collection in January 1669 and Tweeddale appointed three collectors, two of whom, his cousin Sir James Hay of Linplum and Lord Elibank, had been in the tax farming syndicate that had lost money on its bid in 1666. The third member was Archibald Murray of Blackbarony, the Sheriff of Peebles.

In England, Charles pressed the commissioners to expedite union with a single bicameral Parliament where Scotland would have 30 MPs in the Commons; the number of peers was left open and would be determined later by the king. England would contribute 70% of taxation raised, Ireland 18% and Scotland 12%; and the legal system of Scotland would remain separate. Lauderdale was first and foremost the king's man, and the interests of Scotland were always secondary to this. He wrote to Charles: 'All your commands are to me above all human laws.' As long as Charles needed union, Lauderdale would do all he could to secure it, but he realised that he had to go to Scotland himself to drive it through. Tweeddale, despite his commitment for union, warned Lauderdale that getting support for it would not be easy, telling him that it was 'mightily spoken against here'. Lauderdale was relaxed and replied: 'What you say of the cabal which is forming against the union troubles me little.' The two Parliaments were to meet in October to debate the issue and one of the first concerns was to decide who should choose the commissioners, the king or Parliament. Lauderdale, as ever, was for the king, and he sent Tweeddale a list of the key matters that Parliament needed to vote on. The main one was union but an Act of Supremacy was also needed to establish the king's authority over the Kirk. Tweeddale sent Yester south with the drafts of the proposed legislation, reminding Lauderdale that this was the first official responsibility of '*Notre Fils*' and suggesting he be given £50,000 as a reward.

Lauderdale left London in September, having been voted a budget of £250,000 for all his expenses, including the refurbishment of the Palace of Holyrood. He told Tweeddale he wanted to be met on his arrival at Morpeth, just south of the border, by him 'and no one else'. He opened Parliament in October and read out the king's 'desire to settle union between our kingdoms'. He reported on the failure of the trade negotiations: 'They produced no effect, unless it were a conviction of the difficulty, if not impossibility, of settling it in any other way, than by a nearer and more complete union of the two kingdoms.' Parliament voted on union and 'without any alteration unanimously agreed to, excepting one lawyer'whose long speech against had been angrily interrupted by Tweeddale. Lauderdale did however recognise the reality of the Scottish peoples' mistrust of union and he advised Charles that the next steps must come from England.

Whilst the king was delighted at the success of the vote, he was slow at moving matters on, probably because he was now deep in his secret negotiations with the French over what became the Treaty of Dover. In reality, his eagerness for union would only remain if his discussions with the French failed. Moray sensed his reluctance and, in order to keep the process moving, suggested that the Scottish Parliament should pass an Act giving Charles the right to issue a commission from Scotland to initiate negotiations on union, thus avoiding the need to wait for the English Parliament to act. Lauderdale was furious with him for suggesting this without first discussing it with him. He had always wanted England to lead the process, as he would then be sure of pushing it through the Scottish Parliament. Lauderdale knew how sensitive the matter was in Scotland and how great was the mistrust of England. He wrote in fury and despair to Moray:

> You cannot imagine what aversion there is generally in this kingdom to the union. The endeavour to have made us slaves by garrisons and to ruin our trade by severe laws in England frights all ranks of men... what is done is purely in obedience to his Majesty... But to press more before England take notice of the matter would render the proposer more odious as the betrayer of his country. For God's sake let his Majesty lay another punishment on me, no command could be more grievous. This I must say, yet if he do command it I shall... obey come what can come. Yet I must assure you it does quite overthrow the service and render the union here impossible.

A week later, Lauderdale received an order from Charles to have Parliament endorse the proposal. This letter was sent by special express post, which in itself raised much conjecture about the letter's content. Lauderdale asked Charles to consider his objections and told him, if he still decided to press on, that he would obey him but would 'disclaim all promises of success in this or in the treaty'. He told him that he had consulted with all fifteen members of the Articles, including Tweeddale, and that they all opposed the blank authorisation. Charles agreed that he would await Lauderdale's advice as to how to proceed. Lauderdale then wrote to Moray that he was pleased 'that I shall not be chidid for not obeying the command you sent me BY THE EXPRESS'. He explained to the king: 'I was afflicted above measure to have so great a business miscarry in my hand by precipitation.' Charles prorogued the English Parliament in December with no further discussion about union.

Lauderdale had much greater success in religious matters. Parliament passed the Act of Supremacy in 1669, which declared that the king 'hath the supreme authority and supremacy over all persons and in all causes ecclesiastical within this his kingdom'. Parliament also approved severe punishments for those participating in conventicles, including instant execution for preachers and severe fines and deportation for worshippers. The Earl of Dumfries told Tweeddale that 'the king had now got in between God and the bishops,' and Sharp wrote to Tweeddale that 'all King Henry the 8th ten years' works was now to be done in three days'. The passing of the Act enabled Lauderdale to get rid of Burnet, who resigned as Archbishop 'being sensible that my service... hath not been... acceptable to his Majesty.'

However success in Parliament was not mirrored on the ground, as religious dissent grew. Lauderdale wrote to Tweeddale: 'I am desperate... They are unsatisfiable; what they would have begged before they will reject when offered. Oh, they are a terrible insolent generation.' Tweeddale could only agree: 'The grounds for your hope are I confess rational... yet when I consider the insufferable humour of these unsatisfiable cattle I confess I can not hope.' Another Act of Indulgence had been passed in July 1669, only to be declared illegal by Sharp and Burnet, and by March 1670 only seventeen ministers had returned to their parishes.

Parliament passed the Act creating the militia and Lauderdale wrote to Charles: 'In a word this Church... nor ecclesiastical person in it can never trouble you more unless you please; and the other Act settles you twenty thousand men to make good that power... That if you command it not only the militia but all the sensible men in Scotland shall march when and where you shall please to command, for never a King was so absolute as you are in poor old Scotland.' Charles later declared that 'now Scotland hath the best laws in the world and the completest'.

Lauderdale was at the peak of his powers and this began to provoke envy and mistrust, both in England and in Scotland. He wrote to Tweeddale about 'the strange prejudices' that the Militia Bill had aroused in England but felt they would pass. One commentator wrote that 'many talked that he deserved an halter rather than a Garter'. Another wrote: 'The members were rather overawed than gained to a compliance; for Lauderdale was become so lazy, and was naturally so violent, and by his Majesty's favour and his own prosperity so far raised above all thought of fear, that he never consulted what was to be done... he would oft times vent... that such Acts should be passed in spite of all opposition.'

Lauderdale was delighted at his success in Parliament but was still realistic about the problems confronting Scotland. He wrote to Charles in November: 'I hope you will allow us to do something for our trade,' and Tweeddale agreed, hoping that Charles 'be well pleased with what is done is the height of our ambition and desire'. He wrote to Moray about the prospects of creating a fishing company 'Let see we mind not the union so much as not to provide as if it were never to be.' The company was established, with Charles subscribing £500,000, which would come out of taxation rather than his own pocket, and the three cousins contributed £100,000 between them.

By the end of 1669 Tweeddale's energy was spent; he wrote to Moray saying he longed for solitude and a retreat and his mood was darkened further after Christmas when his baby son Gilbert died. He and Jean had seven children living with the youngest not yet one, having been born eighteen years after her eldest brother, John. However he was well pleased at the successes the triumvirate had achieved and felt that Lauderdale deserved the nation's thanks. He wrote to Lauderdale in January telling him he was 'leaving Scotland in as good and quiet a condition as it has been these 40 years'. In addition, he told Moray that Lauderdale should be paid an additional £200,000 to cover his expenses and that he should be made a Knight of the Garter. Lauderdale was eager to leave Scotland, saying he was 'weary of this grinning honour; fain I would be at Whitehall again'. He considered that the king was 'now master here over all causes and all persons,' and this was also reflected in England, where his fellow Cabal member, Arlington, complained that Lauderdale's success was 'cried up to the skies' at court and that the king 'said everything there is wonderful as well as he can wish'.

This was the peak of the relationship between the cousins and the decline thereafter was swift and very unpleasant. Lauderdale was enjoying his triumphs and increasingly sought total control over Scotland; his cousins were less important to him now he felt they had become too independent of him. If Scotland was to be Lauderdale's home, then Moray and Tweeddale seemed an actual impediment to his ambitions. In addition, Lauderdale grew increasingly uncomfortable with union as he saw now how unpopular it was in Scotland. He very much wanted to be accepted by its nobles and its people and he felt, unfairly, that both Tweeddale and Moray had let him down in not advising him fully about the strength of feeling against union.

However it was the death of Sir Lionel Tollemache in March 1669 that set in motion events that were to significantly affect Lauderdale and transform the relationships he had with those closest to him. Just before he died, Tollemache wrote to his eldest son describing how to choose and treat a wife. His letter must have been conditioned by his own experience of living with Elizabeth, for it said: 'All wifes are but too apt to take advantage of the fondness of their husband, and upon it grow insolent and imperious, and inclined to pervert the laws of nature by endeavouring a superiority over the husband, and if she gets the reins in her own hands, away she will run with it, you scarce ever will stop her in the whole course of her life.' Burnet goes into more detail in his own description of Elizabeth as 'a woman of great beauty, but of far greater parts. She had a wonderful quickness of apprehension and an amazing vivacity in conversation. She had studied not only divinity and history, but mathematics and philosophy. She was vehement in every thing she set about, a violent friend, but a much more violent enemy. She had a restless ambition, lived at a vast expense, and was ravenously covetous; and would have stuck at nothing by which she might compass her ends.'

Lauderdale's wife, Anne, had continued to live at her house in Highgate with the Yesters and their children but, as Lauderdale had earlier written to Tweeddale, 'though my wife be rid of both fever and pain, yet she recovers but slowly'. Lauderdale took a house for her in Paris and paid her a comfortable allowance. She left for France in March 1670, ostensibly to seek the cure for her long-lasting illness but more probably because of the humiliation heaped on her by her husband's open adultery. She took with her her own jewels and the jewels of the Lauderdale family. Lauderdale does seem to have eased her passage and it is clear that neither Mary nor any of her grandchildren could have gone with her. But there is absolutely no doubt that the arrangement suited both Lauderdale and Elizabeth, and they took full advantage of it.

Tweeddale was now effectively governing Scotland by himself and had no time to enjoy the successes he had achieved. Conventicles were increasing rapidly in the west and now in the east, reaching even Edinburgh. He told Moray: 'We shall fill prisons as fast with them as we do pulpits [and have] a magazine of ministers for foreign plantations.' He felt he was increasingly being held responsible for this and that his reputation was at stake. Lauderdale tried to reassure him: 'I wish sober men's eyes may be opened to see at last what those people drive at, when they refuse so reasonable offers.'

Lauderdale wrote in February 1670 asking the Tweeddales to come south because, since Anne had gone to France, he needed Jean to live at Highgate to look after Mary and her children. The Tweeddales arrived in April and Elizabeth gave a dinner for them at Lauderdale's official Whitehall residence. There they met Lauderdale's nephew Richard, Halton's son, who Elizabeth was considering as husband for her eldest daughter. The Tweeddales stayed with her at Ham House and had to extend their stay because Charles was conducting his final negotiations with France through his sister Henrietta. Jean took Yester, Mary and the children back to Scotland in July, leaving Tweeddale behind in England.

The English Parliament had sat in February and approved a bill to move towards union, ordering that commissioners to negotiate it be appointed before the Scottish Parliament sat in July. Charles told Lauderdale that the Scottish Parliament should be called to approve only a limited agenda consisting of the meeting between the commissioners, the approval of three months' supply and the legislation against conventicles and that he should be back in England by September. Lauderdale and Tweeddale left for Scotland in mid-July with Lauderdale complaining that 'no galley slave hath a worse life than I have from morning to night save that I am not beaten,' but he drove all the required legislation through by the end of August. The key measures passed were for Supply and the so-called Clanking Act, which was the toughest yet introduced against conventicles. It enabled those preaching to be condemned to death and those attending to be heavily fined.

Lauderdale also took advantage of his time in Scotland to conduct private business. There was no doubt that his motivations had changed and that his hunger for power and wealth had greatly increased, not only for himself, but for his family. As this coincided with his passion for Elizabeth, it is likely that her own ambitions were a powerful influence on his. Burnet wrote in his *History of the Reformation* of her plan to marry her daughter to Halton's son, Richard, and noted that this would be to the detriment of the Yesters' fortunes. Richard, however, had to be a good catch and Lauderdale enabled this by improving both his and Halton's positions.

Before Lauderdale left for England, he stayed the weekend at Yester House to see his daughter and his grandchildren. Earlier in the year, Yester had had some difficult conversations with his in-laws, as Lady Lauderdale had written to him from France, complaining about his support of her husband's liaison with Elizabeth. Lauderdale had warned him, Yester later wrote, that she might 'out of the pique she had at me defraud my wife and children' out of their inheritance. Lauderdale also suggested that as it was likely that he, Lauderdale, would predecease her she could be 'preyed upon for that end by strangers and by people about her'. Lauderdale said he had therefore consulted with the Lord Advocate, who had suggested that Lauderdale give Yester a bond for £1.2 million, which would indemnify him for the value of the jewels if Lady Lauderdale disinherited Mary and her children. Yester should, in return, give Lauderdale a back-bond for £850,000 'only for the fashion, that being the usual form in such cases'. The back-bond would be payable to Lauderdale, or another person named by him, and would cover the payment of Lauderdale's debts. These bonds would be drawn up in Scotland so that Lady Lauderdale would not find out about them.

Lauderdale now told Yester that he wanted the bonds to be exchanged and Yester duly handed over his bond. Lauderdale made a play of searching his pockets and said he had forgotten to bring his own bond but that he would deliver it later, but he never did; he had deliberately set out to cheat Mary and her children of their inheritance. In addition, Tweeddale found out later, and only by chance, that Lauderdale had paid the rose noble in England which allowed him to change his will and allow Halton or Richard to inherit his titles and estate, thus depriving the Yesters and their children of what was originally due to them. Despite all this, Tweeddale and Yester still did not grasp the depths of Lauderdale's deviousness and Elizabeth continued to write friendly letters to Jean, who had written expressing her concerns, promising 'there seems to me to be no sort of ground of suspicion, you have not a better nor a firmer friend than E. La and he is not easily to be lost'.

Tweeddale went to London for what he hoped would be the final negotiations on union between October and December but it became clear that the English had lost interest in pursuing discussions. The signing of the Treaty of Dover in June had obviated Charles's need for union, as the alliance with France meant that Charles should have plentiful revenues both from King Louis and from the planned destruction of the Dutch Empire and he thus no longer needed to rely on Parliament for the provision of finance. He would not oppose union, but if he did not get exactly what he wanted from it, he had no interest in pursuing negotiations.

Lauderdale had also lost interest, writing to Yester 'for zeal to a union I am as far from betraying the rights of Scotland as any of them'. He said that he did not think Tweeddale should stay long in London and added, rather graciously if not honestly, 'I hope it for Lady Tweeddale's satisfaction and fear it for my own.' It was actually Lauderdale himself who, supported by Tweeddale, had brought discussions to an end by insisting to the English commissioners and to Charles that the two Parliaments be fully merged. That ended the discussions as far as the English were concerned and Charles gave no further support to any idea of union. Tweeddale stayed in London until December, trying to salvage something, but got nowhere and seemed to have succeeded only in irritating Lauderdale by his efforts. He said Lauderdale had 'called me in derision his tutor, saying he would not be tutored in England as he had been in Scotland'. Sir George Mackenzie wrote: 'Lauderdale began to shift Tweeddale and professed that he was ashamed to have it believed that he was yet under tutory; which was instilled in him by my Lady Dysart and the Earl of Rothes: nor was Lauderdale himself unwilling to be freed of a person, who was an enemy to his amours with her... when Tweeddale was to go out to Ham... Lauderdale told publicly at table, that he could not go without his governor.'

Tweeddale returned to Scotland, where Mary was expecting another child. Her mother wrote to Jean from France, expressing her concern that Mary was so far from a doctor and Jean tried to reassure her, saying they were only three hours from Edinburgh and that they had, in any case, a good male midwife. Lauderdale was less gracious and told Jean she should ignore his wife's impertinences. A boy, John, was born safely in March.

Despite all the pressures of work, Tweeddale pushed on with his plans to rebuild Yester House. He engaged Lauderdale's architect, Sir William Bruce, whose Edinburgh house he had bought in 1670 and he consulted Moray, who told him: 'Sir W. Bruce and I are to hold a consultation about your new house at Yester.' He had decided not to build a completely new house, preferring to add two new wings and a nursery to the existing building. He created a formal park and gardens by enclosing the estate within a seven mile wall and he demolished the old settlement of Bothans near Yester House and built new houses in the village of Gifford. He asked Yester to look for some paintings in London, adding the somewhat cynical comment: 'These may be all either landscapes or ruins... I think the burning of London would do well for one.' He later wrote to him: 'My park will be closed within this month and I am designing some long walks in it, if you please to send me the breadth of the walks in St James Park, both the largest as that be the Pall Mall, and that we walked in beyond the canal, and also of the narrower, it will help me much.' Three weeks later he reported that he was laying out a walk 900 feet long and 50 feet broad, and proposed during the following year to add flanking walks of lesser breadth, the trees in all three walks to be planted at 25 feet intervals.

A Flemish artist, James de Witt, painted five pictures of Yester House, the gardens and the park around 1690 and one shows that wings of four storeys had been added to each side of the tower, as well as a nursery extension for the grandchildren. The other paintings show an elaborate formal garden to the south side of the house with a fountain, a cascade running into a lake, a maze and extensive avenues and plantations. Marilyn Brown considers this cascade 'the earliest known in Scotland, is perhaps the outstanding feature of the garden'. Formal gardens with marble and lead statues stand either side of a long avenue, at the end of which stands a gate leading into parkland and an extensive range of well-ordered fields. The avenue from the village had been planted with limes and other trees were planted on the banks on either side of the drive leading to the house, whilst the fields beyond them were meticulously quartered by long, straight hedges and avenues. A deer park was made on the east side and behind the house rise the hills leading to the Lammermuirs.

৯

Lauderdale made his move against Tweeddale public in March 1671 when he significantly increased Halton's power by giving him Bellenden's post as Treasurer-depute, a position Tweeddale wanted. Halton was also given the estates of the Earl of Dundee, who had died without heirs; he was appointed to the Court of Session and he was confirmed as Master General of the Mint, where his son Richard was also given a position. These appointments were received very badly by Tweeddale, and by most of his colleagues, as Halton was not held in high regard. Burnet described him as 'weak and violent, insolent and corrupt'. His lawyer, the Lord Advocate Sir John Nisbet, was offered the post of Lord President of the Session, but he declined and the post went instead to Sir John Dalrymple, Lord Stair, who was Kincardine's and Rothes's candidate. Tweeddale was now in danger of being isolated; Kincardine was becoming Lauderdale's greatest confidant and was often writing to him about a whole range of matters. His manner can be seen in a letter he wrote to Lauderdale telling him of the birth and naming of his daughter Elizabeth, remarking, 'you may guess after whom'; if it had been a boy, he added, 'I guess it had been called John'. Burnet was, however, complimentary about Kincardine: 'He was both the wisest and the worthiest man that belonged to his country and fit for governing any affairs but his own... he had a noble zeal for justice... and solid principles of religion and virtue... he was a faithful friend and a merciful enemy.'

In his despair, and demonstrating his occasional naivety, Tweeddale wrote to Elizabeth complaining that Lauderdale's 'way with me is altogether changed and growing to a distance scarce consistent with friendship'. She replied urging him not to worry any more; he said he would try, but she did not allay his concern. He wrote to Moray, his one true friend in England, complaining that he could not be as useful in undertaking the king's business as he had in the past. Moray wrote to his great confidante Lady Hamilton, who did not like Tweeddale, telling her how Tweeddale's problems would affect the management of Scottish affairs and that 'things, I am afraid, will go the worse for it'. This came true in February 1671 when Halton advised the Treasury Commission that Charles wanted to stop Tweeddale's system of direct collection of taxes and revert to tax farming. He had got Kincardine's support for this, unsurprisingly, as Kincardine would benefit greatly from such a change, given his substantial interests in coal and salt. Tweeddale was justifiably angry that he had not been consulted and he wrote to Lauderdale: 'I have known that to be no bad character with you and I am conscious to myself not to have offended you in the least... I have kept a friendship the most exact and most sincere that mortal man may be capable of.' As he had selected the current tax collectors, he wanted to know why Lauderdale would 'expose me thus, for so I account the using of those I trusted and was answerable for'. He wrote to Moray: 'I have an uneasy life here, and all my designs and endeavours are broke and overturned with all the obloquy imaginable.' Lauderdale replied, all innocent of any intention to mislead: 'I dealt frankly with you and thought I had satisfied you. Now you express greater jealousies but I cannot imagine any ground.' Tweeddale answered, pointing out how well the collectors had performed the previous year, and wrote on the same day to Moray saying that the king's revenue was 'the best collected and counted for revenue... as is in Europe, and whatever change is made I am very sure shall be to the worse.' In the vote taken in the Commission regarding the change, Tweeddale's was the only vote against. He now understood how completely isolated he was. 'Canny men,' he told Moray, 'will hardly be seen with me, especially in a coach.' His mood was not helped by Jean having another miscarriage.

Maurice Lee writes of Lauderdale that 'with advancing age and steadily worsening health his methods grew more brutal and less conciliatory, and so did his arrogance towards his personal friends and political allies'. Burnet agreed, commenting: 'Lauderdale's way was to govern by fits, and to pass from hot to cold ones always in extremes.' Lauderdale did, however, go through the motions of trying to appease Tweeddale, who told him he would acquiesce in whatever the king wanted. However, he voted against salt being made a monopoly, he was again in the minority and it was awarded to Kincardine for a rent of £250,000 a year. This was an important award, as the import of foreign salt had just been banned and the price of domestic salt was expected to soar. The cost for Kincardine was not unduly high as he expected to cover his costs from his handling of the king's revenues from the Isle Orkney alone.

Correspondence between the two cousins diminished as the year advanced. Tweeddale offered to sell Lauderdale Pinkie House, so that it would remain in the hands of a grandchild of Lord Dunfermline, whose favourite house it had been and the sale would have allowed him to buy the estate of Linton for Yester and Mary. Lauderdale declined, saying he already had too many houses. This at least was certainly true as he had focused on making Thirlestane magnificent which had left Lethington somewhat neglected. Macky wrote of it in 1723: 'It is an old tower full of very good conveniences and one good apartment made by the Duke of Lauderdale. There are some beautiful avenues in the park and a great deal of old planting round the house but the Duke having no sons of his own and being a little Wife Ridden left the seat to his lady's son.'

Monmouth came of age in 1671 and he removed his existing curators, including Tweeddale, and appointed new ones who included Rothes, Bellenden and Wemyss, none of whom were friends of Tweeddale. Margaret Wemyss was also spreading rumours that Tweeddale had enriched himself as a curator but Lauderdale reassured him that the king was 'very sensible of the causeless malice against you'. The king was also sensitive about other matters and he initiated an inquiry as to whether Jean Tweeddale could invalidate Monmouth's marriage if it was considered that his wife Anna had violated her father's entail. Tweeddale feared that Monmouth was being told, probably by Margaret, that he could never be comfortable about his financial position unless this question was finally resolved. Tweeddale amazingly still believed he had Lauderdale's support and wrote to him: 'Consider the club, a malicious mother seeking the ruin of the family, a stepfather who refused to be curator with other honest men, Lagshaw an old ignorant knave... and the Chancellor [Rothes] to supervise and laugh at other men's misfortunes if he make his advantage of it.' A formal process to consider the Buccleuch entail began in April 1672, Charles was advised that Jean had a case and Tweeddale received a formal summons to produce whatever documents he had relating to the entail.

The Lord Privy Seal died in October and Tweeddale asked Lauderdale to recommend him for the post. He wanted it not because it was 'invidiously lucrative, but a mark of the king's favour, which I design chiefly in it'. He offered to give up his position in the Treasury if he were appointed. Unfortunately, his uncle Dunfermline also had a claim to it, having been promised it by Charles I, and the king duly gave him the post, which must have been particularly upsetting to Tweeddale, given his history with Dunfermline and his uncle's character.

Lauderdale was in an increasingly emotional state, his wife was very ill and he was desperate to marry Elizabeth. Moray wrote the Duchess of Hamilton a ten-page letter telling her of his moods: 'A very small provocation will make him fly quite off the hinges... the turning over of a straw may serve to lose his friendship, so little is he master of his humour... what humours not her [Elizabeth] will certainly put him out of humour.' This was shown to be prescient advice, which Tweeddale should also have heeded, if Moray, as would seem likely, had also warned him. Burnet visited Tweeddale and relayed a message from Lauderdale 'that it should be my [Tweeddale's] fault if it were not as well betwixt us as ever'. Tweeddale wrote to Lauderdale to complain but admitted he had made mistakes and that he had tried to correct them 'after I have suffered all I can by them. Jealousies I remit to God.' Lauderdale replied, saying: 'I am far to seek for an understanding your discourse of mistakes... that you have suffered all you can by them, for I am wholly ignorant of those sufferings... Certainly I have never been the cause of them, nor do I comprehend what those jealousies are... which you commit the removal to God.'

Lady Lauderdale died in December 1671. She had sent Lauderdale a message by a French cleric saying she departed her life in a state of loving friendship towards her husband, regretting only the cause of the froideur between them. The cleric added: '*Elle mourut pleine d'amitie pour vous et fort touché de souvenir des tendresses que vous avez eu autrefois pour elle.*' Lauderdale gave her a splendid funeral but his behaviour towards others was deplorable. He wrote to Yester of her death, saying that he felt his daughter would 'overgrieve' but that he would write to her soon; meanwhile he would be 'taking physic at Ham'. He wrote to Halton on January 23rd: 'I told you to yourself alone my resolution by the blessing of God to marry and now we have resolved it. Her fortune is double and more to what I had by the last.' Tweeddale's half-brother, William Hay of Drumelzier, who was in France, had written to Yester about Anne's death, before even Lauderdale had, and Tweeddale asked him to protect Yester's and Mary's interests. He sent Yester to London, leaving Mary at Yester House as she was again pregnant, and told him his task was to protect his wife's and his children's inheritance.

But he was too late, as the schemes Lauderdale had long planned were already in motion. He had sent two of his men to France, where they forced his wife's companion, Lady Boghall, to hand over Anne's jewels, which were valued at £200,000 and which Anne had left to Mary in her will. Lauderdale then claimed that a wife's will was only valid under French law if it had been made with her husband's consent. Sir George Douglas, who was commanding a regiment in France, helped him arrange this with the French lawyers and he was rewarded with Lady Lauderdale's coach and horses. Douglas's mistress also arranged for Elizabeth's wedding clothes to be made in Paris and he wrote sarcastically to a friend: 'What fine lady his lordship intends to regale is not known, but it is probable that she will be of my Lady Dysart's stature, for I am told for certain that the gowns were made to her measure... It seems that my L.Lauderdale intends that somebody shall rejoice, mourn who pleaseth.' Yester wrote to his father that he had met Lauderdale on February 3rd and had been told of his impending marriage: 'He assured me it should not lessen his kindness to my wife and our children and that he intended when he came down himself to give her a large share of those things were left her than she could have expected while her mother lived.' Lauderdale later told Yester that he wanted to give Mary the jewels himself and that she would benefit more from her father than she would have from her mother. Yester believed all this and returned to Scotland, where he was criticised by his parents for his weakness and gullibility. Lauderdale and Elizabeth were married on February 17th and she wrote to Jean Tweeddale, defending her new husband:

> That Pack... have spread fine reports of me and they do so much defame ye best of men: our Good friend [Lauderdale]: that at present he is made guilty of all his Lady's faults... her trials under his Tirany pitied, and her going to France said to be against her will forced upon her by her lord's anger who they report took from her all her jewels... and does not let her live here withal, it is further added that this lady was passionately earnest to have one of ye children with her but it was refused:as all other things were purposedly to make her break her hart.

Moray urged Tweeddale to come to England so that he could act as a mediator with the king to sort out his problems with Lauderdale, whom he blamed for all the disputes 'groundlessly made and unjustly kept up'. Moray himself had now lost Lauderdale's friendship, due increasingly to Catherine's 'contempt of him' and he complained to Lady Hamilton: 'You know well enough the Commissioner stands as high in his pride as any creature can do and turns on all those who are not sufficiently deferential to his brother.' Tweeddale did receive one piece of good news, as Dunfermline died in May, thus enabling him to secure and sell his estate. Charles again did not appoint him Lord Privy Seal, appointing Atholl instead. Moray was also humiliated when Kincardine was appointed Secretary in London when Lauderdale left for Scotland to attend the new sitting of Parliament, having been made a duke and a Knight of the Garter.

England's second war with Holland began in April 1672 and Charles demanded that Scotland supply an army of 3,000 men. Parliament passed all the measures required by the king and also passed an Act abolishing the monopoly of foreign trade, historically held by the royal burghs. This was of great benefit to the other burghs, which were controlled by nobles, including Lauderdale, whose burgh was Musselburgh. He handed out other benefits to his supporters: Halton became Sheriff of Edinburgh for life; Rothes received a new pension; and Halton's new son-in-law, Elphinstone, was given the monopoly on brandy; Hamilton was allowed to reimburse himself £1.65 million of the Crown's debts owed him, but only after he had supported the vote of supply; Kincardine was given £500,000; Argyll was forgiven non-payment of taxes; and the heirless Wemyss was allowed to pass on his titles to his daughters. Even Tweeddale had his tax reduced on his Haddington parkland, but probably only because Lauderdale also enjoyed the same benefit.

Whilst in Scotland, Lauderdale summoned the Yesters and formally told them that he had altered his will by the payment of the rose noble, thus removing Mary and her children from their inheritance, but he said that he had not named any other heir. He told Mary he wanted her to renounce any claim she might have over her mother's estate, other than on the houses in London, and all her claims on his own estate. He told her she had no claim over her mother's jewels because the Court of Session had ruled that they had been held to cover her mother's debts, and he refused to hand over the back-bond. There was an underlying threat that he would take Yester and Mary to court if they did not sign so they capitulated and gave him everything he wanted. Despite this, Lauderdale wrote that his daughter 'should have a considerable share of all, and that the bond and back-bond should be destroyed,' and that he wanted Mary's inheritance to come as a gift from him. Tweedddale later wrote to Yester that Lauderdale was 'valuing himself upon his overreaching [him and Yester] by their exuberant trust of him'.

By September Lauderdale was back in England and saw how Scotland was increasingly irrelevant to Charles. Tweeddale felt this too, but for very different reasons. He had almost given up taking part in government, merely going through the motions of attending Commission meetings, which now had little relevance.

Moray continued to press him to come to London to sort matters out but Tweeddale stayed in Scotland. He brooded over the winter but spring seemed to have invigorated him and he went on the offensive. He wrote to Moray in April 1673, setting out his concern about Lauderdale's activities, and comparing them to Middleton's excesses. Tweeddale was sure his letters were being intercepted and suggested he and Moray wrote in cipher. Moray was now Tweeddale's only friend in England and he was tireless in his efforts to restore Tweeddale's reputation. This really could only be done by discrediting Lauderdale, which was perilous as Lauderdale was becoming increasingly irascible and unpredictable. Tweeddale gave Moray an example of this, quoting Lauderdale's view of the Presbyterians: 'Would to God they would rebel, that so he might bring over an army of Irish Papists to cut all their throats... but after he had let himself loose into these fits for near a month, he calmed all on the sudden.'

Tweeddale tragically lost his key supporter in England when

Moray died in July, after dining with the Lord Chancellor, Shaftesbury. Lauderdale's only recorded comment on the news of his old friend's death was 'one use I shall make of it: I shall be very unwilling to dine with the Lord Chancellor, seeing his meat digests very ill'. He also wrote to Kincardine complaining: 'You know I lent him £100,000 five and twenty years ago. Indeed he paid me the principal when the king gave him money, but I have payed interest for it for 25 years, of which I never had a penny... So I lost my money, and one I once thought my friend.' He did not, of course, remember his letter to Tweeddale in 1667, where he had said that Moray should only pay the interest when he could afford to.

Matters grew even more serious for Tweeddale as in September he learnt that Monmouth was going to take him and his wife to court over Jean's claim over half of her brother David's estate; and in October the Monmouths refused to ratify the 1667 agreement over Tweeddale's debt to the Buccleuch estate. The king had approved this settlement and agreed that the Monmouths would ratify it when they came of age, but he based their refusal on the agreement which stated that Jean's younger brother Francis, was over 25 when he had given up his claim to his brother David's estate. Unfortunately, Francis was only 24 when he died and his renunciation was therefore declared invalid, as were all subsequent agreements, so Tweeddale was due to pay the Monmouths £1.2 million.

Hamilton had become an ally of Tweeddale as a result of their mutual dislike of Lauderdale and they believed that, if Charles knew how unpopular Lauderdale was in Scotland, he would remove him. Tweeddale felt confident that the king trusted him and said he had been told that Charles had laughed at the Duke of York and Lauderdale when they had urged Charles to fire him. He wrote to Alexander Murray: 'Laud is not so well with the king but that the king believes he can not do his Affairs here without him, he be the darling and delight of the country.' Unfortunately, neither Tweeddale nor Hamilton had a reliable ally in England and they misread the situation. Burnet was not complimentary about Hamilton or his judgement: 'He wanted all sort of polishing, he was rough and sullen but candid and sincere... he was mutinous when out of power and imperious in it..but a narrow and selfish temper brought such an habitual meaness... that he was not capable of designing or understanding great things.' However, not everything was going Lauderdale's way in England; he may have had Charles's support but he was disliked and feared by a number of important figures. English politicians were also becoming nervous about the Catholic Duke of York, and Parliament voted against both his marriage to a Catholic and to the proposed alliance with France. Lauderdale had left for Scotland and he now came under heavy attack in the Commons, who voted unanimously to ask the king for his removal. Shaftesbury led the attack and Lauderdale was named as an 'evil counselor', but Charles prorogued Parliament and dismissed Shaftesbury instead.

Lauderdale had no real need to go to Scotland but Charles had probably felt it were better were he away from London. When the Scottish Parliament met in October, Lauderdale read out the king's address saying that purpose of the sitting was to prevent the further spread of conventicles. Watching him was his duchess, who had broken all conventions by attending Parliament. Burnet wrote about her increasing influence over Lauderdale, who 'delivered himself up to all her humours and passions... she took upon her to determine everything... and was wanting in no methods that could bring her money, which she lavished out in a most profuse vanity. As the conceit took her, she made him fall out with all his friends.' Lauderdale proposed that the Lords of the Articles immediately meet to reply to the king's letter, but instead Hamilton rose and proposed a redress of grievances be debated first; he had agreed this with Tweeddale and he was supported by a majority vote. Hamilton's supporters became known as The Party, Tweeddale was a member but not openly as he still wanted to regain Lauderdale's favour, who, however, had noted that Tweeddale had 'spoke very ambiguously' in Parliament.

Lauderdale also had to give way on the salt, brandy and tobacco monopolies which he had given to Kincardine and Elphinstone, but he wrote to Charles blaming the situation on Shaftesbury and Tweeddale, the 'contriver and counsellor', and on Hamilton, who was acting as their figurehead. He accused them of wanting 'to hinder the Parliament from paying their duty to you, and to make it appear that the kingdom is not united in your service... if they be suffered to prevail you will quickly see what work they will make.' However he realised he would not achieve his objectives so he adjourned Parliament until January 1674.

It was the last Parliament Lauderdale would attend and he had been badly shaken by his reception, which he blamed Tweeddale for not preparing him for. He told Charles that Hamilton and Tweeddale would visit him in London but that 'they have no authority. They shall only come as private men.' Charles replied that Yester 'comes but seldom and in my eye looks but melancholy upon it'. When Yester did meet Charles he sought to explain the misunderstanding between his father and Lauderdale, and he told his father the king had replied 'he concerned not himself therein, but that he expected you would have a care of his service... and bidding me beware of believing some persons who would be for the making his kingdom a province of the republic of England'. The latter was a pointed remark, given Tweeddale's Cromwellian background and his continuous support of union. Charles seemed to be angrier about Hamilton's behaviour and Yester asked Charles for permission for Tweeddale to visit him, but Charles 'put it off... saying you had better stay there to advance his service'.

When Tweeddale and Hamilton did meet the king in London they were careful not to blame Lauderdale directly but rather unnamed people who sought to further their own interests. Tweeddale set out how well he believed he and Moray had served him as they had 'ordered the affairs of the Treasury to the advantage of the Crown and the Kingdom so the king's old debts contracted in Scotland paid, the expense of Government fully satisfied, fees and pensions payed, the King's House and fortresses repaired, the magazines filled with arms and ammunition... and yet no cesse lying upon the country'. They complained to York about the cost of Lauderdale's office, at £2.25 million a year, and said that it was 'against the constitution of Scotland to be governed by a Commissioner'. York replied that 'all kings so governed their kingdoms... where they could not be themselves by one man'. Charles criticised them for not having discussed these matters with Lauderdale and York was equally unsupportive. It had not helped Tweeddale's cause that he had chosen to support Hamilton, who was not liked in England for he had opposed the king's wish for union in 1669. In Scotland his reputation was not much better, Moray considered him a drunk and 'not yet a very worthy nor a wise personne' and Halton accused him of being 'overbearing and insolent in the extreme'.

Hamilton returned to Scotland having gained nothing but Tweeddale stayed, principally to lobby all those he could about settling the Monmouth dispute. Charles still valued Tweeddale's advice and reappointed him to his Privy Council. He also accepted his advice to cut Lauderdale's daily fee by 80% when he was not in Scotland and Tweeddale tried to get Charles to agree that no Commissioner of Scotland should serve more than five years. Lauderdale was very angry and 'reckoned it as an unpardonable crime which made him implacable unto him ever thereafter'. Kincardine was also in London and was also briefing the king and his brother on the situation in Scotland and Lauderdale broke his alliance with him. Meanwhile, Halton's corruption was becoming an open embarrassment.

Charles's domestic administration had crumbled and, of the original Cabal, only Lauderdale remained his supporter. Lord Danby had become Lord Treasurer and Lauderdale sought to gain his favour, writing to him from Scotland that the king 'may do what he pleases in parliament or out of it here'.

The attacks on Lauderdale in the English Parliament were renewed in January 1674 with Sir Robert Thomas declaring that he 'has contributed as much to our misfortune as any man'. He was curiously accused of seeking to impose popery and many more feared he would use the Scottish army against them. However, he continued to receive Charles's support, who wrote to him telling him not to worry about Parliament's criticism: 'It is hot at present [but] reason and justice will have the credit it ought to have.' Peace was made with the Dutch in February and Charles had no more need of Scottish support. Lauderdale wrote to him: 'You shall find me readier than all your enemies to rid you of the trouble of Scots Parliaments, which I swear are now useless at the best' and he adjourned Parliament in March. Tweeddale tried to prevent this but failed, whereupon Kincardine advised Charles to dismiss him, saying he was 'beloved by nobody'. Lauderdale told Charles that Tweeddale 'does you much mischief there and here,' and urged the king to 'dispatch him and listen to no more complaints'.

Tweeddale had met Anna Monmouth in London but she refused to accept that she and the duke should abide by Charles's settlement of the dispute in 1667. She had recently lost her only child but was again pregnant with a child she had in May. Jean Tweeddale wrote fondly to her but her answer made her realise that Anna was being driven on her course by Lauderdale and thus there was little hope, as Jean knew 'I shall never expect right or justice from him'. Jean wrote to her husband regularly from Scotland, telling him his enemies 'vaunt on all occasions their malice and revenge against you,' and wrote of Lauderdale, who was still in Scotland, 'I am astonished to think from whence all this hatred can come'.

Lauderdale decided to return to London and Hamilton wrote to Tweeddale, telling him to stay there to confront Lauderdale 'to show you do not fear to face him'. Lauderdale was, however, becoming even more powerful; he was given an English peerage as Earl of Guildford, the Privy Council cleared him of all charges brought against him and Charles restored his daily fee; in addition, Halton was cleared of any wrongdoing at the Treasury. Secure in his position, Lauderdale then heaped the final humiliation on his cousin. Tweeddale was not reappointed to the Scottish Privy Council; Atholl and Argyll replaced him on the Treasury Commission; Argyll replaced him as an Extraordinary Lord of Session and Kincardine replaced him on the English Privy Council. To complete his humiliation, Charles ordered that his and Yester's militia commissions as Colonel be voided. Jean wrote to him trying to give him comfort, suggesting he should do nothing, as thereby he would gain in esteem and affection. It was probably the right advice, but for the wrong reason.

Matters grew increasingly serious as the Monmouths now formally launched their suit against him, almost certainly encouraged in their timing by Lauderdale. Tweeddale countered the claim on three basic points: first, the original settlement was very much to the benefit of the Monmouths; secondly, the value of Jean Tweeddale's inheritance was now much larger than originally calculated; and, thirdly, Charles had promised that the agreement would be ratified. Monmouth's lawyers focused their case on the error regarding Francis's age and held that the king's promise was based on false information and the court found against the Tweeddales on all points. One judgement was carried by only one vote, that of Lord Pittrichie, a relative of Lauderdale, who was 'brought to the house that day only in a chair for that effect, when he was not in a condition to understand sense, as he never was to understand law, much less the point in question' and he died the very next day. Tweeddale found no support from any side and in 1679 he finally accepted the court's judgements. By then his debt had grown to £1,450,000, the Roxbroughshire estate was valued at only £155,000 and Jean's inheritance was calculated at £480,000, so Tweeddale owed £815,000. In return, the Monmouths agreed to nullify the changes to the entail, which, since they had three children, was an empty gesture. Tweeddale still tried to persuade Anna to accept payment only of the original principal but Anna insisted on full payment. 'I must tell you,' she wrote to the Earl of Cromarty, 'I have never heard of such a way as he has to ask forgiveness, either for debts or injuries, for when he was last in England he printed the basest and falsest paper his overgrown malice could invent.' She would not 'be persuaded to live in debt and miserably all my life to please him'.

In his document titled *The Relation of the Wrangs done to the Ladie Yester*, written by Tweeddale after Lauderdale's death, he speaks of 'Lauderdale's injustice, inhumanity, barbarity and cruelty against me and my nearest relatives, he cannot be thought worth to live in civil society'. Yet Tweeddale maintained his loyalty as a public servant. On the back of a letter from Moray, Tweeddale had written in 1673 that he had always supported Lauderdale's policy 'as long as I understand it the kings even when he was ruining mine'.

Mary Yester continued to suffer from her father's malice. He had finally handed over her mother's London properties, having pocketed the rents, sold the furniture and moved the best fruit trees to Ham House. He made a new will, leaving his valuables to Elizabeth and his title and estate to Halton and he demanded that Mary renounce all the claims on all her and her son's original entitlements from him. Mary tried to fight him but his threat of calling in the back-bond broke her resolve and she accepted his terms. He then burnt both his own bond and Yester's back-bond in the fire at Holyrood.

Lauderdale was, however, not finished with his vendetta against Tweeddale. He took him to court in 1677 over the teinds of Pinkie, worth £10,000 a year, which Lauderdale claimed as Lord of Musselburgh. He persuaded Tweeddale's kinsman, the childless Earl of Erroll, not to leave his title and estates to Tweeddale's second son and he intervened against Tweeddale in his dispute with his half-brother, William Hay of Drumelzier, over lands inherited from Tweeddale's stepmother. Elizabeth, too, waged war against the Tweeddales, writing that 'they have done me so much wrong,' and that Yester was 'a most contemptible creature'. However, she soon found a new target for her scheming, and this time it was much closer to home. Halton's son, Richard, had declined to marry her daughter, Betty, saying that he was not ready and wished to travel; so Elizabeth married her to Argyll's heir, Lord Lorne. Elizabeth's ambitions for her second daughter, Catherine, were equally high but, after long negotiations, Atholl decided that his heir should not marry her. Elizabeth would not accept defeat and within a year Catherine was married to Lord Doune, the heir to the Earl of Moray, who had become Lauderdale's representative in Scotland. In the same year, Richard married Lady Anne Campbell, Lord Lorne's sister.

This was all against a background of increasing religious dissent in Scotland, where there were even discussions about a call for a new Covenant. Archbishop Leighton and Burnet, who had been restored as Archbishop, called for a meeting of the General Assembly, which Archbishop Sharp opposed. Lauderdale supported him but wrote telling him to 'suppress those scandalous and seditious conventicles'. He had no more thoughts of Indulgences.

In 1677 an Act of Council ordered all landowners to sign bonds of religious conformity for all individuals living on their lands, and a body called the Highland Host, consisting of 6,000 Highland and 3,000 Lowland militia, was raised to enforce this. Lauderdale was summoned to London by Charles to brief him on the state of Scotland and Tweeddale asked to travel with him but Lauderdale refused and told him he should visit him at Court when in London. Tweeddale went to Windsor and there he persuaded the Lord Chamberlain, who was ill, to let him carry the sword of state before the king. Charles was not happy about this and reprimanded the Chamberlain. Tweeddale then asked for a royal audience where he stressed his total loyalty to the king and promised to give 'an absolute and entire loyalty to the Duke of Lauderdale in all things'. He dropped to his knees and asked the king's pardon for any wrong he had done. The king was not impressed and reminded Tweeddale of all the promises that he and others had made and not kept, and told him he would now only judge people on how they behaved. Tweeddale then met Lauderdale and complained that he had misrepresented him to the king. Lauderdale's only reply was that he had told the king 'everyman's true carriage'. Hamilton had seen the support Charles gave to Lauderdale and clearly realised that there were no prospects of his being removed from office. His Party began to fall apart and Atholl, who had become a member, complained to Rothes that Hamilton was 'making all the humble address imaginable to the Duke of Lauderdale'.

Another rebellion broke out in southwest Scotland in 1679 and Sharp was murdered near Saint Andrews by Norman Leslie, Rothes's brother. Monmouth was given command of the army and he defeated an insurgency of 5,000 men near Glasgow at the Battle of Bothwell Bridge. This was the beginning of a nine-year period that became known as the Killing Times, which only ended with the Glorious Revolution. Monmouth now insisted on a third Letter of Indulgence being issued in 1679 and this was the beginning of the end of Lauderdale's reign. He had become increasingly ill and, according to Burnet, 'he broke out into the most frantic fits of rage possible... such a fury as this seemed to furnish work for a physician rather than for any other sort of man'. He resigned in 1680 and the Earl of Moray was appointed Secretary of State. Elizabeth Lauderdale, true to form, immediately wrote to him: 'I have only one friend that I rely upon except my own Lord and that is your self.' The Duke of York was appointed High Commissioner and in 1681 Rothes, who had been made a duke, died. His friend the Earl of Queensberry was appointed Lord Treasurer and Lord Haddo became Chancellor.

Lauderdale died in August 1682. Tweeddale wrote of his passing, not without a certain relish, that he had taken 'the salt of Epsom to bring away the waters he had drunk, which worked accordingly upon the old infirm man and gave him a flux of blood so violent that it had almost brought away his bowels, but dispatched him before night, with great pain and torment'. He was buried in St Mary's Church in Haddington; Tweeddale and Yester were invited to the funeral but they chose not to attend. Halton's enemies now took their chance to move against him and he was found guilty of malfeasance at the Mint and of perjury, and was fined £1.2 million, which was later reduced to £330,000 but he was dismissed from all his offices.

Elizabeth, as ever, saw her chance to profit from Halton's problems. She had persuaded Lauderdale, just before he died, to sign a deed which conveyed his title and estate to Yester and Mary's second son, John, but only if she was given the whole of Lauderdale's personal estate and much of his lands, free of any debts, whilst John Hay would be responsible for all Lauderdale's debts. These amounted to £1.3 million and, until they were paid, Elizabeth would head a committee of trustees to oversee the estate. John would receive an income of £48,000 and she would be paid £3.5 million over five years. In addition, she wanted to be given Pinkie to live in and, in return, she would ask Charles to make John a marquis. Tweeddale and Yester rejected the offer, believing 'that she made use of that feint, only to make the better bargain with Halton and his son'. Halton inherited the earldom and was readmitted to the Privy Council in 1686. He died in 1692 and Richard inherited as 4th Earl. He was a supporter of James II, fought for him at the battle of the Boyne and was exiled to France, where he translated Virgil into English and died in 1695, leaving no direct heir.

After Lauderdale's death, Tweeddale presented the king and the Duke of York *The Relation of the Wrangs done to the Ladie Yester*, his history of the Lauderdales's treatment of his family, and with it a petition from Mary setting out her grievances against both her father and Elizabeth. She asked the king for justice to preserve the good name and fortune of her family and for new laws to prevent predatory women from preying on old infirm husbands. Their hatred of the duchess was made very clear: in Mary's petition she wrote of her 'cunning practices and pernicious counsels for promoting her covetous designs... the Conditions proposed by her were so sordid and shameless, and so advantageous for her self without regard to the Duke's family or memory, that he would never hearken to them'.

Charles refused to intervene and so the Tweeddales took Elizabeth and Halton to court. Some of the claims continued well into the next century, and many were dismissed, but Mary did get the £672,000 she was due for the loss of her inheritance and Elizabeth agreed to give her Lauderdale's valuable library in exchange for charges against her being dropped. These included accepting bribes to influence Lauderdale's policies, her acceptance of £48,000 for letting Lord Banff off a charge of having allowed his footman to rape a gentleman's pregnant wife and then of killing her and her baby; and of the charge of overweening pride.

When the Duke of York took over as Commissioner, he proposed an Act ruling that no difference of religion could divert the right of succession to the Scottish Crown. Parliament passed this and also the Test Oath, which required every holder of public office to effectively submit to the king's commands in all matters religious and civil. Many Scots left for the continent rather than swear it and lived there until the Glorious Revolution. York tried to earn the support of the nobles by reviving the Order of the

Thistle and by giving them positions of influence; Tweeddale was made a Privy Councillor and also a Commissioner for the Coinage and the Mint. Only the protestant Earl of Argyll was targeted, being arrested for treason but he was smuggled from prison by Lady Sophia Lindsay and he escaped to Holland, where he began his ultimately disastrous alliance with Monmouth.

When James returned to England in 1684, he left behind a weak administration. There was no High Commissioner and the Scottish Secretary in London, the 2nd Earl of Middleton, removed Chancellor Haddo and replaced him with the Catholic Earl of Perth. James made Middleton his English Secretary of State and the new Scottish Secretary was Perth's younger brother, John Drummond. The Drummonds got rid of all their opponents in office, including the Duke of Queensberry, but Tweeddale managed to retain his positions. James was crowned in March 1685 and he issued an Indemnity to his enemies, but he specifically excluded any Covenanters. In April an Act of Parliament was passed that anyone taking the Covenant was committing treason and in June the rebellions of Monmouth and Argyll were crushed and both men were executed.

Tweeddale had hoped that the rumoured involvement of Monmouth in the Rye House plot in 1683 to murder both Charles and York would have persuaded Charles to reduce the Buccleuch debt. He held this belief even more after Monmouth's execution in 1685 but he achieved nothing as James liked Anna and did not want her punished because of her traitorous husband. Tweeddale finally gave up and he sold his estate in Peebleshire, including Neidpath Castle and the baronies of Linton and Newlands, to the Duke of Queensberry for £390,000, twenty times their annual income of £19,500 and he made his final payment to Anna in 1690. He did, however, gain the satisfaction of receiving from Elizabeth Lauderdale constant letters asking to borrow small sums of money for 'absolute necessities'.

CHAPTER 10 – THE GLORIOUS REVOLUTION

The Glorious Revolution of 1688 provided Tweeddale's polit-
ical life with a *grand finale*. He supported the coronation of
William and Mary and he was charged with taking Edinburgh
Castle from Huntly, who had been made Duke of Gordon in 1684.
He persuaded the duke to cede the castle without a fight and
Tweeddale was made a Privy Councillor in 1689. He was now 64
years old and suffered from kidney stones and frequent headaches.
His beloved wife Jean had died in 1688 and she may have been
buried at St Cuthbert's, as he had its roof plastered 'after the
Gothic manner,' and a panelled balustrade was built in the choir.

He remained in Scotland because of his illness and instructed
Yester to pursue the family's objectives in England. These were
to restore his father's fortune, to gain a seat on the Board of the
Treasury and to ensure that his own family was well provided for;
he wanted Yester to be appointed Governor of the Mint or Sheriff
of East Lothian. Tweeddale knew who the key people were in
England and advised Yester how to go about lobbying them, but
Yester proved inadequate and his father grew increasingly frustrated with him, bewailing his 'abstractions from persons'. Two
other of his sons, David and Alexander, sought careers as soldiers.

Tweeddale continued to fear a breakdown in government or
even some form of coup, so he formed a centre party, consisting

of moderate Presbyterians and Episcopalians, to stand together against the extreme elements on either side and to reintroduce the idea of union. Riley writes: 'It stands to Tweeddale's credit that he concerned himself seriously about the well being of Scotland. He was one of the few Scottish politicians to do so.' He enjoyed a reputation for integrity and moderation and as a man of practicalities rather than one holding strong principles. He pursued his strategy discreetly and in December 1688 wrote an anonymous Address to be sent to the new king. It proposed that union was necessary so 'that we be not hereafter left open by the advantage may be taken of our distinct and different laws and customs and exercise of government whereby methods are taken by the enemies of our peace and tranquility to raise standing armies in either kingdom by which the other may be threatened or enforced to submit to alterations in their religion or diminution of their liberty or foreign forces be brought in either for the subversion of the religion and liberty of both which were a work worthy of your highness'.

He asked Yester to show the Address first to Halifax and to Sir James Hay of Linplum, he wrote directly to other influential nobles in order to gather their support and it was then taken by Yester to King William. Tweeddale also lobbied to increase the number of lairds in Parliament as he felt they were more amenable to union than the nobles. However it proved difficult to organise a party that could properly satisfy both the interests of the English court and the demands of the Scots. Because so many Scots had gone abroad rather than swear the Test Oath, William was advised by men who had not lived in Scotland for seven years. His most trusted adviser was the Earl of Portland, his closest Dutch friend, who had no knowledge at all of Scotland, and his other main advisers were Sir James Dalrymple and Lord Melville. His religious advisers were James Johnston, son of the great Covenanter Warriston and William Carstares, a Presbyterian minister. John Macky wrote of Carstares: 'Few Scotsmen had access to the King but by him, so that he was properly Viceroy of that Kingdom and was called at Court Cardinal Carstares.' William was the first King of Scotland never to visit his realm and, during his reign, neither Portland nor Carstares did either. The most difficult challenges faced by William in Scotland were how to meet the ambition of the nobles and how to resolve the deep-seated religious divide. The nobles were increasingly frustrated as they felt they had been kept out of power since the reign of Charles I and they used all the means they could to change this including the blatant exploitation of religion for their political ends. Their objectives remained the same as ever, the pursuit of power in order to gain influence and wealth and their wish to ensure that their rivals did not become more powerful than they.

The problem of religion was to prove the most intractable. Until the Restoration, the differences between Episcopalians and Presbyterians had not been great. However, under Charles II the Episcopalians had identified themselves with the king and this led the Presbyterians to become the leading opponents of arbitrary rule. This division became even more rigid after 1688 when the Episcopalians moved closer towards the Jacobite tradition and the Presbyterians towards William and the revolution. Paradoxically, William favoured an Episcopalian solution, principally for political reasons, but his Scottish advisers supported the Presbyterians. However, as Riley writes: 'A man's religious allegiance tended to be decided by his relationship to those who comprised the central administration rather than the other way round. But the foundation had been laid of the myth that Scottish political divisions were fundamentally religious.' One writer in 1691 praised William's policy: 'One may say that the middle course which his majesty has chosen, in leaving the government to the Presbyterians on one side, and favouring the Episcopalians with his royal protection on the other, is the surest and only way of preserving the peace in

Scotland.' This seemed true, but it could not cope with the ease with which individuals could move between the two pillars of religion, according to the political advantage they sought to gain.

Parliament met in March 1689 with Hamilton as High Commissioner and as President Argyll, who had supported William and had been restored his father's estates. Parliament demanded the king accept a document containing grievances and a claim of rights. Tweeddale continued to push his dream of union and he succeeded in getting William to support it but the Bill recommending it failed to pass because Tweeddale had been unable to build enough support: the Presbyterians feared the imposition of Episcopalianism and Hamilton's Party could not support union because the Jacobites did not want it and because Hamilton's personal ambitions could not be satisfied by it. Most importantly, the English administration showed no real interest in pursuing union, as it offered no major benefit.

Hamilton soon made his personal ambitions clear by seeking to be appointed Lord Chancellor. When Parliament met again in 1690 he was replaced as High Commissioner by the Earl of Melville who was a moderate Presbyterian who had fled to the Netherlands in 1683, having been implicated in the Rye House Plot. There he befriended William, who made him an earl in 1690. Despite this, Melville gave in to most of the demands of those who opposed the Court: the Kirk was established and lay patronage abolished, as were the Lords of the Articles, which had sat for almost 250 years. William then selected his ministry for Scotland and tried to balance the two factions. He did not appoint a Chancellor, Melville was appointed Secretary of State and John Dalrymple Lord Advocate. Dalrymple's father, Viscount Stair, was made President of the Court of Session and Tweeddale was appointed one of the Lords of the Treasury. He did not like Stair, who he criticised as being one of the high Presbyterian 'violent party'. Stair was a lawyer who had fled to the Netherlands in 1684, he was accused of complicity in the Rye House plot and in Argyll's rebellion of 1685 and he became a trusted adviser to William and returned with him in 1688. His son John had been appointed Lord Advocate by James in 1687, but he was removed a year later for incompetence. Both Dalrymples joined Tweeddale in the Privy Council but they were mistrusted by many in Scotland, who believed they wanted to rule as William's envoys over Scotland. The battle between Melville and the Dalrymples was to dominate Scottish politics over the next two years and their political conflict reflected the religious one as the Presbyterians supported Melville and the Episcopalians supported the Dalrymples.

Tweeddale soon realised that he would gain nothing if he relied on Yester to fulfill his objectives. His health gave him the reason needed to justify a visit to England and in April 1689 he rented an unfurnished house in an unfashionable part of London, and had sent from Scotland all the furnishings needed for it. He was to stay for over two years and the visit transformed his fortunes as he was taken up by a group of disparate politicians who wanted to change the way Scotland was managed and to prevent the spread of radical Presbyterianism. He quickly gained influence in England although this made some in Scotland nervous. George Hume, soon to be made Lord Marchmont, wrote in August 1689: 'Our parliament is basely misrepresented by Tarbat, Tweeddale and folk of that gang. They and the English junto, viz., Halifax, Danby, Shrewsbury, Nottingham and Portland, are taking methods for breaking our parliament, calling a new one, and reducing what is done in our church government.' Tweeddale was made a member of the Treasury Commission in December and Yester was appointed to the Privy Council but, for no known reason, declined so the Jacobite William Johnstone, Earl of Annandale, was made a Councillor in his stead. Tweeddale continued to seek preferment for Yester, writing to Portland and to the king, but achieved nothing for him.

Even though he disliked the Dalrymples, Tweeddale hated Melville more because of a dispute over lands in Midlothian and because his daughter, Margaret, Countess of Roxburghe, was also in dispute with Melville over properties in East Lothian. She had married in 1675, aged sixteen, the 3rd Earl of Roxburghe but he was drowned in 1682 and she was to outlive him for 70 years, dying aged 94. Melville's son, Leven, had his soldiers arrest Tweeddale's son, David Hay, at five in the morning and confine him in the Edinburgh Tolbooth. Hay had resigned his commission in the Horse Guards because he had taken the Test Oath, and this was used as the pretext for his arrest. Yester was also targeted, with the king being told that he was a member of the political opposition in the Privy Council. In addition, Leven had troops quartered on the disputed Roxburghe estate because of rumours of conspiracy.

Tweeddale decided to join the Dalrymples in trying to discredit Melville and his eldest son, Lord Raith, by exposing their misuse of the Treasury, which was headed by Raith, who had recently bought some land for £1.4 million. Melville himself was in dispute over the ownership of a bond for £600,000, given by the town of Edinburgh. Dalrymple set up a commission to examine why the Treasury had allowed the excise duty to be lowered and Tweeddale was asked to head it and to advise how taxes could be raised.

These poisonous disputes encouraged William to change his administration in Scotland and he now turned to Tweeddale, who he had grown to know and like during the two years he spent in England. He saw him as someone who could stand above both factions and who might be able to control them and in January 1692 he appointed Tweeddale as Lord Chancellor. Melville was appointed Privy Seal; Dalrymple and James Johnston were made Joint-Secretaries; Tarbat became Lord Clerk Register; Queensberry's heir, Drumlanrig, was appointed a Commissioner of the Treasury, alongside Linlithgow; and Breadalbane and Raith remained Treasurer-deputes. There were twice as many Presbyterians as Episcopalians in the new Ministry and the magnates had largely been ignored.

Tweeddale's Ministry was riven by the animosity between the joint-Secretaries. Johnston, although a Presbyterian, had promised the Archbishop of Canterbury that he would look after the interests of the Episcopalians, and he undertook to persuade the Presbyterians to moderate their demands but this irritated Dalrymple, as he saw himself as the spokesman for the Episcopalians. He wrote to Tweeddale: 'There's nothing now in Britain that's more the subject of men's observation than whether the Presbyterians will comply with the king's desires in assuming their bretheren or not, if they be obstinate I fear they repent it.'

Tweeddale tried to stand above both factions but found this increasingly isolated him and made him more enemies than friends. He had returned to Scotland after more than two years away, he was hated by Melville, the mutual mistrust between him and the Dalrymples remained and he was looked on by Johnston as a stopgap. In addition to all of this, his appointment had antagonised the magnates, especially Hamilton. He realised that the situation could not continue, so he tried to have Dalrymple removed. He wrote to the king, pointing out the problems, 'but above all the different sentiments of your secretaries gives good occasions of divisions amongst us,' but William decided to do nothing.

During his administration, it is very likely that Tweeddale was living at least part of the time at Pinkie House, as it was only four miles from Edinburgh. Macky visited it in 1723 and his description suggests that it was his main residence.

> The great hall is adorned with the views of the great cities of Italy, and in the drawing room off it is a billiard table both paved with stone. The great staircase is balustrade with iron and crowded with pictures. The first apartment consists of a dining room, drawing room and bed chamber, very spacious in Tapestry. The bed is of crimson vel-

vet in an alcove, neatly supported with pillars. The chimneys are of marble and above that of the dining room is a picture, the finest inside of a church I ever saw. The great gallery is very long and spacious, the ceiling full of Latin inscriptions. It is crowded with pictures, some of them passably good. In the gallery there is a family picture of Lord Seton with his four sons and daughters done by Hans Holbein, Mr Henderson, the famous preacher, by van Dyck, Charles I and the Earl of Dunfermline in his robes by the same. The first Marquis of Tweeddale and his wife with his eight sons and seven daughters[1], as big as the life, takes up almost one end of the room. There is also in this Gallery, well preserved, the Tree of the Family of Tweeddale from 970 to this day, the Giffards and the Frasers. The parterre behind the Palace is very large and nobly ordered with evergreens and on each side of it spacious gardens, the whole in a well planted park of three miles wall round.

It seems that Tweeddale initiated at Pinkie what he was to execute on a much grander scale at Yester. Macky rather amusingly added: 'I must own, if I were owner of Pinkie, I should hardly have built Yester. Pinkie stands nobly and hath a commanding prospect not only of the the adjacent country but also the whole coast of Fife, over the sea at nine miles dist whereas Yester lies in a Bottom and all its views bounded with itself.'

The Jacobites continued to pose a threat in the Highlands and a group was set up to bring that area under control, though Tweeddale was doubtful that any agreement with the Highlanders could be relied upon. Breadalbane, a Campbell, was given chief responsibility for executing the policy and he ordered all the clan leaders to give an oath of obedience to the king on

[1]Macky was wrong - the picture shows Tweeddale's children and their spouses. See portrait on page 167.

New Year's Day, 1692. One old leader, Macdonald of Glencoe, was late in giving his oath and Dalrymple recommended that an example be made of him. He wrote to Tweeddale: 'I am extremely glad that the murderer MacIain of Glencoe did not accept the benefit of the indemnity. I hope care will be taken to root out that thieving tribe.' William signed the order and Argyll's men from Fort William killed Macdonald and 37 others at Glencoe, including two women and two children. The people of Scotland were outraged and the enemies of the Dalrymples sought to hold them to account for the massacre.

Parliament was called in 1693 with Hamilton as High Commissioner but Johnston controlled its programme as Lord Secretary and Dalrymple chose not to attend. Johnston proposed that the Church be unified in law but that the existing Kirk government should remain in place, with all ministers taking an oath of allegiance and the acceptance that 'Presbyterian church government be the only government of this church'. However his proposition was defeated as the Presbyterians considered that the imposition of the oath put them under the control of the king. Tweeddale's ministry became increasingly paralysed as Riley writes: 'More energy and ingenuity went into manoeuvring to score points off rivals than into the conduct of everyday business.' Johnston wrote to Polwart: 'Such a mixture in councils of men directly opposite to one another will never do. I think indeed the king would do better to have them all either white or black.' Tweeddale was unable to resolve the situation and William remained reluctant to intervene. Hamilton, meanwhile, gave his opinions on everything to do with Scotland to anyone he spoke to in England whilst pursuing his grand plans to be appointed a permanent High Commissioner. Johnston wrote of him: 'I would rather be a porter than live such another winter with him,' but the problems he caused were ended by his death in 1694.

Tweeddale was courted and pressurised by both factions during

1694. Johnston's Presbyterian faction was in the majority whilst Dalrymple's Episcopalians had gained the support of Queensberry and Drumlanrig. Tweeddale remained neutral and, like his king, believed inaction was the best policy. He was still trying to get preferment for Yester and was greatly disappointed when the king refused him a place in the Treasury, on the grounds that two members of the same family should not be in it. This was ironic, as the Treasury Commission was so beset with strife between the various members that for many months it conducted no business as it could not establish a quorum while Scotland's financial situation continued to deteriorate. As the year progressed, Tweeddale realised he had to break the deadlock and he recommended to William that his administration be purged because the factions were irreconcilable, 'partly from the differences of their opinions but more from discontent with their share in the government, and jealousies of the firmness of some employed in it which your majesty cannot be a stranger to... but above all the different sentiments of your secretaries gives good occasions of divisions amongst us'. He was increasingly sympathetic to Johnston's faction and he eventually again asked William to dismiss the Dalrymples.

William again did nothing, but he did try to encourage Tweeddale by making him a Marquis. His choice of Coat of Arms reflected those of his ancestor, the 1st Lord Hay: Quarterly 1st and 4th *Azure three cinquefoils Argent* (Fraser) 2nd and 3rd *Gules three bars ermine* (Giffards of Yester) *an inescutcheon Argent three inescutcheons Gules* (Hay). William also renewed Tweeddale's lease of his lordship of Dunfermline to compensate him for the costs he had suffered in his helping that family. Anna Monmouth protested about this but William ignored her. He then appointed Tweeddale High Commissioner for the Parliament of 1695, with Annandale serving as President. Tweeddale was selected as a member of the Commission which held the public enquiry into the Massacre of Glencoe whose Report, which it is thought Tweeddale himself had written, was presented to Parliament and was judged to be 'an excellent digest of evidence, clear, passionless, and austerely just'. Parliament voted the massacre an act of murder but absolved the king and everyone else from blame apart from Lieutenant Colonel Hamilton, the deputy-governor of Fort William, and Dalrymple, who resigned. Breadalbane was charged with high treason and imprisoned but Johnston admitted to Portland that it had only been a device to get him out of the Treasury. William, without consulting Tweeddale, ordered him to be released as he had been angered that the Report had been issued to Parliament without his permission. However Tweeddale had been forced to issue it, as Parliament would otherwise not have voted Supply.

Parliament also passed the Church Act, which gave Episcopalian ministers more time to take the oath, which a large number did. The Presbyterians were also pleased as the Kirk was not forced to accept any Episcopalian ministers. Parliament then passed the Act for the Encouragement of Trade, after which Tweeddale dissolved it. The sitting had passed a significant body of legislation and Tweeddale was largely responsible for its success. Sir James Ogilvy, the Solicitor General, wrote to Carstares: 'I know endeavours will be used to misrepresent our proceedings but, when duly considered, I am hopeful the king will be satisfied... Our party, if well with the court, is able to serve the king to his satisfaction... It is now a proper time for you to do good to your country. Honest men expect your assistance and mistake will soon go over.' Tweeddale also had the satisfaction of angering Melville, who in 1690 had given the Marquis of Lothian precedence over Tweeddale's grandson, Roxburghe. Parliament had voted that not only Roxburghe, but four other Lords, including Haddington, now took precedence over Lothian.

Johnston was delighted at the parliamentary session and wrote to Shrewsbury praising Tweeddale: 'The Chancellor is become 10 years younger than he was... never Commissioner did behave himself with more dignity and consideration, and when he spoke he did it with much weight and precisely to the point... He has been honest and firm in business, like a rock, which has not been his character the former parts of this life, but he says he is going off, and that he is resolved his exit shall be Honourable.'

Tweeddale had advised the king that he wanted to hand over the responsibility of government. He was seventy, he had successfully restored his family's fortunes and he felt he had done as much as he could to support the king, Scotland and the Kirk. William, however, wanted him to stay and this Tweeddale agreed to do. However, the focus on Glencoe and the Church Act had overshadowed the passing of the Trade Act, which was to have momentous and completely unexpected consequences for Scotland, and was one which would cast a dark cloud over Tweeddale's reputation.

CHAPTER 11 – THE COMPANY OF SCOTLAND

Scotland's economy suffered in the latter half of the 17th century with crop failures exacerbating the decline of its basic industries of coal and salt. This period has been described as the most pitiful in Scotland's history and the ending of the union which had existed under the Protectorate was a major contributor to this, as Scotland increasingly relied on supplies from England but had little prospect of earning enough money to pay for them. Following William's accession, however, Scotland's economy had begun a recovery based on trade with the Continent and between 1690 and 1695 47 joint stock companies were established, including the Bank of Scotland in 1695. The most ambitious of these was established in 1695 when Tweeddale approved the Act of Parliament which authorised William Paterson to set up the Company of Scotland, which was given the monopoly of trade with Asia and Africa for all time and of trade with America for 31 years. It also had the right to found colonies in any part of Asia, Africa or America not already occupied by any European sovereign and it was exempted from tax for 21 years. The Act pledged the power of the Crown in support of the Company and its claims. Paterson chose Darien as the Company's first outpost; it lay on the Isthmus of Panama, close to the centre of Spain's gold and silver exports.

Tweeddale had been introduced to Paterson by his neighbour,

Andrew Fletcher of Saltoun and this meeting was to have profound consequences as the three of them were to play significant roles in determining the fate of Scotland over the next twelve years. Paterson was a highly respected financier and had helped set up the Bank of England in 1694. His vision for the Company was compelling: 'Trade will increase trade, and money will beget money, and the trading world shall need no more to want work for their hands, but will rather want hands for their work.' His vision was almost religious in nature, as he saw Darien as a new Eden which would lead to a golden economic future for Scotland.

The Act establishing the Company was drafted by Sir James Stewart, the Lord Advocate, a man of uncertain probity. Tweeddale gave it his official blessing on the same day as the Report on Glencoe was presented to Parliament, probably with the objective of diluting the impact of that Report's findings. The Act specified that at least half the shares should be held by Scottish investors, but subscription started in England in November as capital was far more readily available there. The maximum individual subscription was set at £300,000 and the initial target of half the total capital subscription of £60 million was reached in ten days. The reception was not wholly welcoming, however, as the London merchants generally, and those of the East India Company specifically, were very critical of the issue. Shares in the EIC had halved since August and many powerful businessmen were concerned about the impact 'the Scotch Act' would have on their businesses. Questions were asked in Parliament as to how much English trade would suffer and protests were lodged by the EIC, the Hamburg Company and the Levant Company, amongst others. In December, a parliamentary committee submitted a paper to William setting out 'the great Prejudice, Inconveniences, and Mischief' caused by this Act. The king replied: 'I have been ill served by Scotland; but I hope some Remedies may be found to prevent the inconveniences which may arise from this Act.' Tweeddale was summoned to London and the king accused him of exceeding his authority as High Commissioner, complaining that 'the company had such powers as if there had been no king of Scotland'. Sir James Stewart was also summoned to explain his role and he, true to form, denied having seen Tweeddale's instructions or that he had been involved in the preperation of the Act at all.

Tweeddale's and Johnston's enemies took advantage of this to move against them. Initially, the attack was lead by Tarbat, who had been Chief Minister of Scotland under James II and who had conspired with Middleton to billet Tweeddale in 1662. Carstares had for some time been considering making a change in the Ministry and had even thought of bringing back Melville. Portland's focus, however, was on a completely different area as he considered that the magnates had been denied influence for too long and saw that the new generation offered a group of young men, all of whom were able and interested in politics.

Lord John Murray, the son of the 1st Marquis of Atholl, was 35 in 1695 and he succeeded as 2nd Marquis in 1703. He supported William's coronation and he was a Presbyterian who remained close to the Jacobites. His father had played a major role in the defeat of Argyll's rebellion in 1685 but he was described by Macaulay as 'the falsest, the most fickle, the most pusillanimous of mankind'.

Archibald Campbell, 10th Earl of Argyll, was 37 in 1695. His father and his grandfather had both been executed by the then ruling king but Argyll had supported William and had his estates restored to him. Lockhart said of him: 'In outward Appearance was a Good Natur'd, Civil and Modest Gentleman, but his Actions were quite otherwise, being capable of the worst Things to promote his Interest, and altogether addicted to a Lewd Profligate Life... He was always an Enemy to the Loyal Interest... but what other could be expected from a man that [to curry favour with King James] had renounc'd his Religion and turn'd Papist? Notwithstanding which... he was the darling of the Presbyterians.'

James, 4th Duke of Hamilton, was 36 when he inherited from his father in 1694. He had supported James II, but justified this by saying 'I cannot violate my duty to my master. I must distinguish between his Popery and his Person.' He had been accused of disloyalty to William, imprisoned twice in the Tower, but was released without charge. He saw himself as the rightful king of Scotland if the Stuarts were to be barred from the accession.

James Douglas, 2nd Duke of Queensberry, was 33 in 1695 when he inherited from his father, who had been President of the Privy Council under James II. However the 2nd Duke was, according to Lockhart, 'the first Scotsman that deserted over to the Prince of Orange, and from thence acquired the epithet (among honest men) of Proto-rebel... to outward appearances he was of a gentle and good disposition but inwardly a very devil, standing at nothing to advance his own interests and designs'.

William at last decided to act: he kept Tweeddale as Chancellor but he dismissed both Dalrymple and Johnston and replaced them as Joint-Secretaries by Lord John Murray and Sir James Ogilvy. Selkirk, the new Duke of Hamilton's brother, was appointed Lord Clerk Register in place of Tarbat. Tweeddale was appointed to head the Treasury Commission which was composed of Queensberry, Argyll, Annandale and Raith, whose father, Melville, remained Privy Seal. However, the diligence of these new men did not seem to match their ambitions as, by the end of 1695, Tweeddale reported that there had been no sittings of the Treasury or Exchequer that session because of failure to achieve a quorum.

These changes did little to make Tweeddale's life any easier as they merely replaced the rivalry between the two factions with rivalries between the magnates. Murray at first sided with Tweeddale against Queensberry who was supported by Argyll, who was the most opinionated of them all. He was openly dismissive of Tweeddale, calling him an 'old weather-beaten decayed doge,' and he complained that 'those of the first magnitude are neglected'.

Tweeddale was, however, still highly regarded by William and, after the failed assassination attempt on the king in 1696, he was put in charge of security over the whole of Scotland. Riley writes, though, that: 'by the end of 1695, Tweeddale seemed not to care very much...the stress of age and responsibility had taken heavy toll and he was glad to let events follow their course.' Queensberry and Ogilvy echoed Argyll and recommended to William that priority should be given to the 'nobility of first rank,' so that these would form the basis for a Court Party that would act in his interest. William was persuaded and he replaced Tweeddale with Lord Polwarth, who, as Sir Patrick Hume, had been involved in the Rye House Plot and who had fled to the Netherlands in 1683. Queensberry became Privy Seal in place of Melville, who became President of the Council, Lord John Hamilton was made Master of the Mint and Argyll took over from Queensberry in charge of the Guards. William believed that these appointments would at last bring together the two church factions as Polwarth, Melville and Argyll were Presbyterians, whilst Queensberry was strongly Episcopalian. However neither he nor his advisers really understood the forces driving Scottish politics. Riley gets it right: 'The real nature of the Scottish problem...was not the finding of a *modus vivendi* between Presbyterians and Episcopalians but the satisfying of the growing demands of the magnates and coping with their rivalries'. Murray became a Presbyterian and he was appointed High Commissioner to the Parliament of 1696 as Earl of Tullibardine and he gathered around him the group that had supported Tweeddale and Johnston. The key requirement of William was Supply and Tullibardine achieved this with no difficulty, but Tweeddale had asked to be excused due to his infirmity.

Whilst these changes were taking place in Scotland, moves were underway in England to undermine the funding for the Company. In the spring of 1696 the House of Lords proposed legislation to penalise English citizens who invested in or managed the

Company, and proposed giving the EIC and the Royal African Company privileges to compete with it. The Commons ordered the directors of the Company to be impeached and by July all monies subscribed from English investors had been returned. Paterson and his partner James Smyth turned to Scottish investors to replace them. The nobles were the natural lead investors and Anne, Duchess of Hamilton, the premier peeress of Scotland, was an early target. Yester's eldest son, Charles Hay, had married one of her daughters, Susannah, in 1695. Her younger brother, Lord Basil, wrote to his brother, the Duke: 'Mr Paterson and some others have been with her and say it would be disheartening to the whole kingdome, and might occasion many people far below her... she thought it needless for her to subscribe a greater sum... and they said they would rather pay the proportions of the other two thousand pound than Her Grace should not subscribe it.' In the end, Anne and Basil decided to together subscribe the maximum amount of £300,000. The general subscription opened in February 1697, with investors being asked to pay a quarter of the subscription immediately and a further quarter after one year. By the end of February, £9 million had been subscribed; by March, it had risen to £30 million, the original target from Scottish investors; and the subscription was finally closed in August at £40 million.

This was a huge amount of money, representing four times the government's annual revenue, and the first instalment of cash subscribed represented up to 51% of the total money supply of the nation. The new Bank of Scotland provided a vital role by making loans to investors totalling £2.6 million in the second quarter alone, forcing it to raise more capital. More worryingly, the Company lent £2 million to its own shareholders between July and October. Dalrymple wrote: 'The frenzy of the Scots nation to sign the Solemn League and Covenant never exceeded the rapidity with which they ran to subscribe to the Darien Company.' In total there were 1,300 investors, half of whom invested more than £10,000. The nobles contributed 14%, with Tweeddale subscribing £100,000, as did his daughter, the Countess of Roxburghe, and his half-brother, William Hay of Drumelzier; Yester and two of his brothers together subscribed £190,000. Queensberry subscribed for the maximum amount, as did John Hamilton, Lord Belhaven. Margaret Wemyss subscribed £200,000, as did Argyll and Leven. The lairds subscribed 34% and the merchants subscribed 26%, as did the institutions, including most of the burghs. The first Court of directors comprised two nobles, Lords Belhaven and Ruthven, eight merchants and fifteen lairds, and the Hays were represented by Drumelzier and Yester, who joined the Court in 1698.

Despite the success of the Scottish subscription, the Company's capital was still £20 million short of its original target, so in January 1697 Paterson and Smyth went to raise funds from investors in Amsterdam and Hamburg. Whilst these two cities were together the richest and most experienced in overseas trade, their choice was curiously naïve, given what had happened in England. Amsterdam was the base of the Dutch East India Company and the promoters were not welcomed, so they turned to Rotterdam, Scotland's closest continental trading partner, but there potential investors were directly warned by the magistrates not to participate.

Worse was to come in Hamburg. Paterson had hoped for a favourable reception, as the Company had given Hamburg's shipbuilders orders for four vessels, but he found that Sir Paul Rycaut, the English envoy, had been instructed to obstruct their efforts. Letters had been sent to key German cities in April, saying: 'We Ministers of His Majesty the King of Great Britain have, upon the arrival of Commissioners from an Indian Company in Scotland... Commanded us most expressly to notifie to Your magnificences and lordships, that if you enter into such Conventions with private men, his subjects who have neither Credential letters, nor any otherwise authoriz'd by His Majesty, That His Majesty would regard such proceedings as an affront to his Royal authority, and that he would not fail to resent it.'

These letters had their effect, only £900,000 was subscribed and the overseas funding process was abandoned. The directors in Scotland were furious at this failure because of the shipbuilding commitments already entered into, but worse was to follow. It transpired that the Court had, after the payment of the first instalment of the Subscription, entrusted James Smyth, with £1.7 million. Paterson had encouraged this as, due to the war of Spanish Succession, the English pound had collapsed, and he thought that the Company could profit from its likely recovery using the cash held on deposit. In November the directors were advised that Smyth had defaulted on a bill for £50,000 and two more defaults were reported later that month. In March 1698 Rycaut wrote that 'Mr Smith was lately arrested at Amsterdam for default of payments… it is said that he and Paterson are in contrivance to cheat the stock.' This took place against a background of steep falls in European financial markets as in 1696 and 1697 interest rates had risen steeply, reaching 25% in Scotland; asset prices fell and this resulted in a run on the Bank of England.

Smyth was jailed in London, but he escaped and fled the country. The Company recovered some of the money, but it is estimated that £830,000 was lost. The Court may have escaped blame for the scandal, but they clearly had not done due diligence on Smyth, because it was found that he had been questioned by the Commons in 1695 over an allegation of bribery. In the same year, he had been arrested for trying to dump counterfeit bonds on the Bank of England. Paterson was brought before the Court's inquiry into the affair, he was exonerated of any wrongdoing, but he was criticised for 'easy credulity and folly' and his role in the running of the Company was greatly reduced.

The judgement of the directors over how they spent the Company's money was now seriously called into question. Their greatest expenditure was on thirteen ships, which cost just under £7 million, with the first three ships costing £3.1 million and the flagship alone costing £1.5 million. They had to be commissioned overseas, as the Scottish shipbuilding industry had almost disappeared by the mid-17th century, and the skills needed to build ocean-going vessels was best found on the continent, particularly in Hamburg. Many other trading companies had decided to charter, rather than own, their ships and, had the Court adopted this policy, it would have saved the Company significant expense.

Tweeddale died in August 1697 aged 72. He must have been exhausted and his last years had not been happy. His whole life had, however, been a remarkable succession of triumphs over disasters, with the spectre of financial disaster forever at his shoulder. Somehow he had found time to pursue academic and scientific interests and he was described by John Evelyn as 'a learned and knowing nobleman'. He had been elected a Fellow of the Royal Society in 1664 and achieved a considerable reputation for his improvements to his Yester estate. He kept a fine library at Pinkie which contained a wide selection of books on horticulture and a number of standard architectural treatises, some of which had been Lauderdales. He was acclaimed for his political career, especially in his mature years. Riley wrote: 'Tweeddale's period of office had been marked by a degree of self restraint in the advancement of his personal interest rare in Scotland.' Macaulay wrote of him: 'He was a man grown old in business, well informed, prudent, humane, blameless in private life, and on the whole as respectable as any Scottish lord who had been long and deeply concerned in the politics of those troubled times. He discharged the delicate and difficult duties of his office with great prudence and impartiality.' His contemporary, Bishop Burnet, wrote of him: 'He understood all the interests and concerns of Scotland well: he had a great stock of knowledge, with a mild and obliging temper. He was of a blameless, or rather an exemplary, life in all respects. He had loose thoughts both of civil and ecclesiastical government, and seemed to think that whatever form soever was uppermost was to be complied with. Though he was in all respects the ablest and worthiest man of the nobility, he was too cautious and fearful.' He and Jean had nine children; two had died young and the others all had full lives.

John Yester inherited as 2nd Marquis, aged 52. He may have seen the Company's first five ships sail to Darien from Leith in July 1698 as he had been made a Director of the Company in March. Dalrymple wrote in his *History of the Company*: 'The whole city of Edinburgh poured down upon Leith, to see the colony depart, amidst the tears and prayers and praises of relations and friends and of their countrymen.' On board were 1,200 men and women, including William Paterson and his wife, and £2 million worth of goods, most of which were to be used for building the colony, with the remainder consisting of linen textiles to sell to the natives. They arrived at Darien in November and were delighted by what they saw. 'This harbour is capable of containing 1,000 sail of the best Ships in the World,' wrote one and another wrote: 'It may be made impregnable... if it were all cultivated, to afford 10,000 Hogsheads of Sugar every year.' A third kept a journal detailing the variety of animal life as well as the extensive varieties of trees, which provided timber and fruit and wrote: 'I shall only say of the Country that it is one of the fruitfullest spots of ground on the face of the Earth and best situat for trade.' The local tribesmen, the Tule, told the colonists of nearby gold and silver mines but only later did they find that such variety and richness also came in the form of virulent diseases and that the lushness was a result of the heavy rain which fell for six months of the year. Reality came quickly, Hannah Paterson was one of several who died in the early weeks after landing and ten sailors deserted at the end of November.

A French ship sank as it left Darien in December, killing almost half of its crew and in February 1699 one of the Company's boats was seized by the Spanish, her crew imprisoned for piracy and her cargo confiscated. There was much worse to come as the colonists learned in May that Sir William Beeston, governor of Jamaica, had published a proclamation 'declaring that the Scottish settlement had broken the peace between William and the Spanish, and prohibiting the supply of provisions to the Scots… under severe penalties' and similar proclamations were issued in Barbados and New York. Morale was completely broken and the 900 survivors left in June for New York, where only 550 disembarked, the remainder having died on the voyage. Walter Harries, one of those who made it to New York, later wrote: 'We were sent to the back of God's elbow, where we could see nothing but Death, starving and the Spanish Mines before our eyes… Caledonia, where there's nothing to be had but hard Labour, Sweat, Hungry Bellies and Shallow Graves.'

News of this tragedy did not reach Scotland for some time, so people there remained optimistic. The Kirk had taken up the colonialists' cause and the General Assembly recommended in February 1699 that all ministers 'should pray for the success and prosperity of the trading Company of this Nation and to be fervent in prayer to God for averting his wrath'. The Company was short of money and Tweeddale recommended in April that it should raise new funds but the Court thought that this was unrealistic and decided that an Address should be made to the king about the 'evil consequences' of the American proclamations.

The behaviour by the English caused increasing antagonism in Scotland and this coalesced in an opposition group led by Tweeddale that became known as the Country Party. The political tensions in Scotland came to a head when Tullibardine resigned as High Commissioner because Queensberry's choice, Dalrymple, was appointed as President of the Court of Session.

William appointed Marchmont in his place and Ogilvy was made Earl of Seafield. Parliament was now split between the Court Party, which was supported by most nobles and burghers, and the Country Party, which was supported by the lairds. Its members tended to be Presbyterian patriots whilst the members of the Court Party tended to be Episcopalians but the problems of religion was increasingly overshadowed by the problems of the Company, the question of the Succession and, ultimately, over union.

The Country Party never had more than 50 core Members, and thus could not achieve its objectives without additional support in Parliament. It was increasingly identified with the Company and Tweeddale became its titular leader. Riley writes rather harshly, that: 'The 2nd Marquis made an unhappy debut as the opposition leader, acting with all the rashness of an opinionated introvert under the compulsion to make a mark in public'. The Court Party was dismissive of the opposition, with Argyll writing: 'As for the Marquis of Tweeddale, he has acted a foolish part, for they have made him give in all the foolish proposals.' In Parliament the nobles and the burghs tended to support the Court Party which had a majority of 23 over the Country Party which was supported by the lairds.

One of its members was the Earl of Panmure, a fervent Jacobite who had married Hamilton's sister, and who had been recently elected as a director of the Company. He had opposed the Revolution and had refused to take the oath of allegiance and he was completely open about his motives for joining the Company: 'If it succeeded... it would have been a great advantage to the kingdom and if obstructed by that Prince it would not miss to create him a great many enemies, the most part of the Kingdom being sharers in that Company.' This increased the Country Party bias of the Company, and Tweeddale used it as a powerful platform to pursue his political agenda. He received political support from other directors, including Scott of Thirlestane, Haldane, Scott of Ancrum, Drumelzier and Baillie, most of who were also Members of Parliament.

The General Council of the Company became the forum in which the political battle between the Country Party and the Court Party was fought when Parliament was not sitting. The Council consisted of 46 people, the supporters of the Country Party were in the great majority and they voted off three key Court Party supporters as directors. This focus of Country Party with the Company was, however, a double-edged sword as the news of the disaster at Darien spread, the nation was increasingly divided between those who blamed the directors for the fiasco and those who blamed William and England.

Two ships were sent to Darien with provisions for 300 passengers in May 1699, not realising that the colony had been abandoned. One of the ships contained a supply of brandy and this caught fire and the ship and all its cargo were destroyed and most of the 300 who voyaged out subsequently died ashore. It was, Tweeddale wrote, 'lyke a thunderclap unto us'. Hamilton now followed the example of his father and used this disaster to pursue his personal ambitions and he proposed making a National Address to the king to demand that Parliament be recalled so the concerns of the Company could be addressed. He gathered support for it, focusing first on the Country Party leading Portland's secretary to write to Carstares: 'It must be surprising to you, and all others, that Duke Hamilton proves to be a zealous Presbyterian and that something of great importance must lie at the bottom of his turning that way.' Hamilton's brother, Lord Basil, presented the National Address to Marchmont in November and it was then sent round the country receiving the support of 30,000 signatories. Tweeddale and Hamilton presented it to the king in London in March 1700 but William told them that he had already appointed a Scottish Parliament to sit in May and added 'had you considered this you might have spared the labour of coming here to present the address'. Despite this putdown, Tweeddale and his colleagues received a hero's welcome when they returned.

A third expedition to Darien had set sail in September 1699 carrying 1,300 passengers in four ships, led by Lord Mungo Murray, Tullibardine's younger brother. The Spaniards attacked the colony in February 1700 and the colonists had no chance; Murray was killed and the survivors surrendered in March and sailed to Jamaica in five ships, including the flagship the *Rising Sun* and, again, many died during the voyage. The *Rising Sun* sailed for Scotland in July but she was almost immediately disabled by a storm and anchored off the coast of Carolina, where she was struck by a hurricane and sank as did two other of the Company's ships. 2,000 colonists had died since 1698, representing two-thirds of those who had sailed in thirteen ships of which only three returned; there was no insurance available, so the capital loss was total.

This succession of catastrophes ended the hopes of the directors that Darien could ever be secured as a colony. Queensberry exploited this by attacking the Country Party and he even persuaded William Paterson, with a degree of financial inducement, to persuade Country Party members not to raise the issue of the Company's problems in Parliament. The king wrote that he was willing to repair 'the losses and [support] the interest' of the Company, but said he could not support their ambitions in Darien. Queensberry wrote to the king, pointing out the Company's strong Jacobite connections: 'It was evident that many who set up most of the company... had never taken the oaths and owned your majesty's government.' He did not, of course, remind the king that he had himself invested the maximum allowed into the company. Hamilton, on the other hand, was appealing to Jacobites to support him in Parliament as was Tweeddale. Seafield was not fooled by all this and wrote to Annandale: 'I don't doubt but a great many, especially the ringleaders, have other designs at the bottom.'

This all made the last two Parliaments of William's reign very difficult. Melville summed up the situation well to Carstares, writing that, if William did not assert Scotland's right to Darien, then 'his reasons do either concern Scotland, or are exotic as to Scotland. If the first let us know them; we will be ready to comply with his greater wisdom. If they do not concern Scotland, then, say they, this gives ground for an unanswerable argument, that the crowns of England and Scotland are incompatible, seeing it is not to be supposed that, where the interests of England and Scotland do irreconcilably interfere, the king must act in favours of England.' William told one of his advisers that he considered union 'would be an advantage for it could not be done without admitting a good number of Scottish members into both houses who must depend upon the crown for their subsistence, but he was not desirous the experiment should be made in his reign'.

CHAPTER 12 – THE BATTLE FOR UNION

Queensberry opened Parliament as High Commissioner in May 1700. He and Argyll had managed to have Marchmont's ministry purged of all those connected with the Hamiltons, apart from his brother, Selkirk. Queensberry wanted to secure only the vote on Supply, but Parliament refused to do so unless substantial concessions were granted to those who had lost so much over Darien. Its mood was not improved by the king's letter expressing his sorrow at the 'misfortunes and losses that the nation has sustained' and recommending that they concentrate on improving their 'native product' rather than on foreign trade. Hamilton's Address to the king was voted through by a majority of 35 but it was to no avail as Queensberry adjourned the session several times and Parliament did not meet again until October.

Queensberry considered entering negotiations with the opposition and wrote to Seafield: 'I shall never advise [the king's] calling up of the Duke of Hamilton or his putting any trust in him because I am not persuaded of his integrity for his majesty's interest but if he thinks fit to call any person of that party the Marquis of Tweeddale would be the proper person being a man that both the nation and the company gives a more entire credit to and who having sincere intentions may be better dealt with in what is really designed for the good of his country.'

However, Queensberry was again High Commissioner when Parliament met in October. In his letter of address, William said he was 'heartily sorry for the Company's loss,' and that he was willing to consider 'repairing the losses and supporting and promoting the interest' of the Company, but he could not confirm its right to Darien as 'our yielding in that matter had infallibly disturbed the general peace of Christendom'. The Country Party proposed that the Company be confirmed in its right to Darien but they lost by 84 votes to 108. Marchmont remarked that the session 'was the most clamorous contentious and hot' of any he had experienced since 1665 and, after voting Supply, Parliament was adjourned in February 1701. His success encouraged Queensberry to get rid of Marchmont but he could not form a ministry himself as he had lost the support of Argyll, who had been made a duke, and because he had alienated so many others.

Louis XIV now chose to recognise James Stuart as King of Scotland, England and Ireland, and England prepared for war. The combination of all these factors convinced William that union between Scotland and England was the only solution and he appointed Commissioners to secure it. He did, however, lament to one of his advisers that 'he had not the good fortune to know what would satisfy a Scotsman'. He died in March 1702 and Anne succeeded to the throne, the last Stuart to do so. When her last remaining child, of the eighteen she had borne, died in 1700, the English Parliament had passed an Act of Settlement that excluded Catholics from the throne and named Sophia Electress of Hanover, the granddaughter of James I, and her heirs, as Anne's successors. The Scots were angry that they had not been consulted and it confirmed their belief that England cared little for their interests. They, too, now realised that it was essential to have a resolution to the question of union but they were fearful that they would lose their independence and receive nothing in return. Matters were further complicated by the War of the Spanish Succession, which began in 1701 when England, the Dutch Republic and the Holy Roman Empire allied together against France.

æ

Mary died in March 1702 and she left Tweeddale the barony of Steads, comprising the farms of Snawdon, Carfrae, and Danskine, which were held by the family until the estate was sold in 1967. He had two sons serving in the army: John, who was a Brigadier General and who fought under Marlborough, and William of Newhall, who was also a Brigadier General, and who had married Margaret Hay, daughter of John Hay of Linplum, with whom he had ten children. Tweeddale's two daughters, Anne and Jean, had married the Earls of Ross and Rothes respectively.

Tweeddale resurrected his father's plan to build a new house and began to consider the economics of this. He was well positioned in one respect. Daniel Defoe wrote in 1724 that the Tweeddales had 'planted above 6000 acres all full of Fir Trees'. This was clearly an exaggeration, but it followed the example set by many other landowners at this time, as so many were building new or improving old houses. Timber was very expensive and Scotland imported a large amount from Norway. Tweeddale appointed James Smith and his partner Alexander MacGill in 1698 to design a new house at Yester. Smith was described as 'the most experienced Architect' of Scotland, who had studied art in Italy and who had worked at the building of Holyrood, Hamilton Palace and Dalkeith Palace. He had already carried out two small assignments for Tweeddale and in his dual capacity as architect and building-contractor, he could be relied upon not only to design a grand mansion but also to provide the materials and skilled labour necessary to ensure proper execution. Smith designed an austere Baroque-styled piend-roofed house with two pavilions. Although greatly altered later, his design was much like that published in William Adam's *Vitruvius Scoticus*. Progress was very slow and the pavilions, where Tweeddale lived while the work on the main block continued, were only roofed over in 1704 and the main part of the house was not to be completed for over 20 years. The park and gardens were laid out and St Cuthbert's was closed for public worship. A new church in Gifford was designed by Smith and completed in Gifford in 1710 and the pulpit of St Cuthbert's was installed there.

&

Under an Act of 1696, Parliament had to be recalled within 20 days of a monarch's death but Queensberry knew that the next session of Parliament would bring all these problems to a head, so he chose to keep it adjourned for as long as possible. Anne dismissed most of her Whig ministers, who had been supportive of Queensberry, and replaced them with Tories led by Marlborough and Godolphin. The Scottish Parliament finally sat in June and contained 193 members: 58 representing the peers, 78 representing the lairds and 57 representing the burghs. Queensberry presented Anne's requirements to Parliament: the ratification of her right to rule, Supply, the security of the Kirk, the Hanoverian Succession and the negotiation of union. Hamilton and Tweeddale, despite his having been made a Privy Councillor in 1702, continued to try to block the queen's wishes and made an application for the dissolution of Parliament, since 'all parliaments do dissolve by the death of the king or queen'. They then left their seats and were followed by 74 of their supporters, leaving the remaining 119 to pass the legislation required by the queen.

Chancellor Marchmont was a staunch Presbyterian and was fearful that Queensberry would sacrifice the Presbyterian Settlement to his wish for union. He therefore ignored Queensberry's instructions and proposed an Act of Abjuration whereby Prince

James Stuart would be declared a traitor and officers of state in Scotland would have to take an oath abjuring any support of James's claim to the throne. Queensberry was angry as he felt, if this was voted through, the Scots would lose much of their bargaining power over union, as the Hanoverian Succession would then be assured. He wanted to keep both options open for as long as possible so as to extract the maximum benefit; but for whom one is less sure as he was a man of as great a personal ambition as Hamilton, albeit to a different end. Marchmont's Act passed by a majority of four, and did so without any Country Party votes as they remained outside Parliament; inspired by this defeat of Queensberry, they tried to return but he adjourned the sitting.

He and Anne then made sweeping changes to the government in Scotland. Marchmont was replaced as Chancellor by Seafield, who had been Secretary of State since 1696. Lockhart wrote of his having 'a mean and selfish a soul... a blank sheet of paper, which the Court might fill up with what they pleased'. Tarbat was appointed joint Secretary of State with the Jacobite John Erskine, Earl of Mar against Queensberry's wishes. Burnet described Tarbat as being 'full of ambition... recommending himself to all sides and parties by turns'. Tullibardine, Hamilton's brother-in-law, was appointed Lord Privy Seal.

Negotiations for union began in London in November, but the Tories were not as eager for union as their queen, as they disliked Presbyterianism and they had little love for Scotland in general. Sir Edward Seymour, MP for Exeter, considered by Burnet 'the ablest man of his party,' said that Scotland was 'a beggar, and whoever married a beggar, could only expect a louse for a portion'. Anne wanted 'an indissoluble union between the two nations... to establish the monarchy, secure the peace and increase the trade, wealth and happiness of both nations'. She wanted a United Kingdom and a Hanoverian Succession with no limitations set on it. The Scottish Commissioners agreed to the first point, but also wanted the representations of both kingdoms in one Parliament and mutual trade to be agreed, as well as financial compensation for the losses from Darien. Queensberry wanted to ensure that the Scottish Parliament imposed no further limitations on the royal prerogative and he was supported in this by Seafield and Mar. The priority of Marchmont, Loudon and Annandale was to secure the establishment of the Kirk. The negotiations, not surprisingly, made little progress and Anne adjourned the Commission in February 1703.

A new Scottish Parliament was called in 1703 which produced 237 Members. This was the last Scottish Parliament to be called and it represented a radical change from the previous one. The number of peers increased to 80 out of the 150 who were eligible to vote because Jacobites, such as the Earls of Erroll and Marischal, had decided to attend. There were 58 new members out of a total of 90 representing the lairds, and 43 new members out of a total of 67 representing the burghs; so 64% of those MPs who were not nobles were new, and they tended to be much younger than their predecessors. During this Parliament the numbers voting averaged over 200, an historically high percentage. The newcomers did not automatically support the government, as they contained a larger component of Jacobites and nationalists such as Andrew Fletcher, known as 'the Patriot,' who had represented East Lothian in 1681, but who had left Scotland until the Revolution. Fletcher, now aged 50, had been an early investor in the Company and he had introduced Paterson to Tweeddale's father and he was angry because he considered that the English had both caused the Company to collapse and were not sorry for having done so. He gathered a number of rich young men under his leadership, including four earls: Tweeddale's brother-in-law-Rothes, Rothes's brother Haddington, Montrose and Tweeddale's nephew, Roxburghe, none of whom was older than 23. Roxburghe was described by Lockhart as being 'a man of good sense... perhaps he was the best accomplished young man in Europe'. Another member was George Lockhart from Midlothian, who was equally young and rich and a fervent Jacobite, and he was to write the definitive contemporary history of this Parliament. Together they were loosely grouped under the name of the Cavaliers and were led by the Earl of Home. They supported Anne and the Tories, were tolerant of Episcopalianism, but wanted to see the Stuarts continue to rule in Scotland. To them, Jacobitism represented legitimacy, not just for the rights of the monarch, but for the rights of his people, and for the continuation of Scotland as a sovereign nation. Initially they gave their support to the Court Party because of Anne's support of it, but they were more naturally allies of Tweeddale and many were close to him in blood or through living in East Lothian.

Queensberry opened Parliament in May by reading Anne's Address, saying she 'recommended nothing but what is for your own security and welfare... we confidently expect... you will with concord and diligence bring matters to such a happy conclusion as shall establish a lasting union between us and our people.' His first objective was the vote for Supply which was crucial for Anne as she needed it to finance the war with the French. But the Country Party continued to maintain that the Parliament of 1702 had been illegal and that any future Scottish sovereign must be chosen free of English influence. Tweeddale went further, moving that 'before all other business the Parliament might proceed to make such conditions of government and regulations in the Constitution of this Kingdom to take place after the decease of Her Majesty and the heirs of her body as shall be necessary for the preservation of our religion and liberty'. He wanted to ensure that the succession was settled before the vote on Supply, Tweeddale's motion was passed after fifteen days, therby ruining Queensberry's strategy.

Fletcher supported Tweeddale and proposed an Act of Security, insisting no Supply be voted until other business was finished. He made his position clear: 'We have often had promise of good laws, and when we have given the sums demanded, those promises have been broken,' and asked 'whether this nation would be in a better condition, if in conferring our places and pensions the prince should be determined by the Parliament of Scotland, or by the Ministers of a court that make it their interest to keep us low and miserable.' He made it quite clear where he felt some people's true motives lay: 'He who is not for setting great limitations on the power of the prince... can act by no principle... unless that of being a slave to the court of England for his own advantage.' He finished with the lament 'we have been for so long a time so poor, so miserable, and depending, that we have neither heart nor courage, though we want not the means, to free ourselves'.

His Act of Security proposed that any successor to the Scottish crown, who was also monarch of England, should be subject to limitations designed to ensure the independence of Parliament. His Act was voted down in July but it was followed by four other such Acts, with the last from Tullibardine, who had succeded his father as Earl of Atholl, and which gathered together the core points of the debate. Roxburghe added a key clause, which stated that the successor to the crown of England could not also be the successor to the crown of Scotland unless Scotland's conditions were first met. Queensberry saw that this would effectively mean that Scotland would never be ruled by England and proposed that the clause be changed so that the only condition was that there had first to be a freedom of trade agreement between Scotland and England. Roxburghe agreed to this and the final draft stated that the Union of the Crowns should only continue 'under such conditions in point of liberty and trade secured to us as may preserve our government and Ministry from the influence of the neighbouring Ministry'. It also proposed that, if Anne had no heir, then the Scottish Parliament should chose a successor 'being always of the Royal Line of Scotland and of the true

Protestant religion'. This Act of Security was passed in July by 72 votes and it was hailed by Fletcher as 'an Act that preserves us from anarchy'. Queensberry refused to give it the Royal Assent until Supply had been granted, thus there was deadlock so he adjourned Parliament in September.

That month he met Simon Fraser at the suggestion of Argyll. Fraser was a dreadful man; he was the heir to Lord Lovat but the 9th Lord had settled the family estate on his daughter, Amelia, who Fraser tried to marry, but she rejected him. Fraser then raped and kidnapped her mother, who was Atholl's sister, and forcibly married her and she, surprisingly, decided to stay with Fraser. Fraser was convicted of abduction and rape and was sentenced to death but he escaped and lived in Skye. He received a pardon from King William and went to live in France, where he joined the court of James Stuart. There he became close to the French king and he suggested to Louis that the French should assist a Stuart rising in Scotland. This attracted Louis and he supported Fraser 'since Lord Lovat had been chosen to represent the whole body of loyal Scots, he desired to be understood as from that moment renewing with him all ancient alliances between the two nations'.

Fraser told Queensberry that it was Atholl who was at the centre of Jacobite plotting in Scotland and that he was supported by Hamilton and Seafield. Queensberry had told Anne about Fraser's original approach to him and he now saw a way both to regain favour with her and to attack his enemies, so he passed on to her Fraser's accusations and told her they were probably true. Atholl persuaded the queen they were false and Fraser fled to France. Fittingly, he ended on the scaffold after supporting the uprising of 1745, being the last Scottish peer to be executed.

Queensberry fought back by blaming Atholl, Seafield and Tarbat, who had been made the Earl of Cromartie, for the failures of the last Parliament. The three ministers went to see Anne in January 1704 and they urged her to recall Parliament, to look into

Fraser's accusations and to sack Queensberry. This affair became increasingly contentious and was called the Scotch Plot in England and the Queensberry Plot in Scotland. Atholl was furious about the accusations as he had just been made a duke by Anne. Lockhart wrote: 'Had not Queensberry trump'd up the Plot upon him, which did so exasperate him against the Court, that he joyn'd entirely with the Cavaliers... he became, all of a sudden, a violent Jacobite... tho by Reason of his Proud, Imperious, Haughty, Passionate Temper, he was no ways Capable to be the Leading Man of a Party.'

Tweeddale must have been delighted by all this as those close to him, though not necessarily of his party, had played a major role in defeating Queensberry. Many of his rivals were now discredited by the Scotch Plot. Argyll had died in 1703 and his young heir was only interested in fighting the French. Seafield now considered that Tweeddale was the only man who could bring the Court and Country parties together and he was encouraged in this by James Johnston, Tweeddale's old ally, who was living in retirement in England but who was still advising Godolphin on Scottish affairs. Tweeddale was told there was one condition: he had to propose the Hanoverian Succession. In return, he could negotiate limitations on the power of the Crown to take effect after Anne's death. These would include triennial elections and parliamentary control of public offices which Burnet believed offered 'full security to all their laws and liberties... and brought the Parliament into some equality with the Crown'. As Anne wanted the security of the Hanoverian Succession more than union, it was hoped that the Scots would abandon their Act of Security and accept the Succession in exchange for the English abandoning their proposal for union.

Tweeddale was now 59 and one of the most experienced politicians in Scotland. Lockhart wrote of his having 'never obtained any other Character, than that he was a well meaning, but simple

Man... forced against his Will by his Friends, and those he trusted (who made a mere Tool of him) to enter into many of these bad Measures he pursued; so I may safely say, He was the least ill-meaning Man of his Party, either thro' Inclination or Capacity'. Throughout his life he had not been held in high esteem, by his father, by Lauderdale, by King Charles, by the Darien investors nor by his colleagues in Parliament, but he was more canny than he appeared; he usually had poor hands to play but he tended to play them well, if subtly, and he usually got what he wanted.

Seafield met Tweeddale in Edinburgh but found him very reluctant to serve as High Commissioner. Tweeddale had always been a loyal servant of the Crown, but only if he believed that the monarch was pursuing the interests of Scotland. He told Seafield the Country Party was less supportive of the English because they wanted to interfere with the Scottish legal process by formally examining the Scotch Plot, and that this made it even less likely that the Hanoverian Succession would be accepted. However, he was both realistic and honourable and he agreed to serve his monarch, and protect his country's interests by acting as High Commissioner. A grateful Anne wrote to him: 'Your own modesty and backwardness in the concerns of your own family will always be an argument with me to have the more regard to them.'

Tweeddale sought to distance himself from control from London, but Godolphin wanted to have as many supporters of the Succession in Tweeddale's administration as possible, so he was given very limited scope to change the ministry. Seafield, Cromarty, Atholl and Sir James Stewart all retained their posts and Johnston came out of retirement as Lord Register. However, Tweeddale did get his nephew Roxburghe appointed Secretary of State for Scotland. Tweeddale's direct support base in Parliament became known as the New Party, but it consisted of only 30 members who were principally young followers of Fletcher as well as nobles including Hamilton's brothers Selkirk and Belhaven, Rothes, Haddington, Montrose, Marchmont and Annandale, all of whom were generally united by their support of the Hanoverian Succession, but with the limitations set out in the Act of Succession. Not all of them, however, were considered honourable men. Lockhart wrote of Rothes, who was married to Tweeddale's youngest daughter, Jean, that he 'had not... one good Property to recommend him, being False to a great Degree... extremely ambitious, ridiculous, vain, and conceited, (though of very ordinary Parts and Accomplishments) extravagantly Proud, and scandalously Mercenary... He had neither Sense nor Honesty to resist the first Temptation.'

Queensberry initially gave his support to the New Party as did the Earl of Mar, who had married Tweeddale's cousin, Lady Margaret Hay in 1703, but who was known as 'Bobbing Jock' because of his ever shifting support for those from whom he could gain benefit. Hamilton now broke from Tweeddale because he could not support the Hanoverian Succession as he considered himself the most credible successor to Anne if the Stuarts refused to convert to Protestantism and he was supported in this by Atholl and the Jacobites.

Tweeddale told Godolphin that the Scottish Parliament needed to have its key concerns settled before considering the Succession, but Godolphin ignored his advice and told him to press on with the session which opened in July. Anne gave Tweeddale as much help as she could, telling him to offer Parliament 'unquestionable proof of our resolutions to maintain the government both in Church and state as by law established in that our kingdom, and to consent to such laws as shall be found wanting for the further security of both'. In her Address she could not have been more direct: 'The rent has become wider; nay, division has proceeded to such a height, as to prove matter of encouragement to our enemies beyond sea to employ their emissaries among you, in order to debauch our good subjects from their allegiance and to render that our ancient kingdom a scene of blood and disorder.' She asked for 'the settling of the Succession in the Protestant line, as that which is absolutely necessary for our own peace and happiness, as well as our quiet and security in all our dominion... and for the reputation of our affairs abroad, and consequently for the strengthening of the Protestant interest everywhere [delay] may have very dangerous consequences, and a disappointment of it would infallibly make our kingdom the seat of war, and expose it to devastation and ruin.' She added a small carrot, but refrained from spelling out the consequences of refusal: 'We have empowered our Commissioner to give the royal assent to whatever can in reason be demanded, and it is in our power to grant, for securing the sovereignty and liberties of that our ancient kingdom.'

In his opening Address to Parliament, Tweeddale emphasised the queen's support for Scotland: 'Nothing has escaped Her Majesty's care that can any ways contribute to make you a flourishing and happy people, she reckoning the welfare, peace and prosperity of her subjects the only way to her own greatness and happiness... and yet as if all this were too little, Her Majesty extends her care for you further, in recommending to you... the settling the Succession in the Protestant line.' If Parliament gave her this then, Tweeddale promised, she would accede to all their requirements, including trade, and he ended, showing the essential modesty of his character, 'I have spoke long, contrary to my way and inclination'.

Tweeddale did not have an easy time of it. Hamilton, now sole leader of the Country Party, proposed a motion that Parliament 'will not proceed to the nomination of a successor until we have had a previous treaty with England in relation to our commerce and other concerns with that nation'. This motion succeeded in uniting the opposition to any Court policy put forward by Tweeddale and he told Godolphin that free trade would be 'the most popular handle to throw off the Succession at this time'. He knew an agreement on trade was the key hurdle that England would have to cross if their intentions on treating Scotland with any degree of equality were to be credible.

Tweeddale asked Rothes to answer Hamilton but Rothes proposed that Parliament should first 'rectify our constitution and vindicate and secure the sovereignty and independence of the kingdom'. This was the complete reverse of what Anne had wanted and what Tweeddale was expected to support. It is not known if Rothes had discussed his proposal with Tweeddale first, but it seems likely he had done so. There was long discussion over whether Hamilton or Rothes's motion should be debated first and it was finally proposed that the two motions be combined and they were carried by a large majority of 55. Tweeddale wrote to Godolphin: 'As I have told your lordship in former letters, no other could be expected, considering the ferment the nation is in... I see not what can be done but to adjourn till such time as I can have Her Majesty's direction now that the main point is lost.'

He then wrote to Anne, saying the problem was 'the ill temper this nation has been in for some years through the bad usage they have met with from their neighbours in most of these concerns [which have] been of late mightily increased by the House of Lords' proceedings in the matter of the plot, of which great advantage has been taken, to raise such an aversion in them to the setting of the succession at this time that they could hardly bear even the mentioning of it... but seeing they have entered into a resolve which put that of for this session, things are so far altered, that I know not what I can do, without acquainting Her Majesty and receiving her instructions.' He realised that he could not satisfy his sovereign and his people so he asked the queen to find a replacement 'who may be more capable and so more successful than I have been'.

Anne would not let him go and so he had to handle Hamilton's insistence that the Act of Security be passed before Supply was voted. The passing of his joint motion with Rothes had made Hamilton very popular in Scotland. Lockhart wrote: 'Nothing was to be seen or heard that night, but jollity, mirth and a universal satisfaction and approbation of what was done... the members that had appeared more eminently in behalf of the resolve, were caressed and huzzaed as they passed in the streets, by vast numbers.'

Hamilton now suggested that the Act of Supply be 'tacked' with the Act of Security so that Tweeddale could pass them both together. Johnston advised that this could be done in England but not in Scotland because 'here Parliament sits in one house and tacking of Acts may obstruct voting of them both, [in addition it was] a straitening of the queen, who may possibly consent to the one, and not to the other'. Fletcher accused Johnston of selling himself to the English and said that his 'letter by the queen to Parliament was written when no Scotsman was about her, and so behoved to be by English influence'.

As the mood in Parliament deteriorated, Ross, who was married to Tweeddale's daughter Anne, moved that Supply for two months be voted immediately, and again after four months, but only after the Act of Security was passed but Roxburghe countered that nothing should be done until the Act was passed. It outwardly appears that Tweeddale had no control over his wider family or his friends or he may have been quietly orchestrating them as he refused to do anything, saying in Parliament: 'What hand I had in the Act of Security, that I added more clauses thereto than any other whatsoever, and that I am still in my private opinion of the same mind now as then [I would] have to acquaint Her Majesty before I could do anything.' It was an honest statement bringing his true feelings into the open but showing the hopelessness of his official position. Michael Fry condemns Tweeddale for being 'feeble', but he was no Queensberry; he was not a man determined to grasp all he could for himself by pushing the interests of England over those of Scotland; rather he wanted to protect the true interests of Scotland for as long as possible and to try and get as much as possible for his country before having to bow to the inevitable. Lockhart echoed the view of Parliament that Tweeddale and his ministers 'were obliged to inform the queen that their measures, being quite broke, matters were come to that height, she must either allow the commissioner to grant the royal assent to the Act of Security, or resolve to adjourn the Parliament, without obtaining money to pay her troops'.

Tweeddale did advise the queen to accept the Act of Security, as 'absolutely necessary to quieten the minds of your people' but he also privately proposed to Godolphin another solution. He suggested, as Parliament was so committed to an Act of Security, that it should be 'willing to accept [one] without the clause of communication of trade'. This initially appears very odd, as he had no authority to offer this and it ran explicitly against the wishes of Parliament. However, it shows that he recognised the reality of the situation and that this could resolve an otherwise intractable problem. In addition, he knew that the vote of Supply was becoming increasingly vital for the queen so he felt that this was a clever way to satisfy both parties. Anne's advisers agreed that it would be 'better to satisfy the desires of the people, by allowing that Act the royal assent, than by refusing it to increase the divisions, and be obliged to disband the army'. This was pure *realpolitik* – they had an immediate need that had to be met but they had no intention of allowing the Act of Security to have any meaningful life.

It is, however, unclear how or when Tweeddale was able to alter the text of the Act. Sir John Clerk of Penicuik wrote that the clause relating to the 'liberty of the plantations was by some trick or other left out, for though it was voted and agreed to... yet it seems it never had it'. He added: 'in none of the printed Acts does it appear, though by the by it was chiefly to obtain the benefits of the plantations that the union was agreed to in Scotland, at least it was the chief instrument used for the settlement of the question.'

Parliament was adjourned for a week and when it resumed at the beginning of August Tweeddale announced he was now under

instructions 'to pass an Act of Security that might sufficiently secure the nation'. His wording was interesting and Hamilton
seized on it: 'It was not an Act of Security, but the Act of Security
that they were for.' The Act received another reading, the missing
clause on trade was not commented on and Tweeddale touched
it with the sceptre, giving it the royal approval; he then approved
the Act of Supply for six months. He had succeded in his objectives as the queen had what she wanted and the Scottish people
had their Act of Security. It was a remarkable achievement and
not even Lockhart smelt a rat, believing that Anne's advisers had
told her to sign it as it would be 'better to satisfy the Desires of
the People by allowing that Act the Royal Assent than by refusing
it to increase the Divisions and be obliged to disband the Army'.

The Commissioners to negotiate the Union of the Crowns had
now to be selected, but the animosity between Hamilton and
Atholl prevented any decision being reached and the parliamentary session continued for another month amidst increasing ac-
rimony; Hamilton challenged Fletcher to a duel and Tweeddale
had to exact a promise from each of them to desist. He then, with
what must have been a great sense of relief, adjourned Parliament for six weeks, but it was not to meet again till July 1705.
He was probably the only man in Scotland who could have
achieved the double feat of approving both the Acts of Security
and Supply, but he had gained no pleasure and little thanks from
it, and he again offered Anne his resignation.

The queen again refused this and instead rewarded him by appointing him Chancellor, and allowed him to change his ministry.
He dismissed Atholl and made Roxburghe joint-Secretary with
Seafield. Lockhart, who clearly underestimated Tweeddale, wrote
disparagingly about him: 'They saw the Marquis of Tweeddale
and his party were so insignificant that they were trampled upon
and despised throughout the whole nation yet nevertheless the
Lord Godolphin favoured them, because their scheme of settling

the succession, by the concession of a few deluding limitations would, he thought, be safest for England, and afterwards easily repealed by a subsequent Parliament.' His view was shared by some, but it was both inaccurate and unfair and Tweeddale's reputation grew in the years ahead.

The Act of Security was badly received in England, where the political landscape had changed as the Whigs were enjoying a renaissance of support in the Commons as well as being in the majority in the Lords. Their leadership came from a group of nobles known as the Junto, which included Lord Somers and the Earls of Orford, Wharton, Halifax and Sunderland. The Commons debated Scottish affairs in November and blamed Tweeddale for failing to secure the Succession. Godolphin found himself under attack and was accused: 'By yielding to the Scottish will, the Minister has betrayed the Crown's interest in favour of Hanover.' Godolphin elliptically defended himself, saying 'Whatever ill look it might have at present, it is not without remedy.' Indeed, the Tories' attack on him made the Whigs more eager to give him their support and, as his immediate aim was to secure Supply to continue the war, Godolphin did not mind where his support came from. This criticism of him lends further confirmation of Tweeddale's skill in getting the two Acts through Parliament.

Tweeddale sent Roxburghe to London to assess the situation and he reported back that 'the design of the Whigs... is to force us into the Succession'. He set out realistically the position the Scots found themselves in: 'How shall we be sure but hardships be put upon us, so soon as the succession is over, if we be not secured against them antecedently, as much as a poor nation can be secured against the oppressions of a richer, since it is always in their power, and since they already seem to threaten us with it?' He added his belief as to the reasons why the Scots would eventually chose union: 'Trade with most, Hanover with some, ease and security with others.'

Lockhart blamed Roxburghe as much as he did Tweeddale and wrote of him: 'It was a thousand pities a Man capable to do good, should have proven the very Bane and Cut-Throat of his Country, by being extremely false and disingenuous, and so indifferent to the Ties of Honour, Friendship, Vows, and Justice, that he sacraficed them all, and the Interest of his Country, to his Designs, viz. Rebauce and Ambition.'

The economic problems faced by both Scotland and England because of the war were stark. Total Scottish imports in 1704 amounted to £66 million, twice the level of exports. The war was going well, but at huge cost to the English, who were desperate for cash and troops from wherever they could find them; and to the Scots, who had to contribute and pay for three regiments. The Bank of Scotland stopped paying out coin for notes in 1704 and had to raise more capital. Roxburghe was absolutely right about England's capacity to threaten and the House of the Lords was not prepared to let the Scots resolve the issues at their leisure. Somers lead the attack, which consisted of both carrot and stick. The carrot offered was that the queen would appoint Commissioners to negotiate a full incorporating Union with a single Parliament and a unified free trade area. The stick was the passing of the Alien Act in February 1705 stating that all Scots would be treated as aliens, and trade would be severely penalised, unless Scotland accepted the Hanoverian Succession without limitations by December 25th 1705. Exports to England of Scotland's prime products, linen, cattle, coal and sheep would be banned and the Scots would not be allowed to import English guns and ammunition. Underlying this was the threat of war and overt troop movements in the Borders were begun. These actions succeeded in uniting the Tories and Whigs against the Scots, thus making England's ultimate victory inevitable.

Roxburghe was in regular discussions with all the chief players in Scotland and wrote openly to Baillie about these. He was under no illusions: 'Instead of proposing us favours, as a separate kingdom, if we do settle the same succession with them, they make hard laws upon us, if we do it not within such a time; nor without an entire union will they ever give us any favour in trade. I am thoroughly convinced that if we do not go into the succession, or an union, very soon, conquest will certainly be.' Johnston agreed with him and also wrote to Baillie: 'You may settle the succession upon limitations [or] you may accept of a union. If you will do neither, you may expect all the mischief that can be done you; for you and your independence are not so great but that you must depend either on France or England, and sure they will not suffer you to depend on France.'

Tensions were high and Scottish fury against the English erupted over the affair of the English ship, the *Worcester*, which had sailed in July 1704 into the port of Leith as her Captain, Thomas Green, wanted to join a convoy sailing to London. This came to the attention of Roderick Mackenzie, the Company Secretary. The East Indian Company had seized one of the Company's ships in Dover in January and Mackenzie wanted his revenge. He obtained a warrant to seize the *Worcester*, Green and his crew were accused of piracy and they were brought to trial in March 1705 on the charge of having destroyed one of the Company's ships and Green and seventeen others were found guilty and condemned to death. Johnston wrote of the reaction in London, saying 'they lay it entirely at Tweeddale and the New Party's door'. The queen was lobbied but she felt reluctant to formally interfere in Scottish affairs, so she privately advocated mercy. Tweeddale again offered his resignation and this time Anne accepted it, and reinstated Seafield as Chancellor. Seafield advised Godolphin that Green would have to be sacrificed to placate the mob in Edinburgh and he and two of his officers were hanged, his crew were later released.

The crisis over the *Worcester* severely damaged Tweeddale and the New Party. Even Roxburghe deserted him and turned towards Argyll as his choice to be the next High Commissioner. Argyll had succeeded his father in 1703, aged only 23, and he had fought under Marlborough against the French. Lockhart respected him but had no illusions about his approach to politics: 'as far as I can understand [he] knows nor proposes no way to loose such Gordian knots, but like Alexander the Great to cut them with his sword'. Godolphin liked Argyll and made him High Commissioner in place of Tweeddale. His great weakness was the debts he had inherited, but Lockhart suggested his inheritance went further: 'He succeeded his Father, not only in his Estate, Honours, and Employments; but likewise in his Lewdness and Disloyalty. His sense rather lay in a sudden Flash of Wit, than a solid Conception and Reflexion... his Word so Sacred, that one might assuredly depend on it..he gained the leading of the Presbyterians... and was a very significant Member.' Argyll was indeed an arrogant young man; when Anne and Seafield asked him to include Tweeddale in his ministry he not only refused but resigned and Anne gave way and gave him what he wanted. Roxburghe was discarded and, to the surprise of many, especially Anne, Argyll brought Queensberry into his team. Anne was adamant about rejecting Queensberry: 'a thing I can never consent to, his last tricking behaviour having made him more odious to me than ever... it grates my soul to take a man into my service that has not only betrayed us, but tricked me several times, one that has been obnoxious to his own countrymen these many years and one that I can never be convinced can be of any use.' Lockhart agreed, saying Queensberry was 'inwardly a very Devil, standing at nothing to advance his own interests and designs... he was altogether void of Honour, Loyalty, Justice, religion and Ingenuity; an Ungrateful Deserter of, and Rebel to his Prince, the Ruin and Bane of his Country, and the Aversion of all Loyal and True Scots Men.' Argyll must have been persuasive as the queen was unable to resist him. Queensberry was given the post of Lord Privy Seal and Annandale and Loudon were appointed joint-Secretaries of State.

Parliament was divided almost equally between the Court Party and the alliance between the Country Party and the Cavaliers. Lockhart wrote of Hamilton: 'Never was a Man so well qualified to be the Head of a Party... the Cavaliers, and these of the Country Party, had a great Opinion and Honour for him.' He also presciently noted: 'He was extremely Cautious and Wary in engaging in any Project that was dangerous... but his great Failing lay in his being too Selfish and Revengeful.' Tweeddale's New Party held the balance and its prime objective now was to achieve the Hanoverian Succesion but with limitations. Its strategy was to vote tactically and, because of this, it became known as the *Squadrone Volante*. Sir John Clerk wrote that Tweeddale was:

A very good Man but not properly qualified for Court intrigues. They were for opposing everything which they durst oppose but to keep firmly in their view the succession of the Crown in the House of Hanover. They pretended to be great patriots and to stand chiefly in defence of the rights and privileges of the subjects; in a word, the publick good and the liberty of the subjects were still in their mouths, but in their Hearts they were known to have Court preferments and places in the chiefest degree of veneration. These were the springs and motives of all their Actions, which appeared in a hundred instances thereafter. However I must say that such a *Squadrone Volante* in any Parliament seems to be always a happy means in the hands of Providence to keep the several masters of an Administration in their duty, for people in great power seldom fail to take more upon them than falls to their shoes.

It was easy to criticise such a seemingly opportunistic voting strategy but one commentator wrote more kindly, and truthfully, of Tweeddale that 'he appears as an honest but naive politician devoid of motives of enhancing his personal fortune in his quest to resolve the succession issue'. Macky, in his *Memoirs* of 1705, agreed: 'He hath good sense, is very modest, much a man of honour, and hot when piqued; is highly esteemed in his country, and may make a considerable figure in it now. He is a short, brown man towards sixty years old.'

Parliament opened at the beginning of July to debate the proposed Treaty of Union and the Succession, while Supply remained a key concern. In her Address Anne made her priority clear and told members 'to go to the settlement of the Succession before all other business'. However, Seafield wrote to Godolphin: 'I know the Succession is the most desirable, but I am very afraid it will not succeed at this time... whereas that of a Treaty seems more probable to succeed.' The session was full of tumult, Fletcher and Roxburghe had to be prevented by soldiers from fighting a duel and within a week Argyll showed his ruthlessness by replacing Annandale with Mar because he had proposed that limitations on the Succession be debated before any debate on the Succession itself. Hamilton then proposed a motion requiring that the Treaty be signed and that limitations be voted on before any debate on Succession could take place and this was passed by a majority of 43, despite being opposed by the *Squadrone*.

Queensberry had not attended the session, but he now left London and arrived in Edinburgh on the 23rd. Mar had proposed an Act for a Treaty three days before his arrival and this had been supported by Seafield and the *Squadrone* but only on the proviso that 'if limitations on the successor be voted, though not passed, they will then be for the treaty'. This strange concept was, in effect, very clever, for it allowed full discussion on all points and for agreements to be reached, without necessarily being officially voted on and it again demonstrates Tweeddale's political skills. Fletcher tried to impose a whole range of limitations, but he could find no seconder and thereafter his influence in Parliament diminished greatly. Parliament then passed an Act for a Council of Trade and Argyll achieved further success on a range of other proposals.

The crucial debate on the Treaty of Union, and on the choice of Commissioners to negotiate it, began on September 1st. Hamilton proposed a clause that was standard to all such treaties since the time of James I, 'that the Union to be treated on shall not derogate any ways from any fundamental law, ancient privileges, offices, right, dignities and liberties of the kingdom'. Despite being supported by the *Squadrone*, it was defeated by two votes and this was the Court Party's first key victory of the session. Lockhart said the vote was lost because 'seven or eight of the Cavalier and Country parties were absent'.

The next key vote was on whether Parliament or the queen should choose the Commissioners. Seafield expected that Hamilton would insist that Parliament should appoint them. Lockhart wrote: 'most of the Cavalier and Country parties, and all the *Squadrone* (these last... being inclined to go along with every motion that they thought would obstruct the Treaty's taking effect at that time) did ahere.' He tells what then happened:

> While the Rolls were calling (it being by this Time late) many of the Members... went out of the House expecting... no more business that night; when instantly after the last name in the Roll was called, the Duke of Hamilton... moved "that the nomination of the Commissioners for the treaty should be left wholly to the queen" he gave as his reasons 'the Parliament is too much in heats and feuds and can never agree on proper persons, but the queen, who is free from partiality, may doubtless make a good choice. But if she shall make a bad one, we will be safe, for all must

return to us again, and we may send the Act back to the place whence it came." This, you may be sure, was very surprising to the Cavaliers, and Country party... and never at any time from his Grace who had, from the beginning... roared and exclaimed against it and about 12 or 15 of them ran out of the House in rage and despair saying... 'twas to no purpose to stay any longer, since the Duke had deserted, and so basely betray'd them'... the whole Act was approved... by eight voices... From this day we date the Commencement of Scotland's Ruine.

Hamilton's behaviour was extraordinary, as his action was exactly the reverse of the strategy he had been pursuing since Parliament sat, and was the opposite of what the night before he had told his key party members he would do. One explanation perhaps lies in the secret discussions he had been having with both the French and the English over recent weeks and from which he had been able to assess their objectives and how he could best profit from matching them. He also held the ultimate card in being next in line to the throne were the Stuarts to remain Catholic.

He had met four times an agent of the French court called Nathaniel Hooke, whose instructions were to inspire revolt in Scotland and restore the Stuarts to the throne. Hamilton asked for money to bribe Members of Parliament, but Hooke answered that he only wanted his support for a Stuart restoration. Hooke then asked him: 'You have said you will take up arms. When will that be?' Hamilton answered 'I cannot say but you can count on it that we will act when Queen Anne dies. Perhaps I will be obliged to support the measures put forward by the Court, but my purposes are still the same.' Hooke then challenged him: 'It is said you have come to an arrangement with the Earl of Stair'; Hamilton did not answer but he obviously believed he could become king. He told Hooke: 'A Protestant prince with no pretensions at all to the Crown of England would meet fewer obstacles.'

Hamilton had huge debts and in January 1705 Johnston had written: 'I have had my suspicions, but now I am certain, that Duke Hamilton is tampering… with [Godolphin] He must have his debts paid.' Colonel Graham, an agent of the English minister Harley, wrote to Johnston in March of a conversation he had had with Hamilton who had asked 'to be fully instructed to what point his skill or service may be required and may be plainly informed without reserve how he may be most useful'. Hamilton was clearly playing both sides and believed he would win whatever happened: if the Treaty passed the English would pay his debts and, if it failed, then the French would help him succeed Anne.

After Hamilton's vote the opposition collapsed and, in September, Argyll touched with his sceptre the Acts for a Treaty of Union, for Supply, and for a council of trade. Hamilton now wrote to Colonel Graham, claiming his dues: 'Our Parliament is now drawing to a close. I have done Her Majesty signal service in it.' His formidable mother was, however, most displeased with him, writing to his sister: 'It passes my comprehension to find out a tolerable face for his acting this session… and I am ashamed on his behalf that I know neither what to say or where to look.'

The antagonistic clauses in the Alien Act were repealed in December, but the political situation in England was now more uncertain as the recent elections had resulted in a hung Parliament and the Whigs feared the influx of Scottish Tory MPs that would result from Union. In February Anne named the 31 Scottish Commissioners who were mostly allies of Queensberry and contained only one anti-Unionist, George Lockhart. Hamilton, Tweeddale, Atholl, and the Lord Advocate, Sir James Stewart, were all omitted; however, other members of the *Squadrone* were included, as were three of Argyll's kinsmen, Argyll having returned to his preferred profession of fighting the French, his job in Scotland done. The English Commissioners were named in

April and were dominated by the Whigs, with only two junior Tories included.

Godolphin expressed his feelings in a letter to Marlborough: 'The settling of the government of Scotland and the management of the revenues there is a grievous burden, and the uneasiness of people's laying weight upon every trifle after one has overcome the greatest difficulties to satisfy makes me weary of my life. The English Commissioners made their position quite clear from the start: 'The two kingdoms of England and Scotland be forever united into one kingdom... they be represented by one and the same Parliament; succession to the Crown would be as in the English Act of Settlement.'

The *Squadrone* were uncertain as to what it should do as their preference was still for a Hanoverian Succession with limitations. Baillie put his party's, and the nation's, position in a letter to Roxburghe: 'I cannot satisfy myself which would be more for the New Party's interest. It's hard to know that such a union can be good for Scotland.' But he thought it would happen because of 'the temper of this nation... and how willing to truckle under England for private advantage, I believe wise men will be forced to drink the potion to prevent greater evils'. Tweeddale agreed with this and the *Squadrone* privately gave their support to the English Commissioners' position, whilst publicly representing itself as an honest broker. The Court Party recognised the commercial basis of the need for Union and made this the condition for accepting the Hanoverian Succession. They accepted the English terms on the condition that Scotland was allowed 'full freedom and intercourse of trade and navigation' and the English replied that this was a 'necessary consequence of the entire Union'.

The key factor that secured agreement was, however, money; which perhaps had been the ultimate driver behind the behaviour of many of the key Scottish politicians since the Company collapsed. Sixteen of the twenty-five articles of the final Treaty focused on economic matters and a key consideration was over the combined National Debt. As Scotland had never had a National Debt, it was agreed that England would pay a lump sum, known as the Equivalent, as compensation for Scotland taking on part of the Debt. Lockhart called the Equivalent 'a mighty bait, a swingeing bribe to buy off the Scots members of Parliament from their duty to their country'. But he was unfair, if only because the Equivalent was paid more widely than just to Members of Parliament; it also included repayment, plus interest, of the money invested in the Company, as long as the Scots' agreed to close it. All of the fifteen members of the committee set up to structure it were either from the Court party or from the *Squadrone* and included Tweeddale and three other directors of the Company. They had employed two Scottish professors of mathematics to do the calculations that determined the size of the sum due and in 1702 they had proposed that it should be paid at a rate of £1.5 million per annum, but in 1706 this was changed to a one-off payment of £50 million.

The discussions on Union moved very quickly and the Commissioners agreed everything by July and Scotland was allocated 45 members in the Commons and 16 peers in the Lords. Godolphin authorised a secret payment of £2.5 million to meet arrears of salary to Scottish politicians who held public office. This was not sinister as it was common for politicians to fund public expenditure directly if taxation revenues proved inadequate in the expectation of compensation through pensions or other such means. Mar had discussed Tweeddale's arrears from his time as High Commissioner and had 'assured him of all the assistance in my power,' but added, in rather a Machiavellian manner, 'that much would depend on himself to make it in my power or not'. Commentators, both at the time and later, considered that these payments were used to secure votes for Union from Court and *Squadrone* supporters, rather than to buy votes from their opposition parties. A table drawn up by Allan MacInnes shows that this was, in fact, the case: 27 out of the 48 members of the Court Party who were owed arrears were paid; 7 of the *Squadrone* were owed and 5 were paid; and 16 of the Country Party were in arrears but only 2 were paid. Major recipients were Seafield, with £490,000; Tweeddale, Atholl and Marchmont, with £100,000 each; and Roxburghe, with £50,000. There were 32 recipients in total with 7 receiving £10,000 or less, including £6,000 to the messenger 'that brought down the Treat of Union'. However, it was Queensberry who received the bulk of the money, totalling £1.6 million, both for genuine arrears due to him, as well as for other unnamed reasons.

Queensberry, once again High Commissioner, opened Parliament in October 1706. His key ministers were Seafield and Mar, who proved an extremely efficient President of Parliament. Tweeddale continued his policy of not showing his hand as the *Squadrone* still held the balance of power. He had recently suffered from the loss of his younger son, John, aged only 48, who had fought under Marlborough at Schellenberg in 1704 and at Ramillies in 1706 but who had died later that year of fever 'to the regret of the whole army'.

Much needed to be done to get the Treaty of Union approved. The key Estate Queensberry needed was that of the peers and in this he was successful. Burnet later wrote: 'It was the nobility that in every vote turned the scale for the union... it was said, many of them were bought off to sell their country and their birthright... the poor noblemen and the poor boroughs made a great majority in Parliament, and were easily to be purchased by the Court.' The royal burghs remained resolutely opposed, although the lesser burghs were in favour. The Cavaliers, of whom Atholl had become leader after Home's death, remained firmly against Union. The last important institution was that of the Kirk where Carstares, now Principal of the University of Edinburgh, proved key in convincing its members to support Union. The mood in the country as a whole was, however, very negative and Lockhart believed that 'the whole nation appears against the Union'.

Parliament moved to proceed with the first reading of the Treaty by a majority of 66, and the Court party was delighted by the strong support of the *Squadrone*. Queensberry then began the process of debating and then voting on each of the 25 articles in turn. The first article, providing for the Union of Scotland and England into one kingdom, Great Britain, was the most crucial, if that fell the Treaty would fall. Hamilton argued against the article, but without much conviction but the debate that followed was full of passion and, two days later, the article was passed by 116 to 83.

Mar was disappointed at the size of the majority. The peers voted 46 for to 21 against; the lairds 37 for to 33 against; and the burghs 33 for to 29 against. Two members of the *Squadrone* voted against, the rest for, and they were joined by a further 25 members who had previously voted with the opposition. Throughout the whole process the Court Party rarely enjoyed an absolute majority in the House on any vote and so the role of the *Squadrone* proved crucial. Of the 113 Court members, 59% voted in support in more than 15 divisions and 37% in more than 25 divisions; for the *Squadrone's* 26 members the percentages were 69% and 53% respectively; and for the Country Party's 103 members the percentages were only 27% and 5% respectively. MacInness's conclusion was that 'the voting strength of the *Squadrone* was vital to securing Union. By throwing in their lot with the Court Party, they consistently secured majorities that prevented amendments to all but one of the fifteen articles contested by the division of the house. Yet their actual voting strength was only decisive in securing the majority in two divisions... even with their combined strength, the Court Party and the *Squadrone* only achieved an outright majority on four occasions.' There was, however, a substantial amount of cross-voting in all three parties and much of this was due to Mar's skill in incentivising members, especially of the Country Party, to vote against their own Party's position on a number of articles. They were rewarded for this later with office or other favours.

A major challenge was to pass the Act of Security for the Church. This was achieved by a clause promising 'perpetual security to Presbyterian government,' thus removing the Kirk from the sovereignty of the British Parliament. This was a very fundamental freedom, since the Scots considered Presbyterianism as the 'true Protestant religion,' whereas it was the monarchy that preserved the Church of England. Union was thus not entirely seamless as the General Assembly could also place constitutional blocks on the united Parliament. Parliament voted for the Act by a majority of 75, far larger than that for union. Atholl and Hamilton were among the 38 voting against, but it was the abstainers who constituted the largest group for this, and for any other, vote.

Queensberry could not yet celebrate victory. Debate resumed in November 'that the Crown should pass on the death of Anne to the Electress Sophia of Hanover or heirs of her body'. Hamilton immediately said that settlement of the Hanoverian Succession should include limitations but the vote was carried 114 to 57; Tweeddale and the *Squadrone* having accepted the inevitable and after that everything proceeded smoothly. Hamilton could have derailed the whole process when he proposed that all members who were opposed to the Treaty should sign a National Address and then leave Parliament but on the day it was to be signed he did not attend Parliament, claiming he had toothache, and he became completely discredited. On January 16th 1707 the Treaty of Union and Act of Security for the Church were ratified together as the Scottish Act of Union by 110 votes to 67. Queensberry had retained the support of the *Squadrone* throughout and, whilst he must take the credit for the overall success of the process, Tweeddale must also take credit for his political skill in getting the process to the position it reached under his Ministry, for keeping the *Squadrone* together, for his typical self-effacing loyalty, for the consistency of his support of the queen and for the dignity he showed throughout. The Scottish Act passed in the Commons very swiftly, with the third reading being voted through on February 1707 by 274 votes to 116. In the Lords it passed in only three days and the Act came into force on May 1st. Tweeddale was able to share in the political rewards as he nominated eleven of the 45 Scottish Members to the new Parliament, Queensberry nominated 13 and Argyll 5. Tweeddale was appointed one of the sixteen Representative Peers to sit in the House of Lords and his nephew Roxburghe was made a duke.

In August, a dozen wagons guarded by 120 Scots dragoons brought the Equivalent to Edinburgh Castle. A large mob threw stones at the wagons and the soldiers as they passed. If they had expected that these wagons contained cash amounting to the whole of the Equivalent then they had every right to do so, for the wagons contained only £19 million of the £50 million promised. The balance was paid in paper, principally Exchequer bills and notes, which could not be cashed in Scotland and which paid no interest. The Equivalent had finally been designed to satisfy four purposes: the first was to establish a fund to pay the Scottish contribution to the English National Debt over a fifteen-year period, but no such fund was ever set up; the second was to cover the cost of standardising the Scottish coinage with that of England, which was calculated at £6.5 million; and the third was to compensate the shareholders of the Company for their losses and for the cost of winding it up. The shareholders received £29 million, or 58%, of the Equivalent, and this amount covered 72% of their original investment. Tweeddale and his family received £390,000; Queensberry £235,000; Anna, Duchess of Hamilton £235,000; and the Countess of Wemyss, the Countess of Roxburghe and the Earl of Argyll received £130,000 each. No more than 100 out of the 234 Members of Parliament who voted were shareholders in the Company and no one Party had a dominance of shareholders, with the Court and Country parties each having around 40 shareholders.

The final purpose was to pay, out of any remaining balance, those owed money by the Scottish government. Almost 1,000 soldiers shared £12 million, of which several of the senior officers each received £250,000. The Civil List comprised 935 individuals who collectively received £10 million for arrears of salaries, fees and pensions. Tweeddale received £125,000, on top of what he had already received as a shareholder, and others who benefited included Sir James Stewart, Queensberry, Melville and Atholl. Lockhart summed up his feelings: 'The truth of the matter lies here, a Sum of Money was necessary to be distributed amongst the Scots: and this distribution of it amongst the Proprietors of the African Company, was the cleanliest way of bribing a nation, to undo themselves; and alas! It had the design'd effect.' The Errolls, however, had once more gone against the trend. The 13th Earl had voted against Union and, on rumours of a French invasion in 1708, he was imprisoned in Edinburgh castle. He died in 1718 and his title passed to his sister.

The Exchequer notes that were the large percentage of the payment fell sharply in value as the recipients tried to sell them. Only after the war ended in 1714 were the notes allocated a coupon of 5%, and the amount required to pay this interest came out of taxes raised in Scotland. Indeed, the extra taxes on wines, beers and spirits imposed on Scotland after Union amounted to such an amount that it could be said that the Scots themselves funded the original cash sum of the Equivalent.

CHAPTER 13 – BUILDING YESTER HOUSE

Tweeddale sat in the first combined Parliament of 1707 but, in essence, he had retired from active politics and preferred to focus on the building of Yester. In his last year, 1713, he reflected on the history of his family and how they had achieved their comfortable position, writing:

> It is to be observed, that the whole fortune of this familie came by marriages, and whatever hath been purchas'd, was by the selling of lands that had come in that way, in consideration wherof, Charles Hay, present Lord Yester, made the following verses:
> *Aulam alii jactent, felix Domus Yestria nube,*
> *Nam quae sors aliis, dat, Venus alma tibi.* [1]

He died in April, aged 67, from an attack of apoplexy, leaving two sons, his heir Charles and Lord William Hay of Newhall, and two daughters. He had outlived his great contemporary Hamilton, who had fought a duel with Lord Mohun in Hyde Park in 1712, in which both men were killed.

Charles Hay, who had married Hamilton's daughter, succeeded as 3rd Marquis aged 43 and was appointed President of the Court

[1] Let others boast of court influence. Thou happy House of Yester hast only to marry; for the good things which fortune bestows on others, benign Venus gives to thee.

of Police and Lord Lieutenant of East Lothian on the accession of George I in 1714. At the general election in 1715 he was chosen as one of the sixteen representative peers for the House of Lords but he died the following December, aged only 45. He and Susannah had eight children, two of whom died young. None of his remaining three daughters married and two of his sons succeeded him, John, as 4th Marquis, aged twenty, and George as 6th Marquis. His third son, Charles, gained great renown as a soldier.

The accession of George as King of England had restored the Whigs to government and the Tories were swept from most of their positions of power. George regarded them as traitors because of their friendship with the French and with the Stuarts and they stayed in the political wilderness for 45 years. Not only were they excluded from positions they already held, but their sons could also not hope for advancement in political, legal or military professions. George Lyttleton wrote in 1747: 'We are kept out of all public employments of power and profit, and live like aliens and pilgrims in the land of our nativity.' Cruickshanks believes 'it was this proscription which turned the Tory party into a Jacobite one'; both Bolingbroke and Harley, now Earl of Oxford, had dealings with James II and Prince James Stuart; Oxford was impeached and Bolingbroke driven into exile. It was due to their relationships with the Jacobites in Scotland that rumours of Jacobite rebellion, often with suggestions of French support, continued to surface for the next 30 years.

The first such attempt had been made while Anne was still alive. In 1708 Louis XIV had ordered a fleet carrying Prince James Stuart and 6,000 men to sail to Scotland, but the invasion was easily beaten back by the British. The invasion seven years later was more serious. In 1714 the War of the Spanish Succession had ended with the French recognising the Hanoverian succession in England. The Jacobite Earl of Mar, who had been dismissed as Secretary of State by King George, raised the Stuart standard at

Braemar in September 1715 at the head of an army of 12,000 soldiers, but he had failed to advise anyone in England of his plans.
He was accompanied by John Hay of Cromlix, a son of the 7th
Earl of Kinnoul, whose sister, Margaret, had married Mar. They
took Inverness and Perth, but were defeated by an army led by
Argyll at Sherriffmuir in November. Prince James only landed in
Scotland in December and realised that he had no option but to
return to France with Mar and Hay. Three of Atholl's sons had
joined Mar and his eldest son, Tullibardine, was attainted. The
House of Erroll also suffered, as the 13th Earl's brother-in-law
James, 5th Earl of Linlithgow, had joined Mar's uprising and he
was exiled and his estate attainted and both the 7th and 8th Earls
of Kinnoul were temporarily held in Edinburgh Castle. In 1716
the English and French made a Treaty of Friendship and Prince
James had to leave France for Rome, where he was joined by John
Hay of Cromlix who became known as 'the king's favourite'. He
was made Earl of Inverness and he became James's chief inter-
mediary with the Jacobites in England; James made him a duke
in 1727 and he died in 1740.

King George appointed the Duke of Roxburghe Secretary of
State for Scotland in 1716 and he held that post for nine years.
His cousin John Tweeddale was only twenty when he succeeded
in the same year as 4th Marquis. He had studied law, but his immediate prospects were not good. When he inherited, his mother
wrote to him: 'The circumstances of the family are very low, at
present above [£300,000] in debt so the annual rents and keeping
of our credit and paying them punctually must take some considerable management.' However his financial situation improved
when he was appointed an Extraordinary Lord of Session in 1721,
the last Tweeddale to hold that office, and when he was elected
as a Representative Peer in 1722 and several times thereafter.

Being in office meant he could afford to restart building Yester.
The main roof had been covered with slate in 1714 and the in-

terior decoration of the offices and pavilions, where the family were still living, continued but the main block was largely unfinished. The second floor was laid in 1722 and most of the rooms seem to have been lined and plastered by 1725, but no windows were installed. Smith and MacGill remained responsible for building-operations throughout this period until their final accounts were settled in 1729.

The most detailed description available of the house as it was at this time is that of John Macky, who visited Yester in 1723.

The Palace of Yester, the capital seat of Hay, Marquis of Tweeddale stands in the middle of the best planted park I ever saw. The park walls are about eight miles in circumference; and I dare venture to say, there is a million of full grown trees in it. The Palace stands about half a mile from the park gate, to which you go by a paved coach-way, through a thicket: It is of free-stone, curiously wrought, of 120 foot front, and 60 foot deep; and on each side of the fore-front are two pavilions, by the way of wings, where the Lady Marchioness and her son the Marquis reside, till the body of the house is finished. The offices underground are very noble, and vaulted with paved galleries of communication. You enter the body of the House up six or eight steps into a large hall thirty-six foot high, and behind it a saloon fronting the garden of the same height, and at top is a gallery for music, which opens into both, exactly as at Bleinheim House in Woodstock. The rooms of state, that run on each side of this saloon fronting the garden, are very stately, and of an exact symmetry; and those from the hall have a communication with the appartments in the two pavilions.

There is a mathematical stone stair, balustraded with iron, which leads you up to the appartments above; but they are not yet so much as floored, although the House is entirely covered at top. In short, it is larger, as well walled and more regularly planted than Richmond in Surrey. The parterre and garden behind the House are very spacious and fine. There is a handsome basin, with a *jet d'eau* in the middle of the parterre, with four good statues upon pedestals at each corner. There are abundance of evergreens, and green slopes, regularly disposed: and to the west of the garden, on an artificial mount, is a pleasant summer-house. At the upper end of the garden fronting the Salon, are a pair of iron gates, which open into the park. The green-house joins the pavilion to the west, as does a laundry to the east. The great area before the gate is not laid out yet; but according to the disposition designed it will be very noble, with vistas from it cut through the wood, and statues at the end of every vista to terminate the view. There is a pretty rapid stream runs by the House and by its rustling through the trees as it runs through the park, makes the whole very rural.

There is a pretty bowling green by the riverside and the stables, henhouse and coach house are at a distance in the park, as is the custom in all the great houses I have yet seen in Scotland. Every nobleman's house hath what they call the Mains where their hand labourers, grooms and every body belongs to the stable and poultry reside.

He goes on to talk about the family and makes some interesting observations that show how contemporary Scots thought about the earlier Hays.

This noble family of Yester is very ancient for in the reign of William the Lion there is mention made of John de Haye *Miles* [soldier], brother to William de Haye, Dominus de Arrol [Erroll]. William lord Yester was one of those Peers who joined with the utmost zeal for the Reformation in the reign of Queen Mary and John who opposed all the innovations of Religion in King Charles I's time... [the current Marquis] is a youth of very promising parts.

Smith was in his seventies by 1725 and his partnership with McGill, who had been responsible for most of Scotland's large houses since 1700, was breaking down. Smith had been dismissed by the Government in 1719 from his commission to build Highland forts because of delays and it seems likely that the partnership had taken on too many projects. However, Tweeddale remained loyal and Yester was one of the few commissions Smith continued to work on. By 1728, however, a number of defects had become apparent, particularly in the design of the roof, which leaked. This was unsurprising, as Smith had designed it so that the pitches from the ridges at the front and back sloped downwards, creating a valley where 'lodged a great quantity of snow in the winter season to the great prejudice of the said roof'. Tweeddale decided to replace Smith with William Adam, who was the rising Scottish architect of his time. He was transforming the Earl of Hopetoun's family house into a Baroque palace and he had just returned from England, where he had spent time with Sir John Clerk of Penicuik visiting the latest country houses, including Wilton and Cliveden. He had executed commissions in Scotland for the earls of Stair, Mar and Marchmont, and for Sir John Clerk. Tweeddale was a keen amateur architect and he had subscribed to the first two volumes of *Vitruvius Britannicus*, published in 1715 and 1725 and written by Colen Campbell, the Scottish architect who was the founder of the Georgian style. In 1743 Adam described his projects and the surge of building in Scotland generally: 'For these many years past he had devoted himself to the Service of most of the Nobility and Gentry in this Country who being possessed of plentiful Fortunes Liberally educated and endowed with a genius for Architecture did incline to erect Palaces or houses Suitable to their Rank and fortune in the world.'

Tweeddale asked Adam to draw up his plans for the roof and for remodelling the interior of the house. Adam recommended that the roof be raised by an extra storey on the middle bays of both the north and south fronts and that these be topped by pediments. A sloping roof could then be set across the whole house with small leaded platforms on either side. On the north side of the house, the centrepiece was to incorporate tetrastyle Corinthian columns 'to take off the plainness of the front,' with a similar feature on the garden front where, however, pilasters would be employed instead of columns. Tweeddale had some reservations about the design of the north front, but a letter to Adam setting out his concerns brought an immediate reply: 'Now your Lordship will observe that if this rule as to the spaces betwixt windows and pillasters is not observed, but that the 2 outermost pillasters were placd betwixt the windows exactly, then the spaces betwixt pillasters themselves woud become unequal. This is a coledge on architecture which I'm sorry your Lordship does not like better.' Adam was clearly accustomed to addressing his client with considerable freedom, for at the end of the letter he declares: 'Now I think I have fully answered your Lordships [letter] and will conclude with the reverse of yours, that this is my trade and I like it.' Tweeddale however decided to have pilasters only on the north side 'after the Ionic Order,' leaving the south side plain, and by December 1730 the roof was finished.

The principal changes proposed were that the ground floor hall and garden saloon were to be reduced a storey in height, while the corresponding rooms on the floor above were to reach up into the newly formed attic storey, attaining heights of 29 and 24 feet respectively. A contract for £85,000 for the first stage of the alterations was signed in December 1729 and work was to be completed by November of the following year. As part of the contract, Tweeddale had to cut 'two rows of the fir trees now growing in the garden' for scaffolding, and he was to allow Adam some trees from the park for making a 'hand or horse machine' to lift materials to the roof.

Tweeddale removed 140 paintings from Pinkie House in 1734 and they were hung at Yester. Mahogany panelling and carved capitals were purchased for the Saloon and by 1737 the ground floor was habitable and marble fireplaces, one of which alone cost £10,000, had been fitted to most of the main rooms of the house. Three plasterers, lead by Joseph Enzer, started work in 1736; Enzer lived in a room containing a tent bed with a canvas bottom, a new fir table and a pewter chamber pot, and he was paid £6,500 a year. Tweeddale failed to be elected as a Representative Peer in 1734 and again in 1741 so he cut back on his spending and asked Adam to draw up a list setting out the minor works still to be carried out. These included the erection of a gentlemen's lavatory beside the road leading to the stables, 'a commodious structure of timber, 14 feet in diameter, carefully screened by a hedge'.

❧

The Whigs continued to control the political landscape in England but the Tories remained a cohesive force, united by their hatred of the Whigs and the Hanoverians. From exile, Bolinbroke wrote 'Of all the causes of our present public misfortunes…a principal one is this: the Whigs have always looked on the protestant succession, and the Tories on the restoration of the Stuarts, as sure means to throw the whole power of the government into the hands of one or the other…and to keep it there'. The War of the Austrian Succession began in 1740 and seven Scottish Tory nobles, led by the Duke of Perth, issued an Invitation to Prince James, similar to that originally sent to William of Orange. James had continued to receive substantial funds from England and he replied that he would never again attempt an invasion without first consulting his English friends and he also insisted that France must be asked for support. The Duke of Argyll emerged as a figurehead for the Tories and he led the group of dissident Whigs and Tories who opposed Walpole and called for the formation of a new Government in 1742. Sir Watkin Williams Wynn, a supporter of Prince James, proposed that Argyll be made Commander-in-Chief and Parliament sanctioned this but he resigned the very next day as he did not get everything he wanted. Some months later a Tory member disclosed that Argyll had received two letters from Prince James; this destroyed his political credibility and 'he retired, hardly seeing anybody... as one moped, indolent, dejected and broken-hearted', dying less than a year later, aged only 45.

Walpole was brought down as Prime Minister later that year, transforming Tweeddale's prospects. He was elected a Representative Peer and was appointed Secretary of State for Scotland which office had been in abeyance since 1739, but was revived for him. He was clearly popular at Court and respected in financial circles, as he was also appointed Principal Keeper of the Signet and Governor of the Bank of England for life. The Lord Advocate wrote to a fellow lawyer in 1742: 'You have been mentioned to the King by the Marquis of Tweeddale as my successor. You are happy in having to do with a patron who is a man of truth and honour.' Tweeddale was now at the height of his powers and of his reputation, but both were to be severely challenged over the next four years.

He was now able to accelerate the work on Yester and the first-floor rooms were all finished by July 1743 but Adam also wrote that 'Poor Joseph Enzer died last week. Among the last things he did was altering a trophy he had done over the pediment of the chimneypiece in the garden parlour. I complain'd of it to him and indeed he has put a much better thing in its place, a vase with some mosaick work.' Tweeddale was not satisfied with the design of the steps leading to the entrance in the north front and wrote to Adam: 'I have considered your last plan for this stair, and am still of opinion, as I always was, that it is too large and extensive for the house, besides you have added some further ornaments to it, such as your niches, which I don't like, since I desire it might be done plain without any ornaments. I had a few minutes discussion with my Lord Pembroke, who entirely agreed with me in opinion.' He asked Adam to prepare a fresh plan for a more modest stairway, and added that he intended to employ only estate labour on the work about the forecourt, 'for I am not in such a hurry to carry on great works as you, perhaps, think I should be' and with this letter he sent Adam the plan of the stairway he wanted.

Adam defended his original design at length, but reluctantly agreed to make a new one which Tweeddale approved but asked for the dimensions to be adjusted, adding, perhaps with tongue in cheek, 'providing always that the directions be according to the rules of architecture and will answer'. The stairway was completed in July 1745 but it was hardly modest as it consisted of a hundred single blocks of stone quarried on the estate at Whittinghame. It cost £150,000 but, as Tweeddale's factor Thomas Hay wrote, 'a great house is a great drain'. At the same time, the two pavilions were joined to the main block by covered passages and twin curved colonnades enclosed the lawns on each side to the south.

❧

The War of the Austrian Succession between France and Prussia on the one side and England and Austria on the other had started in 1743. The Tories, led by the Duke of Beaufort and Sir Watkin Williams Wynn, took advantage of the war to conspire with the French to restore Prince James to the English throne. They planned to achieve this by simultaneous invasions by the Scots from the north and by the French from the South. Louis XV told Philip V of Spain in December 1743 of his plans and then asked Prince Charles, then aged 23, to act as Regent for his father and to lead an expedition of 10,000 men to Scotland under the command of Marshall Saxe. Rumours of the invasion swept London and an emergency debate was held in Parliament because only 10,000 troops remained in England. The French sailed in February 1744 and were attacked by the English fleet; both fleets was scattered by a storm and the French withdrew to Brest. Charles was angry that the French would not continue their invasion and wrote to a friend in London: 'I am certain there are many in Scotland willing to follow me though I would go naked and alone among them, and I will try my fortune that way, if I can do nothing better.' His father and the Tories in England were adamant that any rising in Scotland had to be supported by a French invasion from the south, but it seems that Lord Stanhope, who was the liaison between the Stuarts and their Scottish supporters, had persuaded Charles that this was not necessary; so he sailed from Brittany in July 1745 and, after losing one ship to the English, he landed in the Outer Hebrides, where Cameron of Lochiel gave him his support. Incredibly, he had told neither his father, nor the French, nor his supporters in England of his plans.

When the Prime Minister, Henry Pelham, heard of Charles's landing, several weeks after the event, he immediately called for 6,000 Dutch troops and wrote to the new Duke of Argyll: 'I see the contagion spread in all parts... for my part, I have long dreaded it, and am as much convinced... that this country will be fought for some time before this year is over.' Tweeddale, who was in London, disagreed and advised the king there was no cause for alarm, although he had been warned by Argyll that the rising should be taken seriously. Charles had written to King Louis asking for assistance and his brother, Henry Duke of York, had gone to France to lead the invasion from the south. Lord Semphill, Charles's representative at the French court, wrote: 'The City of London...the Duke of Beaufort, and all the English cry loudly and vehemently for a body of troops to be landed near London, as the most effectual means to support the Prince, and the only method by which a dangerous and ruinous civil war can be avoided.' When Charles took Perth in August and proclaimed his father king, Tweeddale personally undertook to direct operations against the uprising from London. He still remained unconvinced about the seriousness of the threat and, even after he was told that the Prince's army had left Perth in their march south, he wrote to the Lord Advocate 'I flatter myself they have been able to make no great progress'. On the very day on which this letter was written, Charles entered the Palace of Holyrood. His army consisted of an equal amount of Highlanders and Lowland foot regiments with four companies of cavalry but only one of Charles's generals, Lord George Murray, who became Charles's chief adviser, was a Highlander. He wrote to his brother, the Duke of Atholl: 'I own frankly now that I am to engage, that what I may do may be reckoned and will be reckoned desperate... My life, my fortune, my expectations, the happiness of my wife and children are all at stake (and the chances are against me), and yet a principle of (what seems to me) honour, and my duty to King and Country, outweighs everything.' The Countess of Erroll was actively recruiting men for the Jacobite cause and managed to conceal her actions, but her niece's husband, the Earl of Kilmarnock, openly joined Charles's army; as did Andrew Hay of Rannes, a descendant of Sir Edmund Hay of Talla.

Sir John Cope, the commander of the Government's army of 4,000 soldiers, was camped in September at Prestonpans, on the coast south east of Musselburgh, when Charles's force of 2,500 men attacked and routed them. The workers on the roof at Yester threw slates at Cope's troops as they fled into the security of the

Lammermuirs and Charles spent the night after Prestonpans in Tweeddale's Pinkie House. The Marquis responded by setting a bounty of £4 million for his capture and he was criticised for his failure to control the situation; in a letter about him written a week after Prestonpans it was said that he had 'laid himself open to the severest censures by the manner in which he treated the rebellion; for within this week he spoke of it to two gentlemen...as a thing no more considerable than the desertion of the Highland Regiment in England the summer before last'.

In October Louis signed the Treaty of Fontainbleau with Prince James, by which he recognised him as King of Scotland, and of England if a free Parliament there voted for him. The French invasion force was due to sail in mid-December and on December 4th, David Morgan, a barrister acting for the Duke of Beaufort, met Charles's generals at Carlisle and advised them: 'It would be an easy matter to march forward for London, for there were not above 3,000 soldiers between them and London.' Manchester was taken by Andrew Hay and Charles's army entered Derby in December. There, Lord George Murray and his fellow commanders advised Charles that they should return to Scotland and, after much argument, he gave in with great regret: 'After this, I know that I have an army that I cannot command any farther than the chief officers please, and, therefore, if you are all resolved upon it, I must yield; but I take God to witness that it is with the greatest reluctance, and that I wash my hands of the fatal consequences which I foresee, but cannot help.' Richelieu heard the news of the retreat and told his invasion force to stand down.

The Duke of Cumberland took effective control of Scotland and destroyed Charles's army at Culloden in April. The Earl of Kilmarnock was captured and later executed and his son, James, Lord Boyd, who had fought for Cumberland, inherited as 15th Earl of Erroll when his great-aunt Countess Mary died in 1758. Andrew Hay of Rannes survived the battle and escaped to France.

Tweeddale continued to be criticised for his handling of the whole episode and he resigned as Secretary of State in January 1746. The Swedish ambassador wrote of him: 'It is true that no evil intents have been laid to his account, but rather a considerable degree of sleepy complacency. Moreover he recommended a number of men, and especially the Provost of Edinburgh, to His Majesty, as being of unquestionable loyalty, whereas the contrary soon proved to be the case.' King George refused to allow Pitt to enter the Administration in February and Pelham resigned. The Earl of Granville and Tweeddale attempted unsuccessfully to form a new government and Pelham resumed office; but Tweeddale was left out and he resigned his office of Keeper of the Signet.

His brother, Lord Charles Hay of Linplum, had been made an Ensign in 1722 and in 1729 he commanded a troop in the 9th Regiment of Dragoons. He served at the siege of Gibraltar in 1727 and afterwards in Germany as a volunteer under Prince Eugene of Savoy. He represented Haddington as MP in 1741, but soon returned to active service and fought at the Battle of Fontenoy in 1745. There was a picture of him in the dining room at Yester, showing him standing well clear of his own front rank and confronting the French Guards. He had pulled out his flask and was toasting the French, saying: 'We are the English Guards and we hope you will stand till we come quite up to you and not swim the Scheldt as you did the Main at Dettingen.' Voltaire wrote a description of the event:

> In the midst of that bloody engagement the British and French officers mutually saluted each other by taking off their hats. The English being fifty paces distant from the French and Swiss Guards, Charles Hay, Captain of the English Guards, steps out of the ranks; Count d'Auteroche, Lieutenant of the Grenadiers of the French Guards, goes to meet him.

"Gentlemen of the French Guards, fire," says the English Captain.

"No, my lord," answers the Count, "we never fire first." The English then gave a running fire. Nineteen officers and 380 soldiers of the French Guard fell dead or wounded.

Hay was later severely wounded and the battle was later claimed as a victory by both sides. He recovered from his wounds and was appointed *aide-de-camp* to the king in 1749, Colonel of the 33rd Foot in 1752 and Major General in 1757. In May that year he sailed for America as second-in-command under General Hopson, and joined the Earl of Loudoun, who was the Commander-in-Chief of the army of 11,000 men. Loudon was not highly regarded, his army was not engaging the enemy and Hay criticised him for this, as did others. 'He is like St. George upon the sign-posts,' said a Philadelphian to Benjamin Franklin, 'always on horseback but never advances.' A council of war was called in 1757 and Hay was put under arrest and sent to England. He faced a general court martial in 1760 and was found guilty of insubordination. The case was placed before the king, but Hay died only two months later. Loudon was recalled in 1758 and his replacement, Wolfe, took Quebec a year later. Dr Johnson later spoke highly of Hay: 'I suffered a great loss when he died, he was a mighty pleasing man in conversation.'

Chapter 14 – The Finest Room in Scotland?

William Adam died in 1748, but his sons, Robert and John, had been working with him at Yester in his latter years. The main part of the house was virtually finished, apart from the staterooms on the second floor, and £45,000 had been spent on hangings, tapestry and other furnishings. Much of the furniture was made using wood from the estate by Charles Douglas, a local carpenter, who had been sent to London by Tweeddale as early as 1732 in order to buy timber, tools and books on architecture.

William Adam had been renting the Pinkie coal works from Tweeddale for many years and offsetting his payments against those due to him from his work at Yester. When the accounts were finalised in 1750, John Adam found that his family owed Tweeddale more than £36,000. Nor did the situation improve, for the coal works soon ran into difficulties and Adam had to ask Tweeddale to remit the annual rent on several occasions. Tweeddale's own finances were bolstered in 1748 when he received £327,000 as compensation for losing the baillery of Dunfermline under the Act abolishing hereditary jurisdictions and he celebrated by marrying Lady Frances Carteret, daughter of his political ally, the Earl of Granville. He was 53 and she 30 and was described by Lady Mary Montagu as being ugly, but Horace Walpole said she was 'infinitely good-humoured and good company who sang a thousand French songs very prettily,' There was a portrait of her at Yester by Alan Ramsay which depicts her as being attractive, confident and elegant. Her sister wrote: 'I think my sister Fanny to all appearances happily established. The Marquis is a sensible reasonable man and quite her lover.'

Her marriage to Tweeddale, and his improved finances, may have led him to reconsider his plans for Yester House. William Adam had originally prepared a design for the great room on the northside first floor which he called the Saloon and Tweeddale asked John Adam to refresh the plans for 'the great room as soon as possible', and in 1750 the floorboards were laid by Charles Douglas. Adam sent his plans to Tweeddale in March 1751 writing that it would look 'extremely genteel without being crowded or overburthen'd with ornament. And I flatter myself the execution of it can be got done to your Lordship's satisfaction by the person who did the two glass frames for my Lady Marchioness, who works also in stucco. He is a Scotch lad, but served his time in London, and my brother and I prevailed upon him when there to come down and settle here.'

Robert Adam left for Italy in 1754 and Tweeddale asked the Scottish painter Gavin Hamilton for his opinion on how the Saloon should look. He replied: 'I am entirely of the Italian way of thinking, viz: that there can be no true magnificence without the assistance of either painting or sculpture and I will venture to say that if this room is finished in the manner I propose it will be the finest room at least in Scotland, and few equal to it in England.' He suggested that the family Van Dycks should hang either side of the fireplace and that he be commissioned to paint a big picture for £36,000 to hang on the wall opposite. While Tweeddale did not accept Hamilton's offer, he clearly liked his ideas.

Robert Adam returned from Italy in 1758 and the Adams and Tweeddale decided on the final design of the Saloon, the responsibility of which was given to John Adam. Alistair Rowan has described the Saloon as 'one of the most perfect examples of the

Adam brothers' early style.' It was based on William Adam's original design, especially its high ceiling and the large door which opened into the drawing room on the south side. His sons designed the octagonal coffering, inspired by the vaults of the Basilica of Maxentius in Rome, which slope upwards to the flat ceiling designed by Robert. The French painter William Delacour was chosen in 1761 to produce the series of seven large landscape panels which fill three sides of the room and which are painted in oil in imitation of tapestry. Their cost was a third of the price quoted by Hamilton for his one painting and their installation signified the completion of the Saloon.

The Tweeddales had four girls and one boy between 1748 and 1753 and this led Tweeddale to focus on alterations and additions to the east pavilion to provide a nursery for the children. This was completed in 1752, the same year that their son, George, died aged only one. Tweeddale also wanted to improve the gardens and the lands surrounding the house. He had always been very interested in agricultural development and he had become an early member of The Society of Improvers in the Knowledge of Agriculture in Scotland, which had been founded in 1723. He brought the great larches that still stand near the west side of the house as seedlings from Blair Atholl in 1739. The gardener there had put the young plants in the hot house, where they sickened and he threw them on to the rubbish heap, where Tweeddale saw them flourishing and took them back to Yester.

Gifford Water was canalised where it ran across the north side of the house and in 1751 John and Robert Adam supplied a sketch for an island temple approached by a bridge with a handrail 'formed in the Chinese manner'. A year later a report was submitted by Mr Bowie, a landscape gardener, who had been recommended to Tweeddale by his neighbour and distant relative Sir Thomas Hay of Alderston as 'the only person I have met with in this part of the world that has a good fancy in laying out ground in a natural way'. Bowie was a follower of William Kent and his proposals for Yester included informal planting of trees, a serpentine lake and the formation of several cascades and a grotto. Some of the suggestions were accepted, as a cascade was under construction in 1752 and George Jameson, an Edinburgh carver, made two heads for a grotto in 1755. Shells and figures to decorate the interior were sent from London.

The Adams remodelled St. Cuthbert's Church as a family burial place, probably because of the early deaths of two of Tweeddale's daughters in 1757. The alterations involved the demolition of the 15th century nave and the conversion of the choir and transepts into a T-plan mausoleum. A new entrance was made on the west side of the building within the former choir-arch, which was re-modelled in the Decorated Gothic style. Bishop Pococke visited Yester in September 1760 and he noted that the church had been rebuilt 'in a very good Gothic taste'. The church had been used for burials in the past but, curiously, the only monuments in the church are the shields of William Hay of Linplum who died in 1614, and of his wife Helen, who died in 1627; the grave of the 11th Marquis; the adjacent grave, which was prepared for Giff's wife Marjorie and where Giff's daughter Daphne was interred; and a small plaque in memory of his stillborn son. Outside there is a row of small grave stones commemorating dead pets, but there are no other marked graves. Excavations were made around the church in 1975 and a number of human bones were found, but no attempt to determine their age has been made.

Work on the entrance gate to Yester, which is flanked by two small lodges, was begun using stone from local quarries. A New-castle smith named Hilkoat wrote to Tweeddale to inform him that the iron gate that he was making would be finished in about two months' time, 'when I hope it will prove an additional ornament to your Lordship's ancient seat and a credit to me as a mechanic'. The walled garden, the gardener's house and the greenhouses were all finished, as were the main rooms in the house, with the exception of the Saloon, which had still 'to be stuccoed and finished in a grand manner'.

The completion of the Saloon brought to an end the building programme upon which Tweeddale had embarked 30 years previously. He must have been extremely pleased at the result, as both the house and the surrounding park were beautiful examples of the classical style. He had lived on the site for nearly half a century, longer than any of his predecessors, but was not to enjoy the fruits of his vision for long. The Tweeddales celebrated the birth of their heir George in 1758 and in 1761 Tweeddale was appointed Justice-General of Scotland, when the holder Argyll died, but he only outlived him by one year, dying in London in 1762, aged 67. He was buried in the family vault in Yester Church and in a letter written after his death, Frances wrote: 'I hope you will not allow any carriage in the park unless they have broad wheels; even though my dear lord is dead I cannot bear to think of his beautiful grass being spoiled. I hope, too, that all the deer need not be sold.'

George inherited as 5th Marquis aged only four so the Yester estate was managed by Lord George Hay of Newhall, the third son of the 3rd Marquis. However, the young Marquis died in 1770 aged only thirteen and Lord George became the 6th Marquis, aged 70. Frances had now lost all her children, save only her daughter, Catherine, who had married William Hay in 1744. He was the son of John Hay of Newhall, a grandson of the 2nd Marquis, who had been a lawyer and who had fallen on hard times. He had married Dorothy Hayhurst, the daughter of a labourer from Lancaster, who was to survive his death as a bankrupt by over 40 years. Catherine died in 1776 leaving her mother completely alone; she lived for another twelve years, suffering from ill health and lack of money. She wrote regularly to the 6th Marquis, who looked after her, but her sadness is captured in a letter she wrote to him in 1774: 'Few have had so many bitter disappointments as myself.' She asked to be buried with her wedding ring on her finger and with all her husband's letters in her coffin.

The 6th Marquis served on of the Board of Police from 1755 to 1771. Very little is known about him, but he added to the Yester estate by purchasing the estate of Catherine's father-in-law, John Hay of Newhall, from his creditors. He also inherited the estate of Linplum from Lord Charles Hay but he seems to have spent most of his time at Newhall, near Penicuik in Midlothian, which he had inherited in 1748 and where he died without issue in 1787, aged 87. At his death the Yester estate amounted to over 40,000 acres, though much of this was moorland. He was succeeded by his cousin George, aged 34, who was the brother of Catherine's husband William Hay of Newhall, and who was the great-grandson of the 2nd Marquis.

George, the 7th Marquis, had served as a naval officer in the East Indian Company. In 1785 he married Lady Hannah Maitland, daughter of the 7th Earl of Lauderdale, resurrecting the relationship with the family that had caused the Hays so much trouble over the previous 250 years. Perhaps encouraged by Hannah, who had grown up at the Lauderdale's magnificent house of Thirlestane, Tweeddale began making further alterations to Yester House, commissioning Robert Adam to design a new approach-ramp for the principal north front, so that carriages could drive right up to the front door instead of halting at the foot of the great stone stairway of 100 steps. Adam was also asked to prepare plans for remodelling the first-floor apartments on the south side of the house so as to create a large drawing room opening off the Saloon. Adam submitted proposals for completely remodelling the front and rear elevations of the house in neo-Classical style, explaining his ideas in a letter sent with the plans in March 1789.

I have always thought Yester House one of the best con-
trived plans I ever saw in this or any country, and that if

the outside elevations had been in any degree on a par with the internal distribution of the apartments, it might be called the most compleat house in Scotland. But those lines of flat ashlers running from end to end and from top to bottom of both fronts of the house dazzle the eye, and render them a mass of confusion... I therefore thought that it would be pity whilst I was doing the design of the ramp of approach, not to try if something could be made of the outside of the house to correspond with it.

Adam proposed to rebuild the north centrepiece, raising the pilasters to first floor level and carrying up the pediment to the full height of the roof. This, he explained, would enable him 'to get three fine broad and lofty windows to light the Saloon, which I think such an improvement as would tempt me to make the alteration, as then that room will be as cheerful as any room to the north can be'. The north pediment was topped by three lead statues, representing a Roman warrior, an athtlete and a female with a dagger which had originally stood in the formal gardens with others, now lost. Francis Menotti found them in the garden sheds and they now stand above the entrance to the north front.

The rebuilding of the north front and the construction of the ramp was carried out by John Hay, a builder from Edinburgh, between 1788 and 1790 at a cost of £51,000. This sum included the cost of repairs to the plasterwork and timberwork of the Saloon and the reinstatement of the coat of arms to the pediment. Tweeddale refused to settle the final account, however, claiming that the work was unsatisfactory and that he had been overcharged and he began a lawsuit in 1792, the year Robert Adam died. John Hay agreed to submit the case to the arbitration of Alexander Ponton, an architect in Edinburgh, and to James Burns, a wheelwright in Haddington. These arbiters failed to agree and the matter was passed to the Edinburgh architect Robert Burn who, after inspecting the work and ordering certain defects to be remedied, ordered Tweeddale to pay Hay £9,000 within ten days.

Tweeddale was elected a Representative Peer in 1796 and was appointed Lord Lieutenant of Haddingtonshire. He and Hannah had fourteen children, including triplets, two of whom died. One other son died in his first year but all the others lived for between 38 and the 90 years achieved by the surviving triplet, Thomas. On the evening of April 3rd 1797, fire broke out in the west pavilion and threatened to engulf the whole house. Tweeddale was away but Robert Somerville, his agent, called out the Haddington fire engine and summoned help from the local military who were joined by some tenants from Gifford and they stopped the fire from spreading by blocking with turf the passage linking the pavilion to the main part of the house. By 4 o'clock the next morning Somerville was able to write assuring Tweeddale that 'the children and every person belonging to the house are in perfect safety... the loss is confined solely to the offices west of the house'. The wing was repaired but was probably never properly refitted. The next year the Hay clan suffered a loss when George, 16th Earl of Erroll, who had served as Lieutenant Colonel in the 1st Guards Regiment and who had been elected a Representative Peer in 1795, committed suicide in 1798, aged only 31, because he had inadvertently passed on a secret entrusted to him by the Prime Minister, William Pitt.

Chapter 15 – The Great 8th Marquis

Tweeddale and his wife went to the continent because of an illness he had developed as he approached his 50th year. There is an extraordinary letter in the NLS archives to Tweeddale from his doctor, recommending the trip to France, in which he says there are examples of men who have lived to 169 and even 185 years old because of its climate and the treatment that was available there. They left for France in 1802, leaving their eleven children at Yester, aged fifteen to five. Unfortunately, France declared war with England soon after and detained the Tweeddales and all other British subjects in the fortress of Verdun. Family friends wrote to Talleyrand and Berthier, Napoleon's Chief of Staff, begging for their release, but to no avail. Hannah died of smallpox in May 1804 and Tweeddale wrote to an English official: 'This melancholy death added to my separation from my family at a moment when the presence of a father is so necessary, the desire of attending the body of my departed wife to England to see it deposited in its native soil, the natural feeling of a father to be restored to a family of eleven young children just deprived of its greatest support and a long and unlooked for absence from my country.' He failed to get any support and he too died of smallpox three months later. Their bodies were kept in ice in Verdun until they were buried at Yester in 1806. The Hays' association with the Maitlands had claimed its most tragic victims.

George and Hannah would have been proud of their children. Their eldest son, George, succeeded as 8th Marquis aged fifteen and had an extraordinary life. Their second son, James, became a Lieutenant-General in the army in 1854 and died in 1862. Their third son, John, entered the Navy and lost his left arm fighting in the Dardanelles in 1807. He served as Commodore of a squadron off the coast of Spain and received the Grand Cross of the Spanish Order of Charles III. He was promoted to Rear Admiral and in 1846 was appointed one of the Lords of the Admiralty, eventually becoming MP for Windsor. Edward, their fifth son, served as a Lieutenant-Colonel in the army and Thomas, their sixth son and surviving triplet, was appointed Rector of Rendlesham, Suffolk in 1830. Four of their daughters married and altogether the children produced more than twenty grandchildren.

The new Marquis was the most remarkable of all the children. He had been taught at Gifford School, where he distinguished himself by his physical strength rather than by the application of his intellect and his father had him tutored by the Scottish philosopher James Mill, who taught him Greek, Latin and history. In particular, Mill made him read the *Life of John Knox* and Bishop Burnet's *History of my own Time*, which would have taught him a great deal about his ancestors, the first two Marquises. He entered the army in 1804, the year in which he succeeded, and received his first training under Sir John Moore of Corunna. He was sent to Sicily in 1806 as *aide-de-camp* to Sir John and then served for six years during the Peninsular War as a staff officer to the Duke of Wellington. He used to bring crates of champagne and claret when campaigning and shared them with his fellow officers, including Wellington. In 1809 he was with Wellington's army in its attack on the French forces at Oporto, where he was wounded and promoted to Lieutenant-Colonel, and he was wounded again at Busaco in 1810 and again at Vitoria in 1813, where he acted as Quartermaster-General. Wellington sent him home, presenting him with the pair of pistols, which were kept on the hall table at Yester. Later that year he rejoined his regiment, which was then engaged in the war with America.

In his *Memoirs*, dictated to his daughter when he was 80, he tells of his roles in the Battles of Chippawa and Lundy's Lane, fought on the banks of the Niagara in July 1814. Prior to these battles he had written to his junior officers that US prisoners should be treated with respect and be given proper treatment. At Chippawa, 2,000 UK troops fought 3,500 US regulars and Tweeddale commanded the 100th Regiment of Foot. Most of his officers were killed or wounded and Tweeddale himself was shot through his Achilles tendon. His wound took ten days to heal and he returned to Fort George near Lake Niagara. There the Governor-General of Canada, George Drummond, had gathered an army of 1,800 men and, as Tweeddale writes in his *Memoirs*: 'My knees plagued me very much but it was a great thing for me to command a Brigade so I bore with these impediments.' General Winfield Scott, the US commander at Chippawa, led the forces that attacked the British at Lundy's Lane, despite having only 1,000 men. The British achieved a strategic victory but Tweeddale was captured and General Scott later described his capture to William Howard Russell of *The Times*. Tweeddale was badly wounded and, his face covered with blood, was standing with his back to a wall keeping his US would-be captors at bay with his great sabre saying 'I will never surrender.' Luckily Scott arrived in time; he had recently captured Tweeddale's brother, Lord John Hay, so he was able to persuade Tweeddale to give up his arms.

He was soon released and spent time in New York when peace was declared. He was surprised how well he was treated until he was told by one of his hosts that his letter telling his subordinates to treat the American prisoners well had been intercepted and published in several American papers, so he was highly regarded.

He sailed to Liverpool and, as soon as he landed, he went to

London to attend Wellington's dinner to celebrate the anniversary of Vitoria. He sat with the Duke who told him about his victory at Waterloo saying that 'his army was principally composed of young soldiers, many were militia men unaccustomed to move in large bodies, but when formed in a position to meet an attack, nothing would move them but the order of their officers.' When Tweeddale asked him why he had not advanced a particular regiment against the French, Wellington told him 'I could not trust them in line, there was no doubt about their pluck but I could not depend upon them if made to move away from their defensive position.' At the end of the evening Wellington said to Tweeddale 'If ever I am employed on active service you may depend upon my not forgetting you.'

Tweeddale married Lady Susan Montagu, the daughter of the 5th Duke of Manchester, in 1816. He was appointed Lord Lieutenant of Haddingtonshire in 1824 and he was a strong promoter of the agricultural revolution then sweeping Scotland. A key driver of this was the improvement in lease arrangements between landlords and tenants, which gave greater security to the tenants, encouraging them to undertake the capital investment required to improve the productivity of their lands. Tweeddale pioneered many changes on the main Yester estate which comprised 967 acres and consisted largely of 'a poor thin wet Moorish surface, resting on a stiff retentive sandy clay subsoil', although Yester House itself was surrounded by a park of 426 acres, divided into grassland and wood. The Reverend James Innes wrote more generally about the parish of Yester in 1791:

> The soil is very different, in the same farm we have rich good land and very poor ground intermixed together; but, by means of lime and dung the greatest part of the parish has been brought into very good order. Some of the best ground is near the foot of the Lammermuir hills; the most

of the arable land is rather a shallow than a deep soil. The air is pure and very healthy. The hill ground is about two miles square and the number of acres of arable land is about 4,000 of which near 2,000 acres are employed in raising corn and roots and in fallow. Wheat, oats, barley, turnips, potatoes and flax were all planted. Much more grain is raised than the people can consume and much is sold in Haddington market and a considerable quantity goes yearly to the west country. More than half the ground in the Parish is in pasture and sown grass; about 200 acres are covered with wood, such as elm, oak, beech and fir; among which are some of the largest and most beautiful trees in Scotland. One oak tree in the wood at Yester was valued at £2,500.[1] A good number of sheep and, of late years, a number of calves are bred in the parish. Some tenants rear in one year about twenty calves each. There may be of saddle and work horses about 200, black cattle about 600 and 140 score of sheep. Prices for produce sold per pound were £3 for beef, pork and mutton; £4.5 for veal, chicken and cheese; and £7 for butter. Geese sold for £16 and lambs for £13 each. A greater quantity of beef and mutton are now consumed by the lower class of people. The fuel commonly used is coal and wood, the former comes from six miles distance; one cart costs £10 at the hill and the the carriage £15 more.

Innes also writes that the wages of 'an ordinary man servant' had risen from £250 a year in 1750 to between £500 and £700 in 1791, with women servants receiving half that amount. The wages of a labouring man, who received no victuals, had also doubled to between £1,500 and £1,800, 'which make him and his family live very comfortably. A common ploughman may earn, including meal, corn, and cow etc. from £1,300 to £1,500 a year.'

[1] All prices within this chapter are in current prices.

The annual land rent of the whole parish amounted to £200,000; there were 150 houses, containing five people each on average and a cottage cost £100 per annum to let. Gifford itself had 400 inhabitants and the main source of employment was the linen industry, until it collapsed in the latter half of the 18th century. Where the recreation ground now stands, to the right of the lime avenue leading to Yester's entrance gate, a canal had been dug which powered a linen mill and assisteted the process of bleaching. One of its products was the paper used for the first banknotes printed by the new Bank of Scotland in 1695. Innes continues:

The parish was much more populous 100 years ago than it is now; the causes of the decrease must be attributed to the demolition of cottages and the union of several small farms increased. There are about five children on an average in a family... not as stout as they were forty years ago, which must be owing... to the different manner of living as the common people now drink a great deal of tea, and not good small beer, which they did fifty years ago. The people are in general very industrious, having plenty of all kinds of labour. Their size varies from 5 feet 5 inches to 6 feet 2 inches. The parish contained: 5 heritors; 1 clergyman; 1 physician; 18 farmers; a good many carpenters, masons and weavers, who have all plenty of work... and live very comfortably; 18 male and 22 female household servants; 30 female and 80 male labouring servants, most of which are married. There is not one lawyer and the people... keep their affairs as much out of the hands of such men as possible, referring all their differences to be determined by the arbitration of neighbours. All the inhabitants are of the Established Church, except 10 Seceders. The number of the poor are from 28 to 32 each of whom receive from £100 -300 yearly.

Money raised from other sources resulted in a further £4,500 being distributed to the poor and Tweeddale's factor ran the impromptu court as Baron Bailie, with two other bailies elected by the tenants, which met three times a year at Gifford Cross.

Yester's three farms were valued at £31,000 per annum when Tweeddale consolidated them in 1841. The land was, however, difficult to manage, as it was poorly drained, and in some years the wheat grown was of such poor condition that it was left to rot in the fields. Tweeddale radically altered the method of cultivation on his estate by focusing on deep ploughing. This could not be effected until the land had been properly drained and Tweeddale's invention of a drain-tile machine in 1836 made this much more economical. The draining scheme he implemented cost £355 per acre, resulting in a large capital commitment of £323,000. Traditional ploughing turned over the earth to a depth of seven inches but this had little effect on the hard, wet, clay subsoil, limiting the growth of grain. Tweeddale therefore invented two ploughs: the Tweeddale plough, which ploughed to a depth of sixteen inches, and the Yester plough, which ploughed the subsoil to a further depth of six inches, thus increasing the depth of land ploughed by three times that of traditional methods. It was also efficient, since the Tweeddale plough turned over an area 50% wider than the traditional plough, using the same number of horses.

The results achieved were dramatic with wheat yields rising 30% and grass and turnip yields doubling. Henry Stephens, writing in 1855, considered that these changes resulted in a fourfold increase to £124,000 a year in the value of the lands farmed. The services Tweeddale had rendered to Scottish agriculture were acknowledged by his election to the office of President of the Agricultural and Highland Society. John Martine wrote of him in 1890: 'The farms he kept were models of agricultural perfection in every respect. He erected an extensive tile-work and made for many years millions of drain tiles and pipes to drain the estate by an ingenious machine of his own invention.'

Tweeddale's enterprise required substantial finance and he began a process of borrowing which the family would continue until 1925. He raised a loan of £3.8 million in 1843 and he borrowed a further £1.2 million through two loans taken out in 1855 and 1870.

The general agricultural labour market in Scotland changed during the agricultural revolution from the traditional form of tied labour to a free market labour based on short term contracts and cash payments. A commentator wrote in 1804 that day labourers were commonly used for 'the fever of improvements, so common and malignant between 30 and 40 years ago'. This reflected the great increase in building and estate improvement that took place after the Restoration and the Glorious Revolution. There was no doubt, however, that this labour market change caused considerable poverty in the countryside generally but those in South East Scotland were less affected as 'the forces of production developed faster than in most other areas of Britain, but the relations of production remained stubbornly traditional'. This was because there were smaller farms and less concentration on cereal production and because day labourers formed a smaller percentage of the total agricultural workforce, who were hired on an annual basis, usually rolled-over, with the men being provided with a cottage and sufficient land 'to sow grain, grazing for two cows, fifteen bolls of oats and 1.5 bolls of peas'. They were generally paid in kind, usually with oats and, in some years, if the harvest had been good, they also received a cash bonus.

The Yester estate employed 21 men each year between 1672 and 1675, fourteen of whom worked throughout the paid year of 220 days. Between 1687 and 1696, the total number of men employed each year had risen to 24, but only ten worked for the whole year and the increase in revenues over the next 150 years did not lead to a significant increase in those employed. During the 8th Marquis's time fourteen ploughmen each used a pair of horses and six men, six women and twelve children worked on general duties around the farms. The overseers and ploughmen were given a house, a garden and the use of a cow, and their wage, consisting of the value of the oats received and whatever additional cash payment was made, totalled about £35 per week, with the women being paid half that. The population of the Yester parish did not change much between 1750 and 1850, and depended greatly on agricultural employment for their livelihood, but in Gifford itself, with a population of 400, there were ten tailors, ten carpenters, nine shoemakers, eight blacksmiths, four masons, four bakers, two millers, one watchmaker, one saddler and six publicans. The villagers were divided between feuars and cottars: the feuars owned their houses subject to an annual payment to the Marquis, and they were bound to attend him on two days a year mounted with arms, at their own expense; they also had the right to graze one cow on the common land. The majority of the villagers were cottars, who were allowed to live in their dwelling as long as they worked on the estate.

Tweeddale employed the architect Robert Brown to effect a series of major alterations to Yester, which resulted in a radical shift in the axis of the ground floor. It is likely that the west pavilion had deteriorated after the damage suffered in the fire of 1797, so it was demolished as were the series of courtyards and offices that had adjoined the east pavilion. The original hall on the north side of the house was converted into a dining room and a new entrance hall was made at the centre of the west front where Brown placed two pillars from the old hall to avoid the expense of having to build a new arch. The glass-lined *porte-cochère* and balustrade were erected outside the new front door. A new drawing room was formed on the ground floor on the south side of the house by joining the garden parlour to an adjacent bedroom, and many of the family apartments were redecorated and equipped with new fireplaces. The new hall extended to the staircase by a wide corridor off which opened doors to the new dining room and the new drawing room.

The work was carried out in two phases, of which the first was completed in 1830 and the second in 1839. Robert Adam's approach ramp on the north front was grassed over and only the entrance to the basement floor remains, set in a stone fronted portico surrounded by a steep, sloping grassed bank. It may also be at this time that a large 300-yard tunnel was built over Gifford Water and covered with earth, enabling a lawn to stretch from the base of the grassed bank all the way to the steep rise of trees 400 yards to the north of the house. Tweeddale and his wife stayed in Geneva while all this work was being carried out, renting *Les Delices*, where Voltaire had lived in 1755.

From 1842 to 1848 Tweeddale served as Governor of Madras and Commander-in-Chief of the Madras Army, a union of offices unprecedented at that period, but specifically created for Tweeddale, as Wellington considered that only he possessed the necessary qualification for restoring the discipline of the army to the standards required by the duke. Tweeddale did much to improve the condition, not only of the soldiers, but also of the native population. It is said that Victoria wanted to make him a duke but he refused, believing he could not afford the expense. He was promoted General in 1854, served as Colonel of the 2nd Life Guards in 1863 and in 1875 was created Field Marshal.

He was renowned for his stature and strength and for his skill with his sword, which was much longer than the regulation weapon. He was a famous boxer and an excellent horseman, known as 'the Prince of the Heavy Bays'. He is said to have driven the mail coach from London to Haddington and to have beaten a train when driving his favourite trotter. A story is told of his driving a pair of ponies along one of the paths through Yester when, at a narrow bridge, he met the village blacksmith in his pony cart. As there was not room for two on the bridge, and as neither would give way, the two men wrestled for the right of way. The Marquis threw the blacksmith into the water and drove on. 'It was either the devil himself,' the blacksmith told friends later, 'or that old devil from Yester House.'

He was also tough with his family. One door of the dining room was reserved for his exclusive use; his wife and children had always to use the other one. Lord John Hay, his younger son, who had been serving as a midshipman in China, forgot this protocol and came in to breakfast by his father's door, and his father drove him from the room with a horsewhip. Lord John commanded the ship which took Lord Ashburton to America in 1842 when he signed the Webster-Ashburton peace treaty, which resolved the dispute between America and Britain's North-American colonies. He also brought the first Pekingese dogs to England after the sack of the Palace at Peking in 1860 and he presented one to Queen Victoria and the other to his wife.

Susan Tweeddale died in 1870 but her husband remained fit and it was only an accident that weakened him. Having been undressed by his valet, he was left alone in his room where he fell between the fender and the fire and was severely burned on his back. He died peacefully shortly after in October 1876 in his 90th year.

Chapter 16 – The last Tweeddales of Yester

The 8th Marquis was the father of six sons and eight daughters, born between 1817 and 1836. His heir, George, Earl of Gifford, was born in 1822, but he predeceased his father. Two of his brothers succeeded as Marquis and the fourth brother, John, was appointed Admiral of the Fleet in 1888 and served as MP for Wick and then Ripon between 1857 and 1871. Two other brothers served in the army and died unmarried; one daughter died young and the other daughters all married. His eldest, Susan, married the Marquis of Dalhousie, who served as Governor General of India between 1848 and 1856; Elizabeth married the 2nd Duke of Wellington; and the youngest, Emily, was the wife of Sir Robert Peel, the eldest son of the former Prime Minister. It was said that Tweeddale disapproved of Emily's choice and that he shut her in her room and fed her on bread and water for a week, but she held firm and he relented.

The marriage and life of the third daughter, Julia, gives an interesting and poignant picture of English life at this time. She married John Cam Hobhouse, Byron's close friend and a Whig politician who entered Parliament in 1820 aged 34. The first reference to Julia in his diary is on June 14th 1828: 'I walked in Kensington Gardens with Lady Julia Hay and sister. A charming day.' Matters moved quickly and on June 26th he writes: 'I dined at Boyd Alexander's. There I met a party of young men and Lady Julia Hay. Going upstairs I sat in the drawing room next to the latter lady and after much conversation made her an offer of marriage which she accepted.' She asked him to visit the Earl of Lauderdale, her uncle, which he did on June 27th. 'In the course of our talk he told me Lady Julia had received, as well as her sisters, a pension from the Crown which would drop at her marriage and he gave me to understand that Lady Julia had no fortune. I said that was neither here nor there and turned the conversation to another subject.'

By the end of July, the marriage settlement was signed and Hobhouse writes: 'Lady Julia Hay will have near [£134,000] a year if I die before her, which I shall most assuredly.' However, Julia was clearly not well, for at her marriage on July 28th at Cumberland Place, Hobhouse writes: 'Lord Tweeddale supported Lady Julia to the sofa, which was filled up like an altar. Poor thing, she was dreadfully alarmed. Spencer performed the ceremony as speedily as might be and I was married. Thus occurred the event which had more influence on my life than any other.' They spent their honeymoon over three months in Italy and France and stayed with the Tweeddales in Geneva. Julia's illness returned in 1831 and it proved to be tuberculosis, and by then she had three daughters. Two years later a blood vessel broke in her lung after 'she was persuaded to try the new quack system' and in August 1834 they travelled to Scotland in a train for the first time and visited Yester. Hobhouse writes: 'I wandered about with my wife as my guide and she pointed out the trees she had planted and she took me to the ruined chapel, the burial place of her family. She showed me the grave of the last Hay buried there. A shudder came over me and I hurried her away.'

Seven months later, on April 3rd 1835, Hobhouse writes: 'My most admirable and devoted wife, the pride and treasure of my heart died at 4 o'clock.' He was to live for another fifteen years and, in that time, managed to favour his father-in-law Tweeddale by helping him secure his position as Commander-in-Chief in India when he, as a young Major-General, had many more senior competitors for the post. Tweeddale had answered Wellington's offer by saying 'I will go anywhere the Queen commands me to go.'

The Earl of Gifford was not the same man as his father; he was shy, insecure and suffered from a serious stutter. He went to Trinity, Cambridge, and in the summer of 1842, aged twenty, he was sent by his father to Italy. There he met Helen, Lady Dufferin, the granddaughter of Thomas Brinsley Sheridan, the great playwright and famous MP. She had two sisters and they were known as the Three Graces because of their great beauty and charm. The eldest was Caroline Norton, who was a novelist and champion of social reform, especially for women, and who was rumoured to have been the mistress of Lord Melbourne, the Prime Minister. The youngest, Georgiana, married the Duke of Somerset. Helen told Disraeli: 'Georgy's the beauty and Carry's the wit, and I ought to be the good one, but I am not.' Helen was being too modest; she wrote novels and poetry and had several plays performed in London. She was the widow of Lord Dufferin, who had died in 1841 from an accidental overdose of morphine when she was only 33. Gifford found her very charming and he told her how misunderstood he was by his father, how he could not make friends at Cambridge and how much he disliked the tutor his father had imposed on him in Italy. She listened to his problems and gave him sympathy and advice and he, inevitably, fell in love with her, but she did not return his affections, as these were focused entirely on her son, who was only four years older than he.

After graduating from Cambridge, Gifford joined the East Lothian Yeoman Cavalry in 1850 and served as private secretary to Lord Newcastle, the Secretary of State for War, in 1854. He was elected as MP for Totnes in 1855 and held the seat until his death, but his shyness and stutter prevented him taking much part in debates in the House. His love for Helen, however, remained constant. He had proposed to her in 1854 but had been rejected so he asked her again in 1859 and this time she said she would only consider him once her own son was married. This he was in 1862, but in that same year Gifford was severely injured by a falling tree during excavations to open the stairway into the Goblin Hall at Yester Castle. He was taken to London for treatment but there was nothing that could be done for him. Helen agreed to be his wife, they were married at Dufferin House in October and he went home to die in her house in Highgate. Tweeddale was furious, believing she was taking advantage of his condition to make claims on the family. Gifford had, however, accumulated large debts and Helen was fearful of being held responsible for them, so she agreed to take on only those incurred after their marriage, and his younger brother, Arthur, took responsibility for the rest. Gifford died two months later, fulfilling the prophecy made by Sir Hugh Giffard back in the 13th Century that any member of the family would die if they excavated Yester Castle. Helen survived him by only five years and was buried beside him in the church at Friern Barnet in London.

Arthur did not adopt his brother's title of Earl of Gifford but chose to remain Viscount Walden until he succeded as 9th Marquis in 1876, aged 52. He had been educated in Geneva and had joined the Grenadier Guards in 1841, aged seventeen. He was promoted to Colonel in 1860 and served in India and the Crimea and transferred to the 17th Lancers in 1866. When he retired from the army he moved to Chislehurst and studied ornithology, and was President of the Zoological Society from 1868 to 1878. He donated a large collection of insects, reptiles, birds and mammals to the Natural History Museum. In 1881 Arthur's nephew privately printed a 760-page volume of his ornithological works, with an introduction by the famous *Times* reporter, William Howard Russell, who Arthur had met during the Crimean War. He married Helena, daughter of Count de Kielmansegger, the Hanoverian ambassador in 1857 but she died in 1871 and two years later Arthur married the beautiful Julia Stewart-Mackenzie, who was 27. Her sister was the famous literary hostess Lady St Helier, at one of whose dinner parties Winston Churchill's parents met. Julia and her sister were also very active philanthropists and suffragettes.

A year after succeeding his father, Arthur borrowed £2.2 million and a further £1.5 million two years later. He had asked the ambitious young Edinburgh architect Robert Anderson to prepare a report on Yester House. Anderson produced plans involving not only extensive additions, repairs to the roof and ceilings and the remodelling of the attic storey, but also the erection of three new wings at each of the available corners of the main block; he also said the Saloon needed a new floor. In his report to the Marquis, he estimated that these operations would cost £850,000 and added disarmingly 'this amount is greater than I anticipated and probably more than your Lordship thought of'. Anderson ended his report by suggesting that this sum would be better spent on the erection of a completely new house. Tweeddale approved a fairly modest programme of repairs, which were not completed until after his early death in 1878, aged 54. Anderson was, however, proved right about the Saloon floor, as we were told in the 1960s we should not run over it, and it was finally replaced in 1982, 230 years after it had been first laid by the estate carpenter.

Arthur's brother, William, succeeded as 10th Marquis in 1878. He had served in the Bengal Civil Service from 1845 to 1862 and was a great friend of Hodson, who in 1857 raised the famous Bengal Lancer Regiment, Hodson's Horse. When Hodson captured the King of Delhi, after the fall of the Red Fort in 1857, he sent the harnessess of the king's elephants to his friend at Yester. They have disappeared, but rumours remain of hidden treasures encrusted with gold and jewellery. William was appointed Deputy Commissioner of Simla and superintendent of the Hill States of Northern India. After completing his Indian service, he served as Liberal MP for Taunton from 1865 to1868 and for Haddington until his succession to the title in 1878. In the same year, aged 52, he married Candida Louise, the daughter of Vincenzo Bartolucci.

He was created Baron Tweeddale in 1881 for his support of Gladstone and this enabled him to sit in the House of Lords. He served twice as High Commissioner to the General Assembly of Scotland, he was created a Knight of the Thistle and made Brigadier-General of the Royal Company of Archers. He was one of the principal pioneers in buying prairie land in America and many of the Scottish nobility followed him. Tweeddale was, however, the biggest of all the British landowners there, owning 1,750,000 acres by 1884, four times that of the second largest owner, the Duke of Sutherland. Tweeddale did not, however, forget those less fortunate than he and three days a week he provided food for the poor from the Yester kitchens. Unlike his predecessor, he did not need to borrow any money until in 1896 when he took out a loan of £700,000; he died in 1911, aged 84.

His Will gives interesting reflections of the social changes of his time. It was witnessed by his butler, Arthur Whitby and by his footman, Ralph Evans and its first bequest stated: 'I direct the Trustees to allow my said wife to select for her own use one motor Brougham and one Napier or Spyker motor car…also three of my carriages.' The probate value of his furniture, paintings and books was set at £572,000; his jewellery at £640,000; the farm stock at £597,000; his stocks and bonds at £812,000; and his life policies at £2,900,000. His taxable estate excluded the entailed lands of 'Tweeddale, Yester, Newhall, Keirsbaath, Hopes and others lying in the Counties of Haddington, Berwick, Fife and Roxburgh'.

He and Candida had five children between 1879 and 1884: William, Arthur, Edward, Clemmie and Candida, who died at birth. William, always known as Giff, succeeded as 11th Marquis aged 26, having been educated at Eton and at Christ Church, Oxford. His Eton housemaster wrote of his time there: 'Lord Gifford has accumulated a vast amount of totally useless and unrelated knowledge'. After leaving Oxford he spent most of his time shooting and fishing. He went on safari to Kenya in November 1909 to April 1910 with Hugh Grosvenor where they shot 94 animals, ranging from lion cubs to elephants. He shot at many great estates in Scotland and England when thousands of pheasants and partridges were killed, including at Yester, and in August 1910 he and five other guns shot 2,900 grouse over five days in Ayrshire. In 1912 he married Marguerite Ralli, known as Midge, who Giff's granddaughter Vicky Morley-Fletcher describes: "Granny was small, dark, beautiful and vivacious and was loved... and adored by all...Sir George Kennard told me he adored her so much that he used to follow her from room to room smoking the stubs of her cigarettes-cigarettes which alas eventually killed her.' They had their first child, Helen, in 1913 and their second, Georgina, in 1916. Death duties were initiated in 1894 and they may have caused Giff to borrow £600,000 from each of his brothers in 1913.

Giff and his two brothers fought in the First World War where Giff served in the 1st Life Guards but he was severely wounded and was invalided out in 1917. His brother, Lord Arthur Hay, who had married Midge's cousin, served as a Captain in the Irish Guards and fought in the battle of Mons in August 1914 and at the Marne in September. He was killed at the battle of the Aisne a week later on September 15th, aged only 25, leaving one daughter. His youngest brother, Lord Edward Hay, served in the Grenadier Guards and fought with them in France, Gallipoli and in Egypt and he served as Staff Captain to General Ironside, the High Commissioner in Palestine in 1921.

Giff and Midge had two more daughters, Daphne in 1919 and Frances in 1926. Giff was desperate for an heir and Midge became pregnant again in 1928, but she did not have an easy time. She was told she should not travel south as her condition was not good but she decided to go and her train had to be stopped at Newcastle, where she was delivered of a boy, who lived for less than an hour. Giff could not forgive her for ignoring the doctor's advice and a family friend advised me that 'it killed Giff's love for her'; however the friend adds 'but she always went her own way, not only was she full of charm and looks but she was also brimming with charisma.' Giff worked in the 1930s for the British Government in the Consular Service in Prague where Midge's step-father, Lewis Einstein, worked in the American Embassy. Some consider that Giff's work there was of a rather secret and important nature.

The Yester estate was not economic and its cash flow was not helped by the payments that had to be made both to Arthur's widow, Julia, who received £25,000 a year between 1873 and 1923, and to Giff's mother, who lived till 1925. Giff and Midge also took grand houses in England where they entertained their friends in great style and all this meant that Giff had to borrow almost £2 million between 1914 and 1925- the cumulative amount borrowed between 1843 and 1925 was almost £14 million.

Giff loved his life in Scotland and was an expert fisherman and shot, as was Midge, and throughout the season they used to host numerous shoots of grouse, partridges and pheasants. *Vanity Fair* wrote in 1938 that his moors of Kilpalet, Hopes and Priestlaw were amongst the top five in Scotland and he used to rent them out to rich Americans to shoot grouse for £150 a brace or £240,000 for the sixteen weeks' season. He may, however, have lost money in the Great Crash since he broke the entail of the estate sometime in the 1930s, with the agreement of his brother Eddy, and this was to have significantly negative consequences when he died.

During the Second World War he commanded the local section of the Home Guard and he gathered a number of young friends and relations in Yester for its duration. These included two relations of General Alexander; Churchill's niece, Sally; Oliver Walston, the son of Graham Greene's lover; and various nephews and nieces of Giff's and of my grandmother, Marjorie, who had come to Yester to help nurse Midge, who was suffering from cancer. Giff lost one distant relation when his kinsman, Josslyn, 22nd Earl of Erroll, met an undistinguished death in Kenya in 1941, but 1944 was to prove a much worse year as in June his beloved brother Edward, who was a Lieutenant Colonel in the Grenadier Guards, was reading the lesson in the Guards Chapel in London when it was hit by a V1 rocket and he and 120 others were killed. The Bishop of Maidstone survived unhurt, as the altar was the only part of the Chapel undamaged. Giff's grandson, Hugo Morley-Fletcher, tells that Hay's wife, Audrey, was sitting with Midge and other ladies in Yester when they heard a loud noise. She immediately said 'something has happened to Eddy' and his death was soon relayed to them by telephone. Then in October Midge died leaving Giff devastated by his double loss. In addition, his financial position had deteriorated further due to the war and he was forced to sell two farms, raising £390,000 and take out a loan of £4 million.

In 1945 he married my grandmother, Marjorie. He was appointed Lord Lieutenant of East Lothian in 1946 and he served on the County Council. He took a special interest in the war-blinded and made a major contribution to the reorganisation of their workshops at Linburn and he succeeded his father as Brigadier General of the Archers. He raised almost £500,000 by land sales and took out a loan for £450,000 in 1953, but within five years he was forced to face the reality of the poor economic environment and he raised almost £3 million from selling 7,263 acres of farmland and moorland. In 1959 he sold the farm and sporting estate of Priestlaw, and a further 8,000 acres, including 5,675 acres of the Hopes and Brookside, raising another £3 million. He may have lost interest in battling against such adverse economic circumstances to keep the estate intact, as he had no close heir to whom he would leave it. He died at Yester in March 1967 and was buried at St Cuthbert's in spring sunshine; as his coffin was lowered into the grave, a cock pheasant crowed loudly from within the woods nearby.

Epilogue

Lord Edward Hay's son, David Hay, inherited as 12th Marquis. He was born in 1921 and, at the beginning of the Second World War, he joined the Merchant Marine, aged only seventeen. He was awarded the Albert Medal, because he had swum back from a lifeboat to rescue a crew mate from their sinking ship. In 1946 he married the Hon. Sonia Peake, by whom he had twin boys, Edward and Charles, who became the 13th and 14th Marquises in 1979 and 2005 respectively; and a third son, Lord Alistair Hay, who is the heir to the title. After divorcing Sonia, he married Nella Dutton in 1959, by whom he also had twin boys, Andrew and Hamish.

David was not close to his uncle which was due, in part, to his disobeying the three cardinal rules that Giff laid down to the young people who gathered together to live out the war at Yester: dress properly, do not get sexually involved with the guests and do not upset the head gamekeeper, John Brown. David, I am reliably informed, once came down to breakfast dressed only in a kilt; he seduced a young female relation of one of Churchill's top generals; and he went shooting without telling John Brown, so Giff asked him to leave Yester.

At Giff's death his estate was valued at £3.3 million, comprised of Yester House and Mains and the buildings in Gifford valued at £2.1 million, and his 'moveable estate' in England and Scotland at £1.2 million. A deduction of £600,000 was allowed for items of National or Historic reasons but he seems to have been poorly advised by his professional team as the estate was subject to the full 60% Estate Duty. He left the estate to Marjorie for her lifetime and it reverted on her death to his four daughters. There is a curious parallel here with the death of Sir Hugh Giffard over six hundred years earlier, who also died leaving four daughters and no male heir, and who was also the last of his male line to live at Yester Castle. Giff left the Village Hall and the land of the golf course to the inhabitants of Gifford and he made two small legacies of £1,000 per annum to Edward Mullins, his butler, and to John Brown, his gamekeeper, both of whom he had grown up with. His executors considered that Yester House and estate were not viable so they sold them to a local landowner, Dr James Lumsden, for approximately £3.5 million. He immediately sold Yester and the buildings in Gifford to Peter Morris and Derek Parker who were Edinburgh-based interior designers and they allowed Marjorie to continue to live at Yester.

She tried to make the house viable by opening it to the public and by having paying guests to stay for the night and have dinner with her, with all the silver on the table and a butler to serve them. Hugo Morley-Fletcher tells a touching vignette of Marjorie towards the end of her time at Yester when he asked her why she had sold the portrait of the 1st Marquis and Marchioness to the National Gallery of Scotland and she replied 'I cannot live with their eyes looking down at me and blaming me for what happened.' The cost of running the house could not be covered and she left Yester in 1970 and moved to Moreton-in-the-Marsh where, on a typically cold dank Christmas day, the vicar in his sermon remarked that some of the congregation would be unlikely to be around in a year's time. Her sister Vivian, who had been visiting Morocco, was staying and she brought some photographs of her holiday. One of these was of David Herbert, the second son of the Earl of Pembroke, who was living in Tangier. Marjorie was very taken by what she saw and decided to rent a house on the mountain near where David lived. After six months she bought a house nearby and she lived there happily, sharing many parties and holidays with David. She died in 1977, with her last drink being a glass of champagne. She had planned to be buried beside Giff in St Cuthbert's, and a grave had been prepared for her, but she was buried instead in St Andrew's Church in Tangier.

Parker and Morris sold Yester to the composer Gian Carlo Menotti who had fallen in love with the house and with the silence surrounding it. He wanted to build an international theatre school in the gardens with a theatre designed in the classical style by Quinlan Terry, but it was not possible to secure funding. Menotti's adopted son Francis and his wife Malinda lived with him at Yester. She died in 2005 and Menotti in 2007, aged 95, and both are buried in Yester Church; in 2014 Francis sold Yester.

પ્

In his 17th century book *Genealogie of the Hayes of Tweeddale*, Father Hay, Prior of St Pieremont, writes

The present Marquis of Tweddale bears in his scutcheon, quarterly, first and fourth, Azur, three Cinquefeuilles or Fraziers; for the name of Fraser, second and third gules, three Barres Hermine for the name of Gifford, above all, in a shield of Pretence, his paternal coat, which is, argent, three escutcheons, gules for his crest, ane goat's head erased, argent, armed, Or, for supporters, two Bucks proper, collaced and armed with seven Tynes, and for motto, these words, Spare (when thou has) nought.

This description of the family's Coat of Arms, so redolent of the history of the Hays and of the Giffards, resonates like Arnold's sea's 'melancholy, long, withdrawing roar'.

One evening, I stayed at the Goblin Ha' Hotel in Gifford and walked down the Yester drive after dinner. A full moon filled the sky and the towering trunks of the beech trees glowed silver in its light. I could hear the burn as it chattered and tumbled over the rocks in spate and the occasional haunting cry of a peacock from the gardens beyond the bank of trees to my right. On reaching Adam's bridge over the burn I stopped, marvelling at the sight of the great house bathed in the full moonlight, looking majestic and serene. I walked further until I stood on the grass circle around which the gravel drive ran. The house was totally dark, the shutters were closed and no light shone from behind. It felt empty and sad and I realised then that a house has no real meaning or purpose without the presence of a family living within, filling it with their dreams, loves, worries and all the wonderful complications that drive every family in any dwelling. As I turned and walked back down the drive, I decided to write about the families who had lived there, and wondered whether Marjorie's empty grave in St Cuthbert's would ever be filled by a descendant of the Giffards or the Hays.

THE DE HAYAS

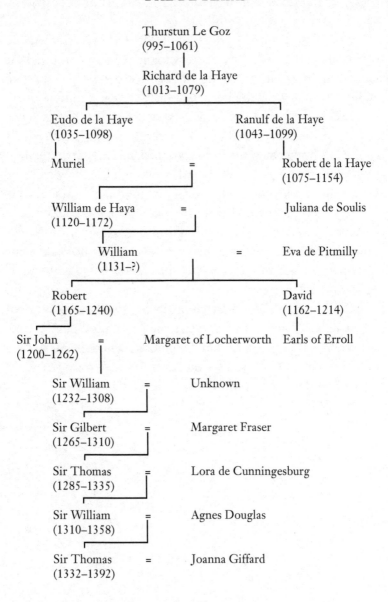

Thurstun Le Goz
(995–1061)

Richard de la Haye
(1013–1079)

Eudo de la Haye
(1035–1098)

Ranulf de la Haye
(1043–1099)

Muriel   =   Robert de la Haye
(1075–1154)

William de Haya   =   Juliana de Soulis
(1120–1172)

William   =   Eva de Pitmilly
(1131–?)

Robert   David
(1165–1240)   (1162–1214)

Sir John   =   Margaret of Locherworth   Earls of Erroll
(1200–1262)

Sir William   =   Unknown
(1232–1308)

Sir Gilbert   =   Margaret Fraser
(1265–1310)

Sir Thomas   =   Lora de Cunningesburg
(1285–1335)

Sir William   =   Agnes Douglas
(1310–1358)

Sir Thomas   =   Joanna Giffard
(1332–1392)

THE DOUGLASES AND THE HAYS

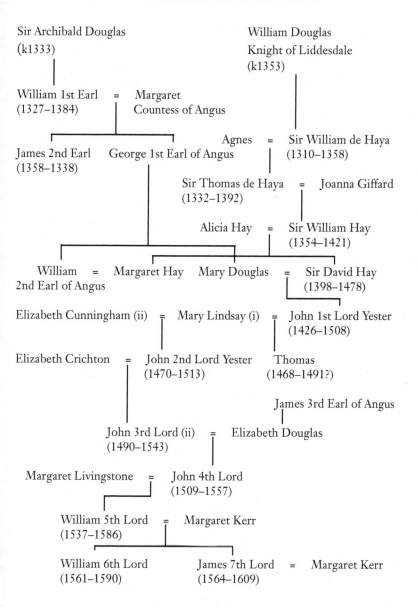

Sir Archibald Douglas (k1333)

William 1st Earl (1327–1384) = Margaret Countess of Angus

James 2nd Earl (1358–1338)   George 1st Earl of Angus

William Douglas Knight of Liddesdale (k1353)

Agnes = Sir William de Haya (1310–1358)

Sir Thomas de Haya (1332–1392) = Joanna Giffard

Alicia Hay = Sir William Hay (1354–1421)

William 2nd Earl of Angus = Margaret Hay   Mary Douglas = Sir David Hay (1398–1478)

Elizabeth Cunningham (ii) = Mary Lindsay (i) = John 1st Lord Yester (1426–1508)

Elizabeth Crichton = John 2nd Lord Yester (1470–1513)   Thomas (1468–1491?)

James 3rd Earl of Angus

John 3rd Lord (ii) (1490–1543) = Elizabeth Douglas

Margaret Livingstone = John 4th Lord (1509–1557)

William 5th Lord (1537–1586) = Margaret Kerr

William 6th Lord (1561–1590)   James 7th Lord (1564–1609) = Margaret Kerr

THE GIFFARDS

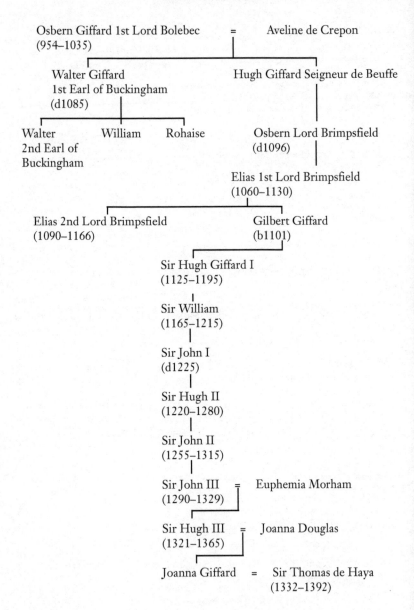

Osbern Giffard 1st Lord Bolebec = Aveline de Crepon
(954–1035)

Walter Giffard   Hugh Giffard Seigneur de Beuffe
1st Earl of Buckingham
(d1085)

Walter   William   Rohaise   Osbern Lord Brimpsfield
2nd Earl of   (d1096)
Buckingham

Elias 1st Lord Brimpsfield
(1060–1130)

Elias 2nd Lord Brimpsfield   Gilbert Giffard
(1090–1166)   (b1101)

Sir Hugh Giffard I
(1125–1195)

Sir William
(1165–1215)

Sir John I
(d1225)

Sir Hugh II
(1220–1280)

Sir John II
(1255–1315)

Sir John III = Euphemia Morham
(1290–1329)

Sir Hugh III = Joanna Douglas
(1321–1365)

Joanna Giffard = Sir Thomas de Haya
                           (1332–1392)

EARLS AND MARQUISES OF TWEEDDALE

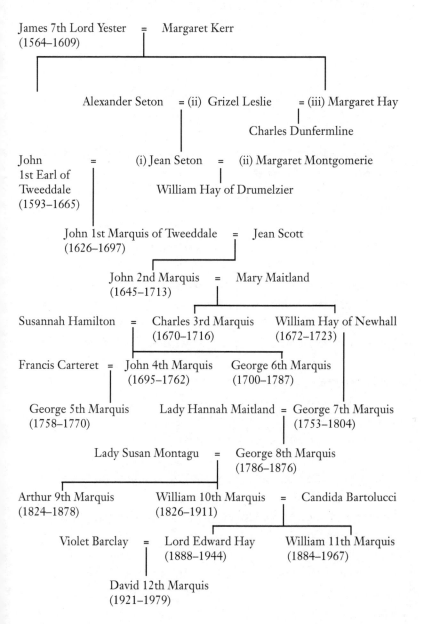

James 7th Lord Yester (1564–1609) = Margaret Kerr

Alexander Seton = (ii) Grizel Leslie = (iii) Margaret Hay

Charles Dunfermline

John 1st Earl of Tweeddale (1593–1665) = (i) Jean Seton = (ii) Margaret Montgomerie

William Hay of Drumelzier

John 1st Marquis of Tweeddale (1626–1697) = Jean Scott

John 2nd Marquis (1645–1713) = Mary Maitland

Susannah Hamilton = Charles 3rd Marquis (1670–1716)   William Hay of Newhall (1672–1723)

Francis Carteret = John 4th Marquis (1695–1762)   George 6th Marquis (1700–1787)

George 5th Marquis (1758–1770)   Lady Hannah Maitland = George 7th Marquis (1753–1804)

Lady Susan Montagu = George 8th Marquis (1786–1876)

Arthur 9th Marquis (1824–1878)   William 10th Marquis (1826–1911) = Candida Bartolucci

Violet Barclay = Lord Edward Hay (1888–1944)   William 11th Marquis (1884–1967)

David 12th Marquis (1921–1979)

Acknowledgements

My thanks to Hugo Morley-Fletcher for giving me so many leads and for allowing me to photograph his portraits of the 1st Earl, the 1st Marchioness and the 7th Marquis. My thanks also to Victoria Morley-Fletcher, Catherine Larthe, David Starling, Anthony Wagg, Angus Hay and Roddy Martine for all their input and help and to Roddy for allowing me to use his photograph of the Goblin Ha'. Also to Lady Elizabeth Benson for taking me round Neidpath Castle and to Charles Tweeddale, who entertained me and allowed me to photograph his portrait of the 2nd Marquis. I am also very grateful to Francis Menotti, who welcomed me as a complete stranger with such kindness and who gave me so much of his time. He also allowed me to take many of the photographs used in this book.

I owe great thanks to both Angus Hay and to Alan Hay for their scholarly input in correcting mistakes in the first edition. Those that remain are entirely my responsibility.

My great thanks are due to Andrew Duncan, who has given me such invaluable help and advice as to the publication of this book, and to Tara O'Sullivan for her excellent editing, to Claire Rogers for her patience and excellent design and to Alex Douglas for her excellent work on both editions.

Finally, I must thank my darling wife Henrietta, who has patiently read the book and given me much valuable advice on style and content and who has supported me throughout the writing of it.

Sources

General

The Yester Archives. National Library of Scotland.
The Calendar of Writs preserved at Yester House 1166-1503. ed.
   Charles Harvey, Scottish Record Society (1916).
The Scots Peerage. Sir James Balfour Paul (1904).
The Clan Hay Society
Oxford Dictionary of National Biography
The Works of the English Poets. Samuel Boyse, ed. Alexander
   Chalmers (1810).

Chapter 1 The Origins of the Hays and the Giffards

Scotorium Historia 1525. Hector Boece.
The Genealogie of the Hays of Tweeddale. Father Hay.
The Origin of the Giffard Family in Scotland. G Charles-Edwards,
   Scottish Genealogist, Vol. 27. Edinburgh (1980).
The Giffards of Brimpsfield. J. Langton, Transactions of the
   Bristol and Gloucester Archaeological Society (1944).
The Giffards from the Conquest to the present time. General
   Wrottesley. William Salt Archaeological Society.
'The Origins of the Hays of Erroll' by Sir Anthony Wagner.
   Genealogist Magazine Vol.s 11 and 12 (1955).
Scottish Hazard. Beryl Platts. Procter Press (1985).
Family of Hay. Charles Colcock. Pelican (1998).

The Story of the Hays. Kenneth McLennan Hay. Scotpress (1984).
Community 2. Bruce and Barbara Morrison. http://community-2.webtv.net.
The Battle Abbey Roll

Chapter 2 Entering Scotland

A Companion to the Anglo-Norman World. Christopher Harper. Bill and Elizabeth van Houts. Boydell (2002).
A Short History of Haddington. W. Forbes Gray. SPA Books (1995).
Scottish Annals from English Chronicles. Alan Anderson (1908).
'The Last of the Brimpsfield Giffards, and the Rising of 1321-2' by R.F.Butler. *Transactions of the Bristol and Gloucester Archaeological Society* Vol.76 (1957).
A History of Scotland. J.D Mackie. Penguin (1964).
Scottish Kings. Gordon Donaldson. Barnes and Noble (1967).
From Domesday Book to Magna Carta. Austin Lane Poole. Oxford (1951).
Marmion. Sir Walter Scott.

Chapter 3 Robert the Bruce

Robert Bruce. Colm McNamee. Birlinn (2006).
'The Boyd Tomb at Kilmarnock' by Andrew MacEwen. *The American Genealogist Magazine* Vol 24 (2010).

Chapter 4 The Douglases

The Black Douglases. Michael Brown. Tuckwell Press (1998).
Neidpath Castle. Lady Elizabeth Benson.
Blood Stain'd Fields. Arran Johnston. Prestongrange and Cuthill Press (2013-08-05).
The Country Houses, Castles and Mansions of East Lothian. Sonia Baker. Stenlebe.

The Castles of Lothian and the Borders. Mike Salter. Folly (1994).
'The Boyd Tomb at Kilmarnock' by Andrew MacEwen. *The Genealogist* (Spring 2010).

Chapter 5 The Covenant

The Last Years of a Frontier. D Tough. Sandhill Press (1928).
John Maitland of Thirlestane. Professor Maurice Lee. Princeton (1959).
Flodden A Scottish Tragedy. Peter Reese Birlinn (2013).

Chapter 6 James, King of Scotland and England

Government by Pen: Scotland under James VI and I. Professor Maurice Lee. University of Illinois (1980).
The Inevitable Union. Professor Maurice Lee. Tuckwell (2003).
The Road to Revolution. Professor Maurice Lee. University of Illinois (1985).
The Scottish Revolution 1637-1644, *and*
Revolution and Counter Revolution. David Stevenson. John Donald (2003).
The Early Stuarts 1603-1660. Godfrey Davies. Oxford (1959).
The Royal Stuarts. Alan Massie. Jonathan Cape. (2010).

Chapter 7 Civil War

'Autobiography1626-1670' by John Hay, Earl of Tweeddale, ed. Professor Maurice Lee. *SHS Miscellany XII*. Edinburgh (1994).
A History of His Own Time. Bishop Burnett, ed. M.J.Routh. Oxford (1823).

Chapters 8–9 The Restoration of Charles II and Tweeddale in Government

The Heiresses of Buccleuch. Professor Maurice Lee. Tuckwell (1996).
Dearest Brother: Lauderdale, Tweeddale and Scottish Politics

1660-1674. Professor Maurice Lee. Birlinn (2010).

'Relation of the Wrangs done to the Ladie Yester, 1683' by John Hay, Earl of Tweeddale, ed. Professor Maurice Lee. *SHS Miscellany XII*. Edinburgh (2004).

King Lauderdale. Raymond Campbell Paterson. Birlinn (2003).

Elizabeth of the Sealed Knot. Doreen Crips. Roundwood (1975).

The Later Stuarts. Sir George Clark. Oxford (1934).

No Tragic Story. Raymond Campbell Paterson. John Donald (2007).

'Lady Sophia's Visions' by Frances Harris. *The Seventeenth Century* Vol. 24 No. 1 (April 2009).

Chapter 10 The Glorious Revolution

King William and the Scottish Politicians. P. Riley. John Donald (1979).

The Cabal. Professor Maurice Lee. University of Illinois (1965).

The Lost Gardens of Scotland. Marilyn Robinson. RCAMS (2013).

A Journey through Scotland. John Macky (1723).

Chapter 11 The Company of Scotland

The Price of Scotland. Douglas Watt. Luath (2007).

Chapter 12 The Battle for Union

Union and Empire. Alan MacInnes. Cambridge University Press (2007).

The Union. Michael Fry. Birlinn (2007).

The Union of 1707. Paul Henderson Scott. Saltire Society (2006).

George Lockhart: Memoirs. J Baker (1714).

Chapters 13–14 Building Yester House and The Greatest

Room in Scotland?

'The Building of Yester House 1670-1878' by John Dunbar.
*Transactions of East Lothian Antiquarian and Field Naturalists
Society*. Vol. 13 (1972).
'Yester House' by Alistair Rowan. *Country Life*. (August 1973).
Political Untouchables. Eveline Cruikshanks. Holmes and Meier
(1979).
The '45. Christopher Duffy. Phoenix (2007).
Famous Scottish Houses. Thomas Hannan. A&C Black (1928).

Chapter 15 The Great 8th Marquis

'George Hay, 8th Marquis of Tweeddale: Autobiography' ed.
Lewis Einstein. *Recollections of the War of 1812 American
Historical Review*. Vol. 32 (1926).
Yester Deep Land Culture. Henry Stephens. William Blackwood
(1855).
Gifford 1750-1850. Rev. John Muir. W.M. Sinclair (1913).
'Parish of Yester' by Rev. James Innes. *The Statistical Account of
Scotland*. No. 36 (1791).

Chapter 16 The last Tweeddales of Yester

Recollections of a long life. John Cam. Hobhouse (1865).
The Children of Yester. Victoria Fletcher. (2000).
This Too Shall Pass: Reflections on East Lothian. Roddy Martine.
Birlinn (2009).
Sasine Court of Haddington (1922-1990).
Will of William Montagu Marquis of Tweeddale 1912
Will of William George Montagu Marquis of Tweeddale 1967